NEIL FINDLAY was born in 1969, the son of a bricklayer and a primary school teacher. Brought up in the working class village of Fauldhouse in West Lothian, after leaving school at 16 he was an apprentice and tradesman bricklayer for ten years with his father's small business, became active in his local Labour Party and struck up a great friendship with Tam Dalyell MP. After returning to education, Neil worked in social housing before becoming a schoolteacher. A West Lothian councillor for nine years, he was elected to the Scottish Parliament in 2011, serving in various front bench posts and contesting the Scottish Labour leadership election in 2015. He acted as Jeremy Corbyn's Scottish campaign manager in two Labour Party leadership elections. Neil enjoys fishing, golf, gardening and going for a pint.

AF283625

Luath Press is an independently owned and managed book publishing company based in Scotland and is not aligned to any political party or grouping.

By the same author:

Socialism & Hope: A Journey Through Turbulent Times, Luath Press, 2017

Life in the Raws: Memories of a Shale-Oil Village (with Jock Findlay), Luath Press, 2020

If You Don't Run, They Can't Chase You: Stories From the Frontline in the Fight for Social Justice, Luath Press, 2021

Hope and Despair

Lifting the lid on the murky world of Scottish politics

NEIL FINDLAY

Luath Press Limited

EDINBURGH

www.luath.co.uk

First published in 2023

ISBN: 978-1-804250-72-3

The author's right to be identified as author of this book
under the Copyright, Designs and Patents Act 1988 has been asserted.

This book is made of materials from well-managed, FSC®-certified forests
and other controlled sources.

Printed and bound by
Ashford Colour Press, Gosport

Typeset in 11 point Sabon by
Main Point Books, Edinburgh

This book is dedicated to my mum and all the other care home residents whose human rights were violated during the Covid pandemic.

Contents

Introduction

A TIME OF perpetual crisis and scandal is the only way I can describe the last few years of my time in the Scottish Parliament. The aftermath of the 2014 referendum on independence left Scottish politics mired in a constitutional dogfight. Rational analysis of how well or badly the country is being governed became a sideshow.

In Scotland, every issue from dog shit on the streets to international trade was viewed through the prism of the constitutional debate. No matter how poorly the SNP in Holyrood or the Tories at Westminster govern, tribal loyalties to 'Yes' or 'No' provided cover for their respective supporters to trot out prepared lines that deflect attention from dire decision-making.

During this period the political world was in turmoil.

The aftermath of Britain's decision to leave the European Union combined with the failure of Prime Minister Theresa May to secure a parliamentary majority set in train two years of unprecedented chaos at Westminster.

Four decades of civil war in the Conservative Party over Europe reached its crescendo with the removal of May as Prime Minister, only to be replaced by a talentless charlatan in the shape of Alexander Boris de Pfeffel Johnson, the worst Prime Minister in the history of British democracy... at least, until his successor was appointed.

Thankfully, the premierships of the abominable Liz Truss, and then Rishi Sunak, took place outside the timeline of this book. Suffice to say, the chaos of the May/Johnson period intensified rather than subsided with a Truss budget that cost the UK billions in just a few calamitous weeks.

In the US, Donald Trump's reign as president culminated in the storming of the Capitol by armed right-wing militia protesting at his defeat by Democrat Joe Biden. Trump threatens to run again in 2024 (if he doesn't end up in prison). God help us.

In Scotland, the ruling Scottish National Party was plunged into crisis with the arrest of former First Minister Alex Salmond on charges of rape and sexual assault. Salmond was later cleared of all charges by the courts. This caused major schisms in the party and the independence movement, resulting in Salmond setting up his own Alba Party. He remained a thorn in the side of his former mentee, Nicola Sturgeon.

At the time of writing, the schisms in the SNP resulted in the shock resignation of Sturgeon. The ensuing contest to succeed her saw the contenders tear lumps out of each other with the eventual winner Humza Yousaf's first week as leader dominated by the arrest of his party's Chief Executive, Peter Murrell, Sturgeon's husband, a media frenzy and appalling headlines. This was a crisis long in the making with the alleged financial mismanagement potentially bringing the party to the brink of bankruptcy.

Following a decade of underfunding of Scotland's council services compounded by a populist council tax freeze, many public services teeter on the brink. Across the country libraries are being closed, social workers drown in cases and the roads are full of potholes.

In our greatest public service, the NHS, one in seven Scots were stuck on waiting lists. Patients were left lingering in hospitals for months waiting to be discharged, cancer treatment times could not be met, there is a recruitment crisis, a financial crisis and a social care crisis. Our most cherished public institution is facing its greatest ever challenge. This is a very public scandal.

Scotland has the shame and indignity of having the worst rate of drug deaths in the developed world. Mental health services are overwhelmed and underfunded. Our previously acclaimed education system slid down the world rankings, despite Nicola Sturgeon's claim it was her number one priority.

There was a similar decline across public services, including housing, social work and transport, with many working-class families struggling to make ends meet and more of our fellow citizens forced to seek charitable food, unable to heat their homes in one of the world's wealthiest economies. And while communities self-organised and responded magnificently to the plight of their needy neighbours and friends by providing material support and solidarity, despair and hopelessness affected groups of people who previously were just about able to cope.

In the Labour Party, Jeremy Corbyn's surprisingly good showing in the 2017 election struck the fear of death into the establishment. They pulled out every stop to prevent him from taking power. In doing so, they weaponised racism and antisemitism, using their friends in the media to portray one of the foremost anti-racist MPs of the last 30 years as an antisemite.

A section of the Labour Party actually preferred a far-right Tory Party in power, rather than the election of a transformative, unashamedly socialist Corbyn government. An outrageous betrayal of Labour voters and members.

Meanwhile, Scottish Labour continued to burn through leaders at a rate of knots. The party that more than any other brought about the creation of the Scottish Parliament continued to be paralysed by an inability to understand the wishes of the Scottish people for further autonomy.

I was involved in many of the conflicts between the socialist Labour left and the hard unionist right of the Scottish party. This book gives an honest account of these often fierce and visceral debates. It is essential that the history of this period is not rewritten or glossed over.

As if all of this was not enough, then came the global calamity of Covid-19, a worldwide public health emergency that claimed the lives of millions.

Covid saw countries locked down, communities become ghost towns, shops and businesses close, and workers sent home. Freedoms and rights were suspended to a degree unseen outside of wartime.

Every family was impacted in some way. Lives were lost unnecessarily and huge mistakes were made. Covid was the greatest crisis to hit the world since the Second World War. But Covid was also a scandal. Political leaders ignored the warnings, failed to prepare, took some appalling decisions, misled the public and failed to take responsibility for errors that cost many citizens their lives. The UK government used the pandemic to reward supporters with contracts worth billions of pounds – no one will ever know the extent of the fraud that took place.

This book is my account of being an elected politician during these times. My comments convey my feelings and emotions as events unfolded. If they cause upset to some, then so be it. I can only report the truth.

Finally, I do not want to put readers off becoming active in politics. I don't want to have them believe 'politics is a waste of time' or that 'politicians are all the same so, why bother?'

There are many good people in politics – fantastic campaigners, inspirational activists and determined individuals who want to make the world a better place. These are the people who inspire me. I hope they inspire you too, because it's people power that changes the world. But I cannot hide the fact that 2017–2021 was a period that, for me, started with so much hope and ended with despair.

Campaigns

THROUGHOUT THIS BOOK there are references to campaigns that I have been heavily involved in. These are summarised here to help contextualise them for the reader.

Transvaginal mesh – in 2012, when I was Scottish Labour's Shadow Health Secretary, I met with a group of women suffering from chronic pain, disability and ill health. They had all been fitted with polypropylene transvaginal mesh implants to address stress urinary incontinence or pelvic organ prolapse. No one in the Scottish Parliament, the media or the medical profession would touch their case. Senior surgeons claimed mesh was the 'gold standard' treatment and that this was not what had caused their disability and pain. I, along with my researcher Tommy Kane, built up a close working relationship with the women. They refused to be silenced and campaigned relentlessly with the support of Marion Scott, the finest campaigning journalist in Scotland. Together we took on the medical establishment, who closed ranks to defend the appalling behaviour of some of the world's biggest multinational health care companies, and exposed the mesh scandal.

Miners' justice – I come from the mining community of Fauldhouse in West Lothian. I was at school when the miners' strike took place. I was fascinated by it and inspired by working-class heroes like Arthur Scargill and Michael McGahey who led the National Union of Mineworkers in the year-long strike. When I was elected to the Scottish Parliament, I made a pledge to myself that I would try to do all I could to support former miners and the ex-coalfield areas. The screening of a BBC Yorkshire documentary on the strike and details about policing that came from the Hillsborough football disaster inquiry provoked me into calling for a public inquiry into the policing of the strike in Scotland. In 1984–85, Scotland employed 10 per cent of the UK mining workforce, but 30 per cent of those who were sacked after arrest were Scots. These men lost their job and their redundancy pay, and many were blacklisted. The twists and turns of the campaign for miners' justice are recounted here.

Health and social care – The NHS is the greatest social policy we have ever seen. Universal health care, free at the point of need and paid for through our taxes is practical socialism in action. It must be protected and fought for consistently and robustly or the corporations will destroy it, leaving the field open for them to set up a pay-as-you-go Klondike for their shareholders.

As an elected politician, a great deal of constituency work concerned health and social care issues and often these issues grew into national campaigns. The plan to downgrade the children's ward at St John's Livingston, my local hospital, is an example of this. Even today, with the crisis in our NHS, the future of the ward remains uncertain.

Social care is the key to ending much of the backlog in our NHS. The failure to develop a working system that allows people to leave hospital quickly when ready to do so causes major delays for those requiring hospital treatment. Delayed discharge results in hundreds of thousands of lost bed days a year and a loss of around £4,000 per patient per week – much-needed revenue. I raised these issues repeatedly in the Scottish Parliament.

Drugs and mental health – Over the years, I spoke to more and more constituents who were going through a mental health crisis and who could not access the support and treatment they needed. Some of this was a result of drug use and its consequences. Hearing their stories and listening and learning about drugs and addiction made me understand the abject failure of drugs policy over the last 50 years, and turned me from a strict prohibitionist to a campaigner for the decriminalisation of all drugs. I hope I capture some of this journey in the pages that follow.

2017

THE PERIOD BETWEEN the summer and Christmas of 2017 saw the UK, Scottish and Welsh Labour parties led by unapologetic socialists. For many of us this offered great hope and was something we had worked for throughout our political lives. To the establishment, outside and inside the Labour Party, it rang alarm bells and marked the start of an all-out war to bring an end to any notion of socialist change.

Following the UK's decision to leave the EU, Prime Minister Theresa May attempted to negotiate a credible deal that would secure a majority in the House of Commons. Every twist and turn of this tragicomedy was played out on our TV screens.

In Scotland, constitutional politics dominated with the battle between two brands of flag waving nationalism influencing every aspect of our political discourse.

As a campaigning politician, 2017 saw me continue to pursue causes I cared deeply about; justice for miners arrested during the 1984/85 strike, the plight of mesh-injured women, Scotland's failing drugs policy and the growing crisis in our health and social care system.

29 August The news tonight is that Kezia Dugdale is to resign as Scottish Labour leader. She says she wants to get her life back. I have some sympathy for this as without doubt being a party leader is all consuming. She has looked miserable for a while. Social media has erupted. The next Labour leader will be the ninth since devolution. Unbelievable. Anas Sarwar will definitely be a candidate and Richard Leonard might also stand. One thing is for sure: I won't.

30 August I have been inundated with calls, texts and messages urging me to stand in the election. Ian Lavery MP and Karie Murphy, Jeremy Corbyn's Chief of Staff, are trying to coax me, but they have no chance. I dodged a bullet when Jim Murphy won in 2015. The press wanted me to speak but I refused to go on TV.

Alex Rowley is to step in as interim leader.

Anas Sarwar is getting his team ready.

2 September Still getting calls about standing, people don't seem to want to listen – I AM NOT STANDING NOW OR EVER!

3 September Up early for conference call with Richard Leonard's team. They are understandably like rabbits in the headlights with a million and one things to think about and few resources. They will need to get organised quickly if they are going to take on Sarwar.

Later both Sarwar and Leonard declared their candidacy. Sarwar's team is putting heavy pressure on MSPs to declare for him.

Richard has support from me, Paul Sweeney MP, Hugh Gaffney MP and Monica Lennon MSP. Anas has MSPs Mary Fee, Jackie Baillie, Mark Griffin, Iain Gray and Neil Bibby.

4 September Met with Patrick McGuire from Thompsons solicitors to discuss the transvaginal mesh campaign. Thompsons have taken on many of the cases.

5 September Parliament returned today after the summer recess. Anas Sarwar is claiming 14 MSPs have nominated him.

Chaired the Health Committee where the SFA (Scottish Football Association) and SYFA (Scottish Youth Football Association) gave evidence on the latest developments with child protection issues. They came before the committee and gave evidence which showed a dysfunctional relationship between the two organisations impacting on child protection procedures. The SFA came out of this badly. The SYFA didn't help with chaotic record keeping and a creaking bureaucracy.

Went to the Labour Group meeting, which was tense. Sarwar has appointed Alan Roden, Kezia Dugdale's spin doctor, to run his media campaign. Roden is a former *Daily Mail* journalist. Richard hopes to get Simon Fletcher, who ran the Corbyn campaign, signed up.

Nicola Sturgeon announced her Programme for Government today with 14 bills. Some of it is decent, some lifted from Labour and other parties.

6 September Met Kevin Neary and the team from Aid & Abet. Kevin was a year older than me at school. He suffered a lot of trauma in his young life and ended up a heroin user, spending time in jail. He is now in recovery and has set up the charity to help people who want to change their offending behaviour. He is a brilliant speaker and tells his story with honesty and passion. I agreed to do what I can to promote the organisation.

Met Simon Fletcher. He has a track record of having been campaign Chief for Ken Livingstone when he won the London Mayor election, helped Ed Miliband when he ran for UK leader and won, and Jeremy Corbyn when he ran for Labour leader and won. It will be a real coup if we get him to run Richard's campaign.

7 September Brilliant news – Simon Fletcher is on board for Richard's campaign.

Did an interview for the BBC alongside James Kelly, who is supporting Anas Sarwar. Kelly claimed Sarwar was the change we needed to win. I said, 'That's what James said when he supported Jim Murphy and look what happened!'

My daughter Chloe came back from four months backpacking in Asia, great to see her home.

8 September Great news: Labour won Council by-elections at Shotts and Cardonald.

The press is carrying the story of Simon Fletcher's appointment. They now know Richard is a serious candidate.

10 September To Stirling University for the Health Committee away-day. We visited the dementia centre for a tour. In the discussion that followed our sessions, SNP MSPs were very tetchy when we raised the crisis in social care, health inequalities and period poverty.

11 September Met with Royal College of Paediatrics to discuss the ongoing partial closure of the children's ward at St John's. This has been going on for three years. Councillors, MSPs and MPs were present and put on a united front in support of a 24/7 service.

13 September I hosted a screening of the film *Nature of the Beast* in Edinburgh. It is a documentary about the legendary Labour MP Dennis Skinner. We had a good crowd turn up to see a touching, moving and gentle portrait of the man, his politics and his life.

14 September Met with the team tasked with setting up the Lobbying Register, which came about following my introduction of a bill in the last parliament.

This a positive step for openness and transparency.

To Easter Road stadium for a question time panel with a wide range of disability groups frustrated at the lack of action on social care. The sector needs a massive injection of cash, a proper career structure, care work valued, proper pay and decent conditions.

Came home to find 700 copies of my book *Socialism and Hope* in my hall. Great to see it finally arrive.

16 September Richard Leonard launched his campaign at Glasgow College. It went well. The message was that whether you voted 'Yes' or 'No', Richard's politics are for you. His speech was passionate, intelligent and full of commitment.

Later the TSSA (Transport Salaried Staffs' Association) union declared their support for Richard.

Went down to the Miners' Welfare for my book launch. Over 200 family, friends and colleagues were there. Chairman of the Labour Party Ian Lavery MP spoke, we had poetry from Jim Monaghan, songs from Calum Baird, Arthur Johnson, Stephen Wright and Fraser Speirs. It was brilliant.

The after party at our house finished at 4.30am – *oof.*

20 September Anas Sarwar and Richard Leonard were interviewed on *Good Morning Scotland*. Sarwar was asked if someone with £4.8 million worth of shares in the family business was 'one of the many or the few'? And if being a shareholder in a business that doesn't recognise trade unions or pay the living wage makes him 'one of the many or the few'? It really was car crash stuff. Afterwards his spin doctor Alan Roden tweeted saying the BBC was biased in favour of Richard Leonard. Not a good start for them.

Went into parliament for the debate on taxation. Derek Mackay led for the government. He was like a slightly less animated speak-your-weight machine, churning out the Tory playbook with phrases like 'tax bombshell' and 'tax raid' to attack Labour. He called on all parties to publish their tax plans, BUT wait for it… the government aren't going to publish theirs!

I took part in a members' debate on UK government tax office closures and raised the Bathgate office relocation plan. This will see 1,200 jobs moved to a new, expensive office in Edinburgh. It makes no sense whatsoever. SNP MSPs are very vocal on this as it allows them to attack the UK government but they say nothing when it's the Scottish Government centralising services.

Apparently at the leadership hustings in Glasgow the Chair read out a statement saying that there should be no questions about a candidate's personal wealth. What utter nonsense! This is not just about the character of candidates, it's also about their behaviour and values. One thing's for sure, if members don't raise these issues political opponents will.

21 September At FMQs Alex Rowley led on child poverty and his line of questioning was going well until he accused Nicola Sturgeon of 'siding with the millionaires' over taxes. At this, the SNP benches erupted, pointing and shouting at Sarwar (wealthy son of a multi-millionaire). As we left the chamber, the press was there to doorstep him. It is beyond me how his campaign didn't see these issues coming and have a plan to deal with them.

The *Daily Record* ran a story about my wife Fiona walking ten miles per shift at her work in an NHS hospital. This followed a comment I made in committee about pressures of understaffing in the NHS.

24 September Down to Brighton for the Labour Party conference. The city is buzzing with huge numbers of delegates and visitors. My job this week is to drum up support for Richard's campaign.

The *Sunday Herald* featured heavily on Anas Sarwar today. It was brutal, a front page, double spread and editorial attacking him for choosing private education for his family, the family business not paying the living wage or recognising trade unions.

25 September The conference is rammed with long queues to get in. All the fringe meetings are packed. Richard's campaign is getting a really positive response.

Into the hall to hear veteran MP Dennis Skinner rouse the delegates as only he can. John McDonnell gave a terrific speech as Shadow Chancellor. At lunchtime I did a fringe meeting on Scotland at 'The World Transformed Festival'.

In the evening I did a book event with David Clegg of the *Daily Record*. It was busy with over 100 delegates in attendance.

26 September Spent the day signing books for delegates.

Spoke at the Labour Representation Committee fringe with a huge cast of Left speakers. I emphasised the importance of the leadership election in Scotland and urged them to help in Richard's campaign.

27 September Up early for flight home, I missed Jeremy Corbyn's speech as I had to be back in parliament.

The Sun ran a story reporting how they had used a hidden recorder to dupe Alex Rowley into making offhand comments about Kezia Dugdale. Jackie Baillie is claiming it is evidence there was a left-wing plot led by Richard Leonard to topple her. Utter rubbish, but they are using it to divert attention from the failings of the Sarwar campaign. The reality is that since he was elected in 2016, Anas Sarwar has spoken to me in the presence of others about Kezia Dugdale's performance and how she was not cutting it.

28 September To parliament for the Petitions Committee with the Scottish Mesh Survivors Group. Dr Wael Agur was there to give evidence. A surgeon, he was a member of the review group on mesh implants and was outstanding in giving evidence. He came across as honest, straightforward, principled and very credible. I don't think I have seen a committee witness make such an impact. Elaine Holmes and Olive McIlroy, two women disabled by mesh implants, spoke to the petition and were superb. They exposed the scandal, hypocrisy and contradictions of the government's sham review. Tory MSP Jackson Carlaw, the SNP's Alex Neil and I worked together to support the petition.

I asked Justice Secretary Michael Matheson if there was going to be a review of the policing of the miners' strike in Scotland (I have been campaigning for this since becoming an MSP). Matheson said he would make an announcement soon, which sounds promising.

Later, I spoke to a joint meeting of the Dundee CLPs (Constituency Labour Parties) on behalf of Richard. He won the nomination easily.

1 October I watched horrific scenes tonight on the news. There was widespread coverage of the Spanish police using batons and violence against Catalan Nationalists. Police have confiscated ballot boxes and provoked clashes in many towns. The cameras caught them attacking firefighters. The referendum is unconstitutional but the Catalan nationalist government went ahead anyway. This issue has faded into the background as the violence became the big issue. I tweeted condemnation of the violence and said we shouldn't see these clashes through the lens of the Scottish constitutional debate, and immediately got dog's abuse from the cybernats, who are now self-declared experts on the Spanish constitution.

A gunman killed 58 people at a concert in Las Vegas and injured 500 more.

In her column in the *Daily Record*, Kezia Dugdale sniped at the lack of ideas coming out from the leadership election and made it all about who would get her vote. She carries little influence.

3 October *The Herald* today ran a horrific story saying women in Glasgow who have miscarried a child have been getting sent home with antibiotics and told to come back five weeks later to have the dead child removed from their body. I really cannot take this in.

Paul Wheelhouse gave a very nervy statement on fracking today. I raised a point of order, as it should have been Cabinet Secretary Fergus Ewing giving the statement. We all know he would frack under his own arse and wants fracking to go ahead. He sat at the back of the chamber throughout, very glum faced. The announcement was not a ban but an extension of the moratorium – a decent result that has only come about because of repeated pressure being put on the government and Claudia Beamish MSPs Members' Bill which would deliver an outright ban.

4 October Spoke to Hepatitis UK about their idea for a state-owned drugs manufacturing facility that would produce generic drugs at a fraction of the cost charged by the pharma companies. I think it is a great idea.

Theresa May made her big speech at the Tory conference. It was an almighty disaster. First, she was interrupted by a comedian who sneaked in undercover and waited for his moment to hand her a large P45, telling her it was for Boris Johnson. Then the letters started falling off the campaign slogan behind her. Then she started coughing and could barely speak, finding it difficult to finish. It was dire.

5 October Fallout from May's speech is huge, the Tories are in chaos. Gove was quoted as saying, 'The speech showed the Prime Minister at the top of her game'. Some MPs are calling for her to go.

Met Stephen Wright, who has a theatre company, and Elaine Miller, a physiotherapist and stand-up comic who does a show called *Is Pee a Feminist Issue?* – all about incontinence. I am going to sponsor a performance of her show in the parliament as this has great relevance to the mesh women. Elaine advised me she wears a 'fanny suit' for her performance and asked how she would get her big bag of vibrators (which she uses as props) through security? I said to her it was a somewhat unusual question, one I had not been asked before and one I was unable to answer. A politician's answer if ever there was one! She is also going to send every MSP a free sample of vaginal lubricant. Well, I can safely say no two days are the same in this job.

6 October Tommy Kane, my researcher, went to London last year to work for the Corbyn team. Lesley Brennan stepped in, but she has gone to work with Richard Leonard, so I was interviewing all day today for a replacement. Sean Duffy was successful.

7 October To parliament for UNISON public services rally against cuts. Good turnout in the autumn sunshine. Not an SNP MSP or MP in sight.

Heard today that Anas Sarwar has been heavily recruiting registered supporters and members through his business connections. He has also said that he would make it a priority to remain in the single market and attacked Richard Leonard for voting against the Labour whip when he voted to respect the result of the EU referendum.

9 October In the leadership election each constituency party can nominate their preferred candidate. The current tally is Leonard 28, Sarwar 10.

11 October Today Sturgeon gave her conference speech, lambasting Labour infighting and Tory policies. She shamelessly claimed for her own Labour policies on period poverty, a public energy company and social care reform.

12 October I met Derek Milligan, Leader of Midlothian Council today. I like Derek, he is a straight-talking, streetwise former miner who tells it like it is. His Council will have to make £44 million of cuts from now to 2021.

Richard won the nominations from Inverness, Edinburgh East and, astonishingly, Edinburgh South, which is the biggest constituency party in Scotland and has Ian Murray as MP and Daniel Johnson as MSP – both of whom loathe Richard's politics. It is also Alan Roden's CLP. And despite this they couldn't deliver for Anas in their own backyard.

13 October Well, well, well, looks like Murray and Roden were indeed hopping mad. Murray has sent a letter to the Scottish Labour General Secretary. Leaked to the press, of course. In it he called for Labour to 're-consider the validity of the members of the UNITE trade union who had signed up to vote in the contest', ignoring all the sign-ups Sarwar has made. He is also assuming that all UNITE members vote the same way, which they won't. He claimed interim leader Alex Rowley isn't impartial and called on him to be removed as chair of a panel set up to vet new recruits. His cheerleaders joined in, accusing Richard's campaign of leaking Murray's letter to the papers. How on earth could they, when the only people who had the letter were Murray and Brian Roy, the party's Scottish Secretary?

15–18 October Spent three days at my wife Fiona's dad's, in Montpellier.

16 October The *Sunday Herald* ran a story I gave them about the sister of *Guardian* journalist Owen Jones: travelling from Germany to Scotland to attend her grandfather's funeral, she was detained at Edinburgh Airport under the Terrorism Act 2000, forced to hand over passwords for her mobile phone and computer, and interrogated about her political beliefs and her relatives, before being driven from the airport to a police station to have her DNA sample and fingerprints taken. She was detained for four hours and missed her flight back to Berlin, where she lives. The police refused to pay for a new flight.

It is clear to me that the police targeted her for her political activism in Germany and possibly because of who she is related to. I have been in correspondence with Police Scotland about the case, but they are completely unapologetic about the way they handled things.

17 October Jeremy Corbyn was in Brussels to meet Michel Barnier and the European Socialist leaders. He was given a standing ovation by the Socialist bloc.

20 October To parliament to do a 'Festival of Politics' event on drugs policy. The long and the short of it is that the current drugs policy is a disaster. With a record number of drug deaths and drugs more readily available than ever, we have a public health crisis on our hands. I am so pleased I was asked to chair this session as it chimes very much with what is going on in my region. I am going to do much more work on this issue.

I visited Bield Housing Association in Edinburgh to discuss their plans to close 12 care homes. The Chief Executive said it was a financial decision, the care homes charge around £800 a week and would need another £300 to make them viable. There was little empathy for the people about to lose their homes.

21 October Got a phone call from Tom Gordon at *The Herald* to say the Scottish Mesh Survivors are going to be one of the nominees for the Herald Scottish Political Campaign of the Year. Great news.

22 October Patrick Harvie was on the *Sunday Politics* programme saying he will vote down the budget if no taxes are levied on the rich. He comes away with this crap every year, then the SNP give him the equivalent of a few energy-saving light bulbs, which is enough for him to back the budget which will again hammer council finances.

23 October Met with two women from the West Lothian Ability Centre, which supports people with disabilities and is lined up for closure due to cuts.

Today the Royal College of Paediatrics published its report on the St John's children's ward. They are still recommending a 24/7 service but confirmed it can only open when the staff are in place and to date NHS Lothian haven't been able to recruit, so nothing much has changed.

24 October The papers are running a story about Tory MP Douglas Ross missing the Universal Credit vote in parliament because he was acting as linesman at a Champions League match. What a farce, we need to legislate against this double jobbing nonsense.

At the Health Committee, Minister for Public Health and Sport Aileen Campbell gave evidence to our 'Sport for All' inquiry. We tried to find out why they were cutting the very successful 'Jog Scotland' programme then were forced to reinstate it. Her answer was incomprehensible, so I asked again. This time she answered a question I didn't ask. When I went to ask for a third time, SNP committee members got all animated. I then asked about the huge cuts to council services and how they are causing the breakdown of our communities. Well, they really didn't like that. After the formal meeting, they then tried to tell me what I should ask at the Conveners' Group when it meets with the First Minister. I told them it is my prerogative as Convener to ask what I want. I will, of course, take account of their views but I won't be told what to do. I raised the issue of Bield closing care homes and they were totally opposed to us having an evidence session on this; 130 older people are about to lose their homes and they don't want it discussed.

In the fracking debate, all the SNP MSPs who haven't uttered a word against fracking are now gung-ho anti-frackers, because the moratorium has been extended. Totally shameless. The parliament voted to reject fracking and continue the moratorium. Oliver Mundell MSP broke to the Tory whip to support a ban. Good for him.

25 October A leaked paper about the future of the Fire and Rescue service has identified major job losses, station closures and changes to the role of firefighters. Post Grenfell this is a very big story.

26 October Audit Scotland published a report stating seven out of eight of the government's key health targets are not being met. It is a damning indictment.

Nominations were announced for the Scottish Politician of the Year Awards. I was nominated for Debater of the Year and Committee MSP of the Year. The Scottish Mesh Survivors were nominated for Campaign of the Year.

Anas Sarwar published his manifesto, saying in an email to party members he was going to deliver 'for the few not the many', instead of 'the many not the few'. Another balls-up.

At FMQs I asked Sturgeon about the cuts to the Fire Service. She really doesn't like being held to account. This was the exchange:

Neil Findlay (Lothian) (Lab)

Does the First Minister believe that cutting yet more firefighter posts and closing fire stations will a) make our communities safer or b) put more lives at risk? If she does not know the answer, she can have a guess.

The First Minister (Nicola Sturgeon)

Sometimes you only have to listen to Neil Findlay's tone to understand why Labour is in the dire straits that it is in. It is shockingly bad. First, I want to take this opportunity to thank our firemen and firewomen across the country for the essential and vital work that they do. It is in recognition of the importance of that work that the Scottish Government has this year increased the operational budget of the Scottish Fire and Rescue Service. Since reform, there have been no compulsory redundancies and no fire stations have closed. In fact, over the past year, 100 new firefighters have been recruited. However, like any other service in the public sector, the fire service cannot stand still when circumstances change. There are changing risks, changing patterns of demand and changing technology, and it is right that the fire service looks closely at how it deals with those changes. However, as it does so, its priority and the priority of this government is not only to protect the front line, but to enable our firefighters to deliver an even better service for the people of Scotland in the future.

28 October Earlier in the year the Royal Bank of Scotland closed their Whitburn branch. I asked them to pass the building over to the local food bank who are desperate for new premises. During a conference call with them today, it became clear they are not interested in this but will consider a financial donation. Not sure what this means but at least it might be something, we'll see.

Ballot papers are out today in the Scottish leadership election.

29 October The papers are full of lurid allegations of sexual abuse and assault being widespread at Westminster and Holyrood.

30 October Over to Stirling to the 'Rally for Richard' event. We had a big cast of speakers – Danielle Rowley MP, Leah Franchetti, Rhoda Grant MSP, Hugh Gaffney MP, Lynne Henderson of the PCS union and Zehyn Mohammed, a young activist. I spoke and then Richard came on. The supporters left happy.

31 October Sexual harassment stories are all over the media. There is supposed to be a list of 40 Tory MPs who are implicated, and a Labour activist has alleged she was raped at an event. There are said to be two complaints about an MSP.

Party leaders met today with the Presiding Officer to discuss how the parliament deals with these claims. There is a really strange atmosphere around the place.

At the committee today SNP members were still objecting to our short inquiry into Bield care home closures.

1 November Lots of names are being thrown about in relation to sexual harassment allegations. Tory Defence Secretary Michael Fallon has resigned because of past behaviour.

I spoke in the health debate today on the Audit Scotland report. Shona Robison tried to defend the government's record. It looks like she will be replaced soon, probably by Jeane Freeman.

2 November Met Mark McHugh, Ian Hodson and Jim Carlin from the Bakers' Union to discuss the McDonald's strike. I pledged to help in any way I can. They are doing great work with low paid workers.

Today the SNP published their tax plans. Paul Hutcheon in *The Herald* summed it up by saying it was 'not exactly Attlee 1945'. Quite.

The press pack are on the hunt for two SNP politicians who are alleged to have been involved in sexual harassment allegations.

3 November Visited Carmondean Health Centre to meet Dr Des Spence who runs Barclay Health Care. They are taking over failing GP practices and building themselves a chain. They have around five practices and are doing good work reorganising the way they do appointments and provide services. However, there are some things that don't sit well and I can't help but wonder if it was

'Virgin Health Care' or 'BUPA' how it would be perceived.

The sexual harassment allegations go on today with MPs Damian Green, Charlie Elphick, Michael Fallon, Kelvin Hopkins and Ivan Lewis all named in one story or another. Hopkins has been suspended by the Labour Party.

5 November Monica Lennon is on the front page of the *Sunday Mail* saying she was assaulted by a senior Labour Party figure prior to becoming an MSP.

SNP MSP Mark McDonald resigned as the Minister for Children and Young People for inappropriate behaviour. Willie Coffey MSP has been named as having been reported by a civil servant for his behaviour. Questions are being raised about what McDonald has done; all he has said publicly is his behaviour fell below the standard expected.

6 November Met with FBU officials today to discuss the Fire Service. Stations have already closed and jobs gone, with more losses to come. I gave a commitment to work with them.

Went to the Royal Society of Edinburgh dinner. I was the only Labour MSP there and what an interesting night it was. Lord this, Earl that, Lady the next thing were all there, the Scottish establishment in all its glory; professors, business people, charity leaders, etc, discussing how we build and grow the Scottish economy. When it came to questions it was all clubby business speak. I asked how can we talk about 'inclusive growth' when we have such gross inequality and see the appalling revelations contained in 'The Panama Papers?' I don't quite think it was what they wanted to hear but I was very pleased to have attended to see how their network interacts.

This is Living Wage Week, so I wrote to all the shops at Livingston shopping centre asking if they pay the living wage. Marks and Spencer and ASDA were the first to write back saying they pay it but didn't want to be registered Living Wage employers.

Kezia Dugdale has called for the resignation of the all-male Scottish Parliament Corporate Body. She seems to have forgotten that she appointed a male to it when she was leader.

7 November The Foreign Secretary Boris Johnson is in serious trouble. He made a statement saying a British woman being held in Iran was a 'trainee journalist' when she wasn't. The Iranians are saying that this is proof she was working against the government. He has put the woman in real danger.

Today, Nicola Sturgeon gave an apology to gay men who had been convicted when homosexuality was an offence. A number of the men were in the gallery to celebrate the announcement. It was very moving.

There was a security alert today as three packages of 'white powder' were delivered to Tory MSPs.

I hosted an event this evening with Aid & Abet. Kevin Neary and Donald Tumilovicz were there to speak about their experience of being involved with the police at a young age, going to prison, addiction and their eventual rehabilitation. It was very powerful.

8 November I convened a breakfast meeting with Alex Neil, Alex Cole-Hamilton, Oliver Mundell and John Finnie to discuss drugs policy. All of us believe the current system is not working and want to see change. We discussed how we might work together on this.

9 November The train to Edinburgh was packed this morning and had only three carriages. The service is getting worse.

To FMQs Jackie Baillie is leading as Alex Rowley is off, following allegations about his private life. She asked how it could be right that Mark McDonald has resigned as a Minister but remains an MSP. I have disliked McDonald from the day I came into parliament, but being tried by media speculation before there has been any due process is unfair both to the victim and alleged perpetrator. This is an issue that must be taken very seriously and dealt with properly.

Spoke to committee clerks today who are really concerned at how one of the committee members is behaving. They find the member's attitude aggressive, with officials being attacked just for doing their job. The clerks do a very good job and are politically neutral. I will raise this on Tuesday at the committee.

10 November Gordon Brown said on the *Today* programme that Jeremy Corbyn 'was a phenomenon' and that he 'was right on many issues'. Interesting.

13 November Up at 6am to do a *Good Morning Scotland* interview on social care budgets, then into parliament to do more interviews.

Disability charity Inclusion Scotland wants me to take a student on a three-month paid internship. The candidates are really good, it will be difficult to pick from them.

14 November At the committee I raised the issue of members being respectful to staff. The person this was aimed at looked as though they had just swallowed a wasp.

15 November Today a newspaper ran a story about Alex Rowley MSP. It was a one-sided story about relationship breakdown from an ex-partner painting Alex in the worst light. The reality is relationships are messy and things can get acrimonious when they end. Alex has referred himself to the Labour Party to investigate and has stood down temporarily as Deputy Leader. Within a few hours the 'ever supportive' Kezia Dugdale released a press statement saying if she was still leader she would have suspended him. So, irrespective of what has or has not happened and with no investigation, she would immediately have suspended him for a relationship having gone wrong. It must be great to live in a perfect world like that of the saintly Ms Dugdale.

I emailed James Kelly, the party's Parliamentary Party Business Manager, raising my concerns about the handling of this case. No one has given any thought to the impact on Alex or his wellbeing. Have they forgotten what happened to Carl Sargeant, the Welsh government minister who took his own life following allegations made against him?

16 November To Edinburgh Castle for the march to parliament in support of the BiFab workers. The Fife company is capable of doing wind farm fabrication work, but it is all going overseas. The business is about to go into administration. With 1,400 jobs at stake, closure would be a disaster for a place like Methil.

To Prestonfield Hotel for the Scottish Politician of the Year event. I was nominated in two categories but didn't win either. Ruth Davidson won the main award for the second year in a row. It was an enjoyable night.

18 November Got up this morning to a text from a journalist which I thought was a joke, I really did. But apparently Kezia Dugdale is going on *I'm a Celebrity get me out of here*. I shit you not. We are coming up to the budget, public services are under massive pressure, poverty and inequality are causing huge suffering and a Labour MSP is pissing off to Australia during parliamentary time to eat kangaroo tadgers with a bunch of has-beens and wannabes. She will of course be getting handsomely paid for her 'troubles'. This announcement has been deliberately timed to undermine the announcement of the new Scottish leader, which is this morning. The clearest indication that Richard is going to win.

Over to Glasgow Science Centre for the leadership announcement. I wrote my prediction down on a piece of paper: 55 per cent for Richard and 45 per cent for Anas. All the campaign team were there.

When the result was announced it was 57 per cent for Richard and 43 per cent for Anas, a fantastic result. Richard gave an excellent, passionate, gracious victory speech.

Afterwards I gave a number of media interviews saying I hoped this result would now help rebuild the Labour Party's fortunes.

We then went to the pub for a celebration. Richard came in and thanked the team and left for his first visit as leader to the BiFab plant to show his support and donate a £500 cheque to the workers.

Richard's win is an opportunity to move away from the failed strategy of recent years. If handled right, we can now provide a radical alternative to the SNP and shake off the disastrous Better Together legacy. Richard and Jeremy will work together in a more coherent way than under Dugdale, who hated everything Corbyn stood for.

Richard has some big decisions to make very quickly but he must not make the same big mistake as Jeremy did of trying to keep his harshest critics close.

Predictably, his victory is being overshadowed by *the I'm a Celebrity* fiasco. Richard's first action will have to be to suspend her.

19 November Up early to do *Sunday Politics* with Gordon Brewer. He covered Richard's victory and what it might mean for Scottish Labour, the Alex Rowley situation and Kezia Dugdale's impending 'holiday' in Australia. I told him I found it 'utterly ludicrous' that she would do this. I would not demean myself by saying anything different. The newspapers are full of it and even her political allies Blair McDougall, Michael Marra, Daniel Johnson and Leah Franchetti were critical.

21 October At the Health and Sport Committee we heard from a range of health professionals about the impact of the lack of staffing and resources on morale and patient care. We hear this time and again.

To the Labour Group meeting where a discussion about Kezia Dugdale's jaunt took place. Even her close allies like Ian Gray were very angry. The decision was not to suspend her but to wait until she comes back so she can face the music. Given that this was an open and shut case with no credible reason for going and that she did not have permission from the Business Manager I wanted her suspended immediately. Not doing so shows weakness.

I spoke to a woman whose son has Asperger's and is desperate for a job. He was previously taken on at a B&M store and given a 3 day trial after which he was told he didn't get the job and he would receive no pay for his trial. How can they get away with this? I spoke to some media contacts who are going to run a story to highlight this injustice. I also contacted ASDA to see if they can help find this man a job.

In the evening, I hosted Elaine Miller's comedy show about pelvic floor health. She was very funny and got across a very serious subject in a fun way.

22 November Drafted a letter to the Scottish Futures Forum calling for a major piece of research on drugs policy. I got a cross party group of MSPs to sign up along with former Presiding Officers David Steele and George Reid.

23 November To the Petitions Committee to support my constituent Emma McDonald with her petition to regulate family contact centres. Emma is a Church of Scotland minister who went through hell with an ex-partner and then with access arrangements to her children arranged through a family contact centre. The committee will look into these issues.

It was Richard's first FMQs and he led on cuts to Fire Services. He was assured and confident, a decent debut. I raised the St John's Accident and Emergency department where the lack of staffing is causing very long waiting times.

Lesley Brennan has been appointed as Richard's Chief of Staff which is a good appointment, but he must also take on Tommy Kane who is strategic, politically astute and well connected, and Simon Fletcher who is a good all round strategist. It would be a big mistake not to.

24 November Met with West Lothian Council about complaints from staff about violence in schools. I have had teachers and classroom assistants come to me about being assaulted every day by pupils. Some children need a lot of support; however, no one should go to work expecting to be assaulted.

26 November To St Luke's in the East End of Glasgow for 'The Rally for Real Change' with Jeremy Corbyn, Richard Leonard, Stephen Wright, Becci Wallace and Jim Monaghan. Lots of new people in attendance and a real buzz around the place.

I heard from a constituent tonight that Gordon Dewar, the Chief Executive of Edinburgh Airport, who I have clashed with over airport expansion, spoke at a meeting of the West Lothian Chamber of Commerce and made a series of inappropriate 'jokes'. He referred to people traveling from Glasgow to Edinburgh by train as being on the 'Whoreient Express', said public sector workers' sons and daughters 'smoked and drank Buckfast' and mentioned me as someone who would give him a warm welcome in West Lothian. None of this is surprising.

27 November Spoke to ASDA to see if they would take on a young man who was treated badly by B&M stores. They are interested in helping, I really hope they can.

28 November To the health committee for a session on NHS Governance with National Clinical Director Jason Leitch and others. All were defending their territory. The NHS is cluttered with so many levels of bureaucracy, there must be a better way to ensure scrutiny, democracy and accountability. NHS Lothian Board papers often run to over 500 pages, there is no way board members read them all. Officials know this and can hide bad news. This is not scrutiny.

Good news today is that Michael Sharpe has been appointed to head up the Labour Support Unit that carries out our research. Simon Fletcher is doing a communications and campaigning role. Frustratingly, I haven't had a conversation with Richard since he took over.

Watched a bit of *I'm a Celebrity Get me Out of Here*, as I suspected Kezia Dugdale is making zero impact. She has nothing to say and comes over as being pretty dull, she is 3/1 with the bookies to go out first.

29 November Got a call from a journalist. He has a story about Underbelly, the company who run the Edinburgh Hogmanay event recruiting 300 people to work as 'Volunteers.' They will work the night shift for nothing, despite tickets

being £26.00 and 50,000 people are likely to attend. What a brass neck they have. I lodged a motion on this and there was a lot of media interest so I did a few TV interviews and gave quotes to the press. It is a reflection on the nature of our economy that a very profitable organisation, running such a high profile event, thinks that they can get away with ripping off workers by dressing it up as 'volunteering'.

Later, I spoke in the debate on GP practices, raising the fact that out of 122 practices in Lothian 57 have closed their list to new patients. The government took a pounding from all sides but their little helpers in the Green Party once again bailed them out by abstaining in the vote, allowing the government motion to pass.

Just before the debate, Michael Matheson, the Justice Minister, was forced to make a statement on Police Scotland. This follows a series of resignations and suspensions within the organisation including that of Chief Constable Phil Gormley and his Deputy.

Got a call from Paul Hutcheon at *The Herald*. He has been informed of Gordon Dewar's comments from the Chamber of Commerce event and is running a story on them.

30 November Mum's 78th birthday today, can't quite believe it; she is in good health, her mobility is still OK and she is very sharp.

Got word from ASDA saying they can't help the young man with Asperger's with a job before Christmas, which is very disappointing, but they will look at it afterwards.

Got a response back from the Futures Forum. Looks like they are going to do the work on drugs policy. Good news.

Heard today Alan Roden has gone out to Australia to greet Kezia Dugdale as she gets turfed out of the jungle, which from her performances appears imminent. I also heard today that she asked Jeremy Corbyn to make a video urging people to vote for her. I thought this was a wind-up but alas, no! She asked the person she repeatedly attacked and undermined to endorse her ludicrous participation in this charade. The plot has been well and truly lost.

2 December *The Herald* is running a story saying Anas Sarwar's register of interests shows he accepted £80,000 towards his failed leadership bid. Apparently, half came from Kasim Gulzar, who runs a string of pharmacies with Mr Sarwar's brother. The other £40,000 came from an international paper business.

3 December Today is my daughter Chloe's last day working as a cleaner at St John's Hospital. It has been a great experience for her. Now she has qualified as an Occupational Therapist.

Theresa May is under pressure over Brexit with 30 MPs and right-wing businesspeople attacking her.

Damian Green MP is in the news about allegations of porn on his computer.

The Gordon Dewar story is in *The Herald* as is the story about footballer David Goodwillie, who in a civil case, three judges said raped my constituent, Denise Claire. I have been supporting Denise for years in her attempt to secure justice.

Tonight, Kezia Dugdale was voted off and was met by a beaming Alan Roden as she left. The press will now attack her as she has served her usefulness to them.

4 December Met with West Lothian Council to discuss homelessness provision; meanwhile, on the other side of the world, my Lothian MSP colleague Kezia Dugdale drinks cocktails at the Versace Hotel.

Former MP for Lanark Jimmy Hood died today aged 69. Jimmy was a miners' leader during the strike before entering parliament in 1987. He was a big solid, decent, working-class man.

5 December Ayrshire and Arran Health Board senior officers came before the Health Committee for their performance report today. The bullshit meter was off the Richter scale, they couldn't answer the simplest of questions.

NHS Lothian have been caught again manipulating waiting times targets across their hospital sites.

We had a chamber debate on the mesh petition. Johann Lamont as Chair of the Committee led and was excellent, setting out the evidence they have taken and the powerful testimony of the Scottish Mesh Survivors and others. There were excellent speeches from Jackson Carlaw, Alex Neil, Alison Johnstone, Alex Cole-Hamilton and Anas Sarwar. The Minister Shona Robison said nothing new. I put forward a number of ideas about how we should progress whilst maintaining the ban. I said if the government doesn't act we will bring forward a political motion to unite the opposition and force the government into action. Afterwards I spoke to the mesh women who came in for the debate. They were really angry at Shona Robison's performance and will pile on the pressure for action.

To Blackwell's bookshop in Edinburgh to do an interview and Q&A with Henry McLeish. He has written a book called *Citizens United* about Trump, the EU, Brexit and disenchantment in the political process. I get on fine with him but he is a bit of a strange guy.

The DUP scuppered Theresa May's plans for customs arrangements for Northern Ireland. May thought she had the EU, Republic of Ireland and the DUP on board, however the DUP, given their past experience in the Northern Ireland peace process, are some of the most experienced and hard negotiators out there and have the government over a barrel.

6 December I went to West Lothian Council to speak to the Council leader about the latest round of spending cuts imposed by the Scottish Government. I asked for information on the list of cuts and was astonished to be told these were confidential and that officials have advised he cannot share them with anyone. He seems to forget he runs the Council not Council officers. I offered to help raise issues in parliament but got nowhere. It was a complete waste of time.

To the St James Centre development in central Edinburgh for a Blacklist Support Group demonstration against contractor Laing O'Rourke, who are implicated in the construction blacklisting scandal. This is where companies refuse to employ people because of their trade union or political activities.

Still not had a conversation with Richard Leonard about his plans but I heard today Kezia Dugdale has said she will accept a place in the Shadow Cabinet if offered one. What a brass neck.

7 December The Brexit shambles continues for the Tories, the DUP are milking it for all its worth.

At FMQs the Tories led on the 'Named Person' legislation which is in trouble.

Late in the afternoon I got a call from Richard Leonard. I made it crystal clear I was unhappy. I have given him more support than anyone during the campaign and yet he hasn't uttered a word to me for three weeks. I gave him a long list of things he must do quickly, including appointing the right team around him, not giving his opponents in the party a position, appointing a new team at party headquarters and taking control of staffing appointments in the parliamentary team. I said he must listen to advice from those who support him and act upon it. He then asked what role I wanted. The reality is I have never asked any Labour leader for anything and won't start now. I really hope he listens otherwise he will make all the same mistakes Jeremy did.

8 December Following conversations with local firefighters I arranged to meet them at Livingston Fire Station. The Fire service management didn't want the meeting to take place and the Firefighters who asked me were sent an email advising them they shouldn't have invited me.

During the meeting I heard that about 100 fire pumps across the country are out of action because of a lack of staff, shift rotas that cannot be covered, job losses and station closures.

I then met with the Deputy Fire Chief and the Fire Board Chair, former Labour Councillor Pat Watters. They spoke at me for about 45 minutes telling me why there was no alternative, how the claims made by the firefighters were not true and everything would be fine if they were allowed to implement their plan.

10 December Caught the overnight sleeper to London.

Over to the House of Commons to meet with some of Corbyn's senior advisers then to the Scotland Office to join a delegation to meet David Mundell about the relocation of the Bathgate tax office. Some couldn't make it because of the flight cancellations so it was only Hannah Bardell MP, Alan Hamilton from the PCS union and me. We put a very strong case for scrapping this uneconomical and illogical move that will take 1,200 jobs from West Lothian and force workers to travel into the centre of Edinburgh. Mundell said he would speak to the council and others but it was a tick-box exercise; they are determined to push ahead with this daft plan.

Back over to the Commons for the Corbyn 'Core Group' Christmas drinks reception. Spoke to MPs Dennis Skinner, John McDonnell, Ian Lavery, Kate Osamor, Angela Rayner and Andy McDonald, among others. Richard Leonard appeared, having just addressed the PLP meeting.

Over to Euston for the sleeper back home.

11 December Bield Housing Association's Chief Officer came before the Health Committee to discuss care home closures. We had a round table discussion on the sector, where profits are made by keeping the pay and conditions of staff low and contracts insecure. How can we allow this to be the foundation of how we care for the elderly and vulnerable?

The Labour Group meeting discussed the possibility of disciplinary action against Kezia Dugdale. I would suspend her but I know they will do nothing.

13 December Went to St John's with my wife Fiona, for her annual check-up with Dr Barber following breast cancer. All fine – delighted.

The Tories held a debate on taxation. Their speakers made the most dreadful, right-wing speeches on the need for low taxes, without a single word of compassion for those suffering because of their austerity agenda.

14 December I spoke in the lunchtime members' debate on Royal Bank of Scotland closures. I got all of 90 seconds to speak – what a joke. This is where the parliament is so inflexible.

RBS were attacked savagely from all sides. It is outrageous that only a few years ago they received a massive taxpayer bailout and now they are decimating the branch network.

I met with Claudia Beamish MSP, Elaine Smith MSP, Lesley Brennan and Richard Leonard. We advised him to get his act together and sort out his Shadow Cabinet and impose himself on the Parliamentary Group.

16 December Up for a campaign session with hospitality rights campaign group 'Better than zero' at Livingston shopping centre. We had a big turn out from Labour activists.

Alex Rowley resigned as Deputy Leader today. He had referred himself to Labour's NEC but they could not progress the case, as the woman who made allegations refused to provide information or engage with the process so there was no evidence for the NEC to look at. I feel for him personally, as had there been an inquiry he could have defended charges. Lesley Laird has been appointed temporarily.

I heard today Anas Sarwar spent £125,000 on his leadership campaign – that works out about £16 a vote. When I stood, I spent £26,000 in total and felt embarrassed about spending so much.

The newspapers are full of Kezia Dugdale's claim she is being shunned by the party, all because no one sat next to her at FMQs. For heaven's sake we are not in primary school.

17 December In Derek MacKay's tax plans, people earning between £45k and £55k will get a tax cut – very progressive.

I got a phone call from Richard Leonard, who wants me to lead on party campaigns, policy development and Brexit. Brexit? And I'm supposed to be one of his pals! Oh joy. He is keeping Ian Gray, Jackie Baillie and Anas Sarwar in his team. Now, I understand that he doesn't have much to work with in terms of numbers but he is making the exact same mistake as Jeremy Corbyn in trying to keep his internal opponents close. This will come back and take a big chunk out of his arse.

Apparently, Kezia Dugdale is unhappy that I am doing Brexit, what a shame.

19 December After the Labour Group meeting the new Shadow Cabinet came together for a photo call – Jackie Baillie remains in the Economy role and Anas Sarwar Health, two big mistakes. I will shadow Mike Russell on Brexit and be able to develop campaigns.

Richard had limited choices with only 23 MSPs to work with but handing the key roles on the economy and health to Baillie and Sarwar is not clever. As we left the Shadow Cabinet I was doorstepped by the media asking how I voted in the EU referendum. I voted remain and told them so. I have never hidden the fact that I was very conflicted by the EU vote. I loathed what the EU did to the Greeks and have major concerns about the power of the European Central Bank. I hate the lack of democracy and accountability and always thought that if there was a referendum I would vote leave but was swayed at the very last moment to vote remain by Farage's racism and the Leave campaign's vile pronouncements.

Went over to the *Holyrood Magazine* Christmas drinks reception. Mike Russell came over and offered his 'congratulations' on my new role shadowing him adding, half-jokingly, he was 'not looking forward to it.' I replied, 'The feeling is mutual, Michael.' We had a bit of a laugh about it. I will actually enjoy being back up against him. He does love himself; someone once said he had one ambition and that was to 'die in his own arms'.

December 20 Wrote a column for the *Scotsman* on drugs and the need for a national debate on policy reform. Met Carole Ewart from the Campaign for Freedom of Information to discuss the Scottish Government's appalling record on FOI and withholding information, it is an issue I have a lot of interest in, the government really are 'at it'.

Took part in a members debate on Drug and Alcohol deaths led by Monica Lennon, whose father died following his struggle with alcohol. I called for an end to the failed war on drugs.

24 December Spent the day getting ready for Christmas. Went to mass at Addiewell with Fiona before she went out on night shift at the hospital.

25 December Up early to do as much Christmas dinner preparation as possible. Had the family over for breakfast.

All the gang came round for dinner at 3.30pm, 12 in total. It was brilliant. We had food, games, jokes, dancing, singing and plenty of drinks until 4am.

2018

THIS WAS A year dominated by Brexit. The UK Prime Minister Theresa May found herself in an impossible situation. Without a parliamentary majority, she was held ransom by the combined forces of Democratic Unionist Party, who held the balance of power, and the obsessive Brexiteers in the European Research Group of Tory MPs. With every day that passed her plight got worse, something had to give.

Meanwhile, Scots had voted 62 per cent to 38 per cent to remain in the EU. The SNP saw Brexit as a strategic opportunity to build support for independence and they used government time in the Scottish Parliament to hold debate after debate to expose what they saw as the folly of Brexit and promote the advantages of EU membership. As Scottish Labour's Brexit spokesperson, I was involved in many of these debates and cross-party discussions.

While the SNP successfully exploited the Brexit chaos, it soon became embroiled in its own internal crisis with the arrest of former First Minister Alex Salmond on a series of sexual assault charges.

Like the Tories, Brexit caused major headaches for the Labour Party. Internal opponents of Jeremy Corbyn used it and the issue of antisemitism to stoke the flames of division in an attempt to oust him. Similar forces in Scotland cranked up the pressure on Richard Leonard.

2018 was a year of major political turmoil on many fronts.

4 January I did an interview with Andrew Kerr of the BBC on Brexit.

5 January – Shadow Cabinet meeting. James Kelly and Lesley Brennan gave presentations on the budget strategy, Land Value Tax, Tourist Tax, Wealth Tax and more. There followed a good, healthy and generally positive discussion.

6 January *The Herald* ran a story on my call for an inquiry into the policing of the miners' strike in Scotland. It is a year since I went to meet the Justice Secretary to make the case for an inquiry. We still haven't had a reply, so I am going to turn up the pressure.

Jeremy Corbyn refused an SNP invite to attend a Brexit summit. It was of course a trap so he was right not to attend.

7 January Theresa May's reshuffle today had a touch of Laurel and Hardy about it. Jeremy Hunt refused to move from Health, Justine Greening refused to go to the DWP, so Esther McVey was brought back. The entire thing was a PR disaster.

8 January To parliament for my final session as chair of the Health Committee as my new duties will see me with other responsibilities. I don't really like chairing meetings but I have grown into it and enjoyed getting stuck into this hugely important area of work. The committee has been pretty effective and I have always ensured every member got their say. We made a real impact on child protection in sport, prison health care and NHS governance. I regret the lack of progress on social care and health inequalities – these are the biggest issues the country faces.

To the Labour Group meeting, where I led the discussion on Brexit. Jackie Baillie and Anas Sarwar are trying to push us into taking a pro single market position, but I rejected this, calling for us to retain a noncommittal position until we see how the Brexit discussions with the EU develop.

The debate itself was good-natured enough but Brexit will run and run and run and run.

10 January Alison Johnstone, Alex Cole-Hamilton and I met with the Scottish Futures Forum to discuss the piece of work we want them to do on drugs.

Met with Clerks to the Delegated Powers Committee. I will be going onto this committee as it will be examining subordinate legislation relating to Brexit. I have to say, this committee is the Gulag of parliament. It will be pretty dire.

Richard Leonard sacked Neil Bibby MSP from his team today. He threw the toys out of the pram because he was asked to sit on the Environment Committee and refused to move from his current committee.

Kezia Dugdale was nominated as the Labour representative on the Corporate Body tonight. These appointments normally go through on the nod. Had I not been on the front bench, I might have voted against as I don't see why someone who has taken the piss by waltzing off to Australia for three weeks when parliament was sitting should sit on its Corporate Body. When it came to the vote, Linda Fabiani, Christine Grahame and Rona Mckay voted against. I admire them for doing so.

11 January Met Morag Treanor from Stirling University, who has written an excellent report on the myth that 'working class people have a poverty of ambition'. Her findings completely chime with what I see in my community. I have asked her to do an event in parliament.

At FMQs today I raised the fact that it has been 200 days since St John's children's ward was affected by closure.

Neil Findlay (Lothian) (Lab)

This month, the children's ward at St John's hospital will have been closed to in-patients out of hours for more than 200 days. When will it reopen as a 24/7 service?

The First Minister (Nicola Sturgeon)

It will reopen as soon as possible. It is, of course, a matter of regret that the situation – which is to ensure safety for patients – has arisen. Patient safety is vitally important for all patients but all of us would accept that it is particularly important for children. As soon as the recruitment challenges have been addressed – efforts are under way right now to recruit into that ward – the ward will reopen. Neil Findlay previously used to say that our plan was to close the ward permanently. That was not the case. We are determined to make sure that the ward remains open to serve patients in West Lothian, and I look forward to it being open properly as soon as possible.

12 January Today the *Daily Record* had a go at me over Brexit. Andy Philip ran a straight story following his interview with me, but the headline said 'Labour's Ludicrous Stance Over Brexit', with the editorial having a real go. This is without a doubt the influence of Kezia Dugdale and Alan Roden, who are very close to the political editor David Clegg. Kezia is also a *Record* columnist.

The newspapers are reporting that for her jungle capers Kezia Dugdale was paid £70,000, plus £15,000 in flights, hotels and expenses, of which she has donated just £7,500 to charity.

13 January To UNISON headquarters in Glasgow for the 'Save our Bield' public meeting. Lots of families were there representing residents who are being forced out. There is a lot of anger. It is a scandal what is happening.

14 January Nicola Sturgeon was on the *Andrew Marr Show* raising independence again. Jim Sillars attacked her in today's papers. There are clearly tensions in the SNP.

15 January Today construction giant Carillion went into liquidation with 20,000 jobs at risk. This exposes the scam of privatisation. The directors will waltz off with their pockets full and pensions intact, the workers face the dole. Business as usual in corporate Britain.

Went over to West Lothian Council for a cross-party meeting with David Mundell about the Tax Office closures. Councillors, Senior officers and MSPs were there but there was no sign of local MP Martyn Day who has been posted missing all the way through the campaign.

The Scottish Government produced an economic impact assessment of Brexit options, including Single Market membership, a trade deal, or no deal. Of course, Single Market membership is presented as the least damaging option. This is not really about the EU, it is about their independence ambitions.

I met with representatives from the charity Fair Share to discuss a possible Members' Bill on food waste. I have been thinking of introducing legislation similar to what has been done in France, where supermarkets and food producers over a certain size must donate their surplus food for either human consumption, animal feed or to burn for energy. We could do this here.

16 January Went to the first meeting of the Delegated Powers and Law Reform Committee – it was crushingly dull.

To London for a round of meetings, first with Lesley Laird MP and then with Keir Starmer MP, to discuss Brexit. I asked Keir Starmer to come to Scotland as soon as possible.

17 January Met with MPs Ian Lavery and Andrew Gwynne, the Labour election coordinators. We spoke about the forthcoming campaign and made a plea for cash to be directed to Scotland, where we have 20 target seats. Both were very receptive to our appeal. They also get it in relation to the Leave areas in the north of England. These areas are going to be key at the election.

Had a good meeting with the Head of Policy, Andrew Fisher, to discuss policy support in Scotland and the need to build relations between the UK and Scottish policy team. John McDonnell took us through investment plans and the £40 billion additional cash that would come to Scotland from a National Investment Bank and National Infrastructure Fund. This is a huge commitment and could be transformative for the Scottish economy.

18 January Got into parliament just in time for FMQs. The Tories gave Sturgeon a torrid time on Police Scotland and the resignation of the Chief Constable.

Richard did really well raising the case of a 94-year-old woman whose Bield care home is to close.

Last week I sent a party email to all MSPs by mistake – it was meant for only Labour MSPs. Someone has reported me to the parliament for using parliamentary resources for a party email. I put my hand up right away and admitted my mistake. I am not the first to have done so and won't be the last. A report will now go to the Corporate Body.

19 November NHS Lothian confirmed that since 7 July, 414 children have had to be transferred up to 30 miles out of hours to Edinburgh Sick Kids hospital instead of going locally to St John's; 370 of these children had to be admitted. This is the reality of how the closure of the ward affects families.

Over to St John's for a demonstration. About 50 people came along in the freezing weather. Two parents spoke about their experience and the need for the service. Our call for the media to attend went well with excellent coverage on radio and in the local and national press. All very worthwhile to keep the pressure on the government to get this sorted out.

21 January Watched John McDonnell on Andrew Marr, he was clear, confident and relaxed.

22 January My Aunty Rose died today, she was 74 and had been unwell for a while. She suffered from poor health all her adult life.

At my surgery tonight I spoke to a young woman being threatened with the sack because she is expecting a baby. How is this still going on in this day and age?

Had a full day exchanging very tetchy texts with Ian Murray about Brexit and the single market, he really is so bloody arrogant. He hates Corbyn and McDonnell and attacks anyone associated with them.

23 January At the Labour Group meeting, Jackie Baillie, Anas Sarwar, Jenny Marra, Kezia Dugdale raised the Deputy Leadership vacancy and the place for a group member on the Scottish Executive of the Labour Party, there is clearly a move on.

Shona Robison made a statement about the closure of the children's ward at the RAH hospital in Paisley. Local SNP MSPs Tom Arthur and George Adam have said absolutely nothing.

I asked her this:

> In 2016, Nicola Sturgeon said live on TV during an election debate that there were no plans to close the children's ward at the RAH in Paisley. For six years, there have been staffing problems on top of staffing problems at the children's ward at St John's in Livingston, with assurances being given that it would not be closed. How can parents, children,

grandparents and local people who joined me on Friday at a protest at St John's believe a word that the Cabinet Secretary or the First Minister says about the future of children's services in Livingston, given their blatant betrayal of the people of Paisley?

This was Shona Robison's reply:

Neil Findlay would be better focusing on supporting his local hospital in its recruitment campaign than on scaremongering, which could put people off. It is a serious point: are doctors who are considering whether to apply for a post that covers St John's likely to be encouraged by what Neil Findlay is saying? I suggest that he should be very careful and should encourage people to apply for the posts rather than doing the opposite. I am sure that the clinicians at St John's would want him to do that, too.

Desperate stuff.

Also spoke in a members' debate on unpaid trial shifts, raising the case of the young man who worked for nothing at the B&M store and the results of a survey of young people I carried out showing the exploitative nature of work for so many young workers.

24 January I met with Richard Leonard and his Chief of Staff, Lesley Brennan, and made it crystal clear to them that we need to be organised and up for it or the right wing within the party and the parliamentary group will kill us. I am not sure he gets it!

I heard that Jackie Baillie and Anas Sarwar are trying to get Monica Lennon off the party's powerful Scottish Executive Committee.

25 January James Kelly led a debate on the Offensive Behaviour at Football Repeal Bill. His speech was very good and took the right tone. There were excellent contributions from Mary Fee, John Finnie and Johann Lamont.

In my speech I said:

As we debate the repeal of the 2012 act, my main reasons for supporting James Kelly's proposals are not rooted in football; they are rooted in defending the rights of my constituents and the rights of my class.

Ever since the 2012 act was introduced, the response from fans, the legal profession and rights groups have been negative and persistent. I do not support the repeal of the act for opposition's sake; it is about defending the rights of people who choose to go to watch a sport, but have their rights removed for doing so.

As it stands, the 2012 act in the main criminalises young working-class men because of something that they do inside, or on the way to, a football match, but that very same behaviour in other circumstances would either go unpunished or be dealt with under a different law.'

For the SNP James Dornan and George Adam were woeful. Adam said only songs about football should be sung at football so no 'Sunshine on Leith,' 'You'll Never Walk Alone' or 'Penny Arcade', because the bold George clearly finds The Proclaimers, Gerry and the Pacemakers and Roy Orbison offensive.

At the end MSPs voted 64-61 to support James Kelly's proposal.

I met with Michael Clancy of the Law Society to discuss Brexit. I really like him. He is a very straightforward guy with great insight and wisdom.

After the Shadow Cabinet, Patrick Harvie, Willie Rennie, Jackson Carlaw and I met with Mike Russell about Brexit. He said he will brief us regularly on issues and is trying to come over all statesmanlike.

I then met David Martin, who has been an MEP since 1984, the second-longest serving in Brussels. I have met him many times over the years and we get along fine. David is 100 per cent Europhile and has given 28 years of his working life to the EU, he really believes in it. We had a good discussion about a lot of things and agreed to keep in touch.

26 January I attended West Lothian Council's very moving Holocaust Memorial Day Service at Howden Park Centre.

To Hearts Football Club for the Edinburgh South Labour Party Burns supper. I had been invited by Nigel Griffiths, the former MP. Emily Thornberry spoke and was in good form, giving a very strong positive take on Jeremy Corbyn's policy agenda. Ian Murray looked very glum during it. He later came up to me and said loudly so the people at the table could hear: 'I didn't see you come. We are all pals together, good to see you, we are all pals together!' – Aye that'll be right!

29 January I spoke to Vince Mills from the Campaign for Socialism, who told me today that his wife, Pauline Bryan, has been asked by Jeremy Corbyn to go into the House of Lords. Well, that is remarkable. Pauline is an uncompromising socialist and would be a great asset. She will argue from the outset that the Lords should be scrapped. The Scottish Group in the Lords will hate this. The likes of Lord George Foulkes will be spitting mad. I am so pleased.

I went to the West Lothian Drug and Alcohol project to meet with seven drug users who are going through treatment. We had a very frank and open discussion. One man who has taken heroin for 25 years since being made redundant spoke of how he wants off methadone but his GP believes that being crime-free and illicit-drug-free is success. He wants to be free of all drugs. All spoke of getting good support at the beginning then after time it disappears. Others spoke of loneliness. One said no one wants to invite an addict round for dinner or to a party to meet new friends, do they? They spoke of how widely drugs are available. A mother spoke of the heartbreak her drug-using daughter has brought to the family. All raised the need for mental health support, stigma, the prevalence of counterfeit street drugs and how dealers infiltrate support groups and deal outside chemists.

It was a powerful, fascinating and challenging meeting which had a profound impact on me. I gave them a commitment to pursue these issues and I will.

Anas Sarwar said today that a Labour council leader told him 'Scotland wouldn't vote for a brown, Muslim Paki.' Appalling.

31 January Met with Helen Martin of the STUC to discuss Brexit. Their position is very similar to the Labour position.

I went into the chamber for the budget debate. The Green party has sold out again, doing a shitty wee deal to ensure the budget passes.

The Sarwar racism story runs and runs with a South Lanarkshire councillor outed as the person who made the alleged comments.

1 February To St John Ogilvie chapel in Wester Hailes for my Aunty Rose's funeral. My cousin Pat, who is a priest, did the service. It was a small gathering but Pat in his inimitable style lightened the mood. Rose is now at peace.

I heard today that Michael Mathieson is to make a statement on Wednesday about the review of the conduct of undercover police officers. I campaigned for a public inquiry into the role of undercover officers in Scotland but the review was the government's way of pretending they were doing something. It will be a sham, I am absolutely confident of that.

2 February Watched *Politics Scotland* – Ian Blackford couldn't bring himself to support a second referendum on Brexit.

4 February I spoke to my constituent Janice McSeveney, whose son Scott was one of a number of babies who died very young and whose body was used for medical research without the consent of parents. A friend came with her and the story she told was even more shocking. She said her son's coffin was exhumed when similar concerns were raised, only for the family to find that no bones were in it. Absolutely horrific. Janice is convinced her son's organs were taken without her consent. I was stunned by what they told me, it is truly awful.

Anas Sarwar got the *Daily Record* to publish an eight-point plan on how to deal with racism, claiming the Labour Party is going backwards on race issues.

7 February A small group of MSPs who support Richard got together. Some said that Sarwar feels hurt and wounded and is hitting out in frustration at Richard at every opportunity and that Alan Roden and Kezia Dugdale are helping.

Michael Matheson made a statement on undercover policing in Scotland. As expected, he will not initiate a public inquiry despite one being under way in England and Wales. This leaves Scottish social justice campaigners as the only people on the mainland UK not to have access to an inquiry. The review is a whitewash with Police Scotland claiming they did not keep social justice campaigners under surveillance. Of course they didn't. Police Scotland has only existed for the last few years but the report says nothing about the legacy forces. There was little recognition of the wrongs committed by undercover officers from elsewhere in the UK operating here We know things happened during the G8 summit at Gleneagles and it is inconceivable that groups such as the Anti-poll tax Federation, trade unions, CND, the miners and others were not kept under surveillance.

At the evening Labour Group meeting on Brexit I presented a paper setting out our position:

1) Respect the result of the referendum

2) We leave the EU

3) The treaties end

4) We campaign for the best new deal possible on our terms.

I also highlighted areas of policy we want to develop including the impact on Scotland's environment, consumers, workers and communities.

When we went into discussion, Kezia Dugdale claimed she resigned as leader because of Jeremy Corbyn's position on Brexit. Previously, she said it was because of the impact of losing a close friend, then she said it was a left-wing coup against her, then it was because she wanted her life back, now it is Brexit. She also said she was now supporting a second referendum, which is extraordinary given that she has repeatedly opposed a second independence referendum. We then had Daniel Johnson doing Ian Murray's bidding and Anas Sarwar using Brexit to attack Richard without actually having the bottle to mention him by name and all the while Jackie Baillie stirring the pot. I got support from Rhoda Grant, Elaine Smith and James Kelly but really what this is about is an organised attack on Leonard and Corbyn.

9 February Went to the UNITE the union Brexit conference in Glasgow. The speakers were Simon Dobbins, the international officer, Catherine Stihler MEP, Pat Rafferty and me. It was a very good meeting with around 70 shop stewards in attendance. The union has done over 20 different sectoral analyses, which is more than the UK government. There was a mixture of views from the stewards but it was a very mature and informed discussion.

11–18 February spent a week in Tenerife with Fiona.

19 February Met with Paul Sinclair and Richard Leonard to discuss how to approach First Minister's Questions. Sinclair is a right-winger bruiser. He and I disagree on most things but we have always been able to get on.

20 February Over to Clackmannanshire to help in the council by-election. In Alva, went to Keir Hardie Road, Mclean Place and Maxton Crescent. Sadly these streets weren't exactly a hotbed of socialism.

21 February What a farce, today MSPs were given timed slots of one hour to go into the library to read the UK government's Brexit analysis. We were only allowed to take handwritten notes, no photos and we couldn't share information. It was like something from *Yes Minister*. Someone stood watching over us all the time.

I spoke in the debate on St John's children's ward. Parents of children who have had to go to Edinburgh by taxis in the middle of night were in the gallery. This has gone on for six years and we are no nearer to it being sorted out. I did TV interviews afterwards.

22 February I took part in the government-led debate on Brexit, closing for our side. I argued for a flexible immigration policy that meets the needs of Scotland. Surprisingly, the best speech of the day came from Jackson Carlaw of the Tories. It was positive, humane and decent – completely unlike anything I have heard from any other Tory on immigration.

Today I heard Kezia Dugdale has made a complaint to Richard Leonard that Lesley Brennan and I are out to get her. It's pathetic.

I spoke to former *Daily Record* Editor Murray Foote regarding the director of communications job for the party, I hope he applies.

23 February Ian McNicol, General Secretary of the Labour Party, resigned tonight. This is good news as he was a real barrier to the changes Jeremy Corbyn wants to make.

Got a text from Mike Russell tonight to advise of the plans for a Continuity Bill to deal with Brexit issues. I agreed to speak to him on Monday.

Social media full of Pete Wishart and two MP colleagues attending the Brit awards instead of voting on the budget. They kid on they hate London and Westminster when in reality they all aboard the gravy train.

24 February To Penicuik for the by-election. John McDonnell came along. He told us that a Tory MP had settled with Jeremy Corbyn for a large sum to avoid a libel case. The money will be donated to a food bank in Tory's constituency.

The campaign team covered a huge area, an excellent morning.

26 February Jeremy Corbyn made a big speech on Brexit today in Coventry, committing Labour to a customs union and tariff free access to European markets. It got widespread coverage and the speech was welcomed by the CBI and the unions.

I got a phone call from Mike Russell regarding the Continuity Bill. The Tories are playing right into the hands of the SNP.

Today college lecturers went on strike over pensions.

The weather has taken a turn for the worse with the so-called Beast from the East coming with temperatures down to -10.

27 February Mike Russell sent me information on the Continuity Bill marked 'confidential'. I tried to send it to my researcher using my phone but instead managed to send it to everyone on the parliamentary email list. I immediately sent him an apology.

Just as we went into the chamber, the Presiding Officer said the proposed Continuity Bill does not have legal competency. The Welsh Assembly is doing a similar bill which has been judged to be competent. There is a lot of confusion around and questions about what should happen next. Russell says he can continue, despite the Presiding Officer's view. Well, they didn't do that with the Trade Union Bill. The question is, how can the Welsh do it but we can't? Labour cannot be seen to side with the Tories on this. In my contribution in the chamber, I attacked the Scottish Conservatives for failing to resolve this matter.

The 'Beast from the East' continues to batter the country with blizzards and freezing temperatures.

28 February Met to discuss our approach to the Continuity Bill, which the Scottish Government wants to pass as emergency legislation within three weeks. This is such an important piece of legislation, we should not be circumventing normal parliamentary conventions.

In the chamber the Lord Advocate was unimpressive, hesitant and dry, and failed to answer key questions. I raised concerns about the truncated timescale and lack of parliamentary scrutiny for such an important bill and urged the Scottish Government to return to the negotiating table and get this sorted out. Every time an opposition member raises legitimate questions, SNP backbenchers heckle and try to shout them down.

Former Prime Minister John Major put the boot into Theresa May and the extreme right-wingers in her party. Nadine Dorries MP called him a traitor. The civil war in the Conservative Party is raging. If only Labour can get its act together and show some unity.

The country is at a standstill due to snow and extreme temperatures.

1 March Major snowfall overnight and Edinburgh, I have never seen it so bad in the city centre.

Rhoda Grant and I met with Mike Russell. He gave us a long spiel about why the bill was an emergency, none of it very convincing. I pushed hard on why it was needed and called for stage two to be taken in committee and not in the chamber as they want. My position is we should support the government but not on their terms and that they should not be riding roughshod over parliamentary conventions.

At FMQs Richard was excellent. Raising homelessness, he called for a ban on winter evictions. This put Nicola Sturgeon on the back foot. He should take a lot of confidence from this week.

To the chamber for a debate on the Continuity Bill. Mike Russell spoke in the full belief that he is right about everything, however Adam Tomkins got the tone wrong, which didn't go down well. Tomkins is a very clever man who should be a much bigger presence in parliament but he does not for one second believe in his party's Brexit position and fails to land a real punch. I argued that we have a duty to defend parliament and the rights of our constituents, and that a curtailed process is wrong.

Not a single SNP backbencher raised any concern about the shortened process and anyone who did was loudly heckled. The lack of independent-minded backbenchers, especially on the government side, is the greatest failing of the Scottish Parliament.

A survey into sexual harassment in Holyrood was published: 30 per cent of respondents said they have been harassed in some way.

2 March I heard today that Kezia Dugdale, Ian Murray and Catherine Stihler are launching a 'Labour for the Single Market' campaign. It is being trailed in the media.

7 March Met with the Labour team to discuss arrangements for the conference. An Executive statement on Brexit has been agreed with the unions supporting. Starmer will do an article for publication and we should have a good position for Friday. Ian Murray and Kezia Dugdale's Single Market group are trying to organise opposition.

Into the chamber for the debate on the Continuity Bill. Russell was at his cocky, arrogant worst, dismissing genuine concerns. He claims he cannot publish a list of the 25 areas of contention with the UK government that the SNP have identified. I suggested that he publish the 86 areas of agreement instead. Adam Tomkins was patronising and superior. There were good speeches from Alex Neil and Jackson Carlaw and real howlers from Maurice Golden and Christina

McKelvie. Bruce Crawford and Tom Arthur took the brass neck prize, waxing lyrical about Donald Dewar and devolution. They were almost in tears at their own praise for the deceased former First Minister. Their objective is to discredit devolution. I reminded them of this and attacked the Scottish Tories' failure that has got us into this position.

8 March After FMQs I headed to Dundee for the Scottish Labour conference. Tonight, the party executive unanimously agreed to a statement on the EU which supersedes any motions that might come up – result.

9 March Up early to set up a stall I am hosting. It is called 'The Big Idea' and is an attempt to get party members to come forward with their ideas for inclusion in our manifesto. People have life experience, work in different sectors and have a contribution to make, why shouldn't we use their knowledge to develop policy? Tom Gordon of *The Herald* and Mandy Rhodes of *Holyrood Magazine* both got a bit snooty about the idea, suggesting we are asking for 'answers on a postcard'. They think that policy only comes from academics and think tanks – elitist nonsense.

Went into the conference hall for Jeremy's speech, he took Brexit head-on and was solid.

Did The Law Society fringe with Michael Clancy and Martin Whitfield MP, one of Ian Murray's chums. The media were there in big numbers, desperate for a story, so I kept things tight and the event passed off without controversy.

10 March Lots of people came to the stall to engage in 'The Big Idea'. It worked really well. The SNP primed their activists to tweet 'My big idea is independence'. Top banter.

At the lunchtime meeting of Kezia Dugdale and Ian Murray's single market group, Murray outrageously claimed that Jeremy Corbyn's reference to 'migrant labour being exploited by bad employers undermining pay' would have Nigel Farage smiling.

The hall was packed for Richard Leonard's speech. He offered a left prospectus not seen or heard from Scottish Labour for decades:

> Our aim is to fundamentally change the economic system, reject PFI, build homes, care for the elderly, inspire the young, respect the referendum, invest in people and extend common ownership.

Reaction was very positive.

Afterwards I did a TV interview with Brian Taylor alongside Ian Murray. I stuck to our lines on Brexit and set the record straight on Corbyn, saying:

He represents one of the most diverse constituencies in the country, is married to a Mexican woman and has long track record as an antiracist campaigner, it is therefore simply wrong and offensive to suggest that he has any views similar to Nigel Farage.

Poll out today has Scottish Labour on 30 per cent for the Westminster election and the SNP on 34 per cent. This is real progress.

11 March Up early for the EU debate. Claire Baker MSP opened the debate and I closed, attacking the Tories for the Brexit shambles, the SNP for the duplicity of wanting to be in the EU but out of the UK, which has four times the size of market. I challenged those who claimed that Corbyn was anti-migrant and rejected the Norway model. My speech seemed well received. When the vote came, the executive statement was approved unanimously. All in all a good day.

The conference finished with an excellent speech from Shadow Chancellor John McDonnell.

13 March Mark McDonald returned to parliament today after four months away following allegations of 'improper conduct' against women. What he actually did is unclear; the SNP hired a private investigator to look into the case and have handled things very badly. McDonald was subjected to a media scrum and then held a very strange press conference, which only poured petrol on the flames.

There are 232 amendments down for the EU Continuity Bill. Labour, the Greens and the Lib Dems put down a number of amendments and the Tories have submitted 150. Adam Tomkins, Donald Cameron and Murdo Fraser are all excited about their 'clever' amendments designed to destroy the bill. Mike Russell is loving every minute of it.

In the debate over common frameworks, I laid into both the SNP and Tories, arguing that we were being used as pawns in a constitutional game and calling for the UK and Scottish Governments to get round the table and sort out areas of dispute. After the debate, the committee stage went on from 5.30pm until 10.30pm.

I hosted an event entitled 'Skivers, Scroungers, Junkies and Neds – Challenging Working-class Stereotypes'. We had excellent contributions for Kevin Neary and Darren McGarvey. They spoke about their experiences growing up in poverty, their offending behaviour and addiction. Both were outstanding. Darren recently won the Orwell Prize for his book *Poverty Safari*. The discussion and contribution from the big audience was very interesting.

14 March To Edinburgh University to support the lecturers on strike.

In the afternoon I spoke in a debate on public procurement, highlighting blacklisting, umbrella companies, scams by subcontractors and anti-trade union activity by companies on publicly funded contracts.

Huge story today is the poisoning of a suspected former Russian agent in Salisbury, with all evidence pointing to Russian agents and claims that the assassination was instructed by Putin. Theresa May has expelled 23 Russian diplomats in retaliation. Jeremy Corbyn said, 'Nerve agents are abominable if used in any war. It is utterly reckless to use them in a civilian environment.' He also called for there to be clear evidence as to the perpetrators before revenge is taken, and for the lessons of the Iraq war to be learned. Common sense, however the Labour right, cheered on by the Murdoch press, are attacking him. *Newsnight* showed a photoshopped image of Corbyn with an exaggerated 'Lenin style' cap set against a backdrop of the Kremlin to report on the story.

15 March Along with Jackson Carlaw and Alex Neil, met with Tom Freeman of *Holyrood Magazine* to discuss our joint working on the issue of mesh implants. We spoke about the campaign and how coming from very different political perspectives we have worked together on this issue. It is an indictment of the way the parliament works that we are treated as such a novelty for this.

Today was Stage Three of the debate on the repeal of the Offensive Behaviour at Football Bill. James Kelly has done a great job on it. The Minister Annabelle Ewing was woeful, in effect saying that those who support repeal of the bill were bigots. All parties except the SNP support repeal. When the government amendments were defeated it was clear that the bill would pass and when it did there was a majority of two. This is the first bill passed by the Scottish Parliament to go on to be repealed by it. At the vote, police and security officers stopped the 40 or so football fans in the gallery from clapping. This has never happened before. When equal marriage came in there was whooping, tears and applause and no action was taken but because it was working-class football supporters they were treated very differently.

16 March This morning the *Daily Record* carried a story about Dumfries Councillor Jim Dempster making an Islamophobic comment about Transport Minister Humza Yousaf. He was immediately suspended by the party.

19 March Over to Penicuik for canvassing with a big team. It was an utter shambles organisationally. The party has put in a young inexperienced organiser and left him with no support or guidance, all the experienced staff nowhere to be seen. This is just not good enough.

I met Keir Starmer and his advisers in Edinburgh for a long chat about Brexit. We spoke about the many challenges of Brexit, the position of each of the parties in Scotland and the questions the Scottish media will ask. He said he works well and closely with Jeremy Corbyn.

20 March Took Keir Starmer to meet representatives from the Scotch Whisky Association. He did media clips afterwards. Then over to parliament where he addressed the Labour Group and took questions. Kezia Dugdale, Anas Sarwar, Jenny Marra and Daniel Johnston led a coordinated attack on the Brexit position but Starmer played it straight and was well prepared.

Jenny Formby, a regional secretary with UNITE, was appointed the Labour Party General Secretary. An excellent appointment.

21 March Stage Three of the Continuity Bill today. James Kelly, Neil Bibby and I attacked the Tories. Adam Tomkins totally misjudged his speech. This is his area of expertise but his contribution was poor. He simply regurgitated lines from the Tory playbook.

22 March Met with Professor Alison Britton who has been appointed to review the process and conduct of 'independent reviews.' She was impressive and candid and said she will not let the government dilute her report.

At FMQS I raised Scotland's appalling level of drugs deaths in this exchange:

Neil Findlay (Lothian) (Lab)

Scotland has the highest level of drugs deaths in Europe. If those deaths were due to knife crime or flu, there would be national outrage. Carrying out the same policy and expecting a different result just will not work. Will the First Minister take a bold step and seriously consider working across the parliament on a major change to drugs policy in order to end the public health crisis and prevent people from dying?

The First Minister (Nicola Sturgeon)

It is a national outrage that so many people die as a result of drugs. Previously, we have had debates in parliament about one of the issues being the cohort of people who used drugs when they were younger. We should all remember and welcome the fact that drug use among the younger population is falling, which is a good thing.

However, there is still a major challenge around drugs, and that is why we should be bold and innovative. I am very sympathetic to the recent proposal from health professionals in Glasgow, but we do not have the power to implement it. I would hope that there would be some cross-party consensus on asking the United Kingdom government to give us the power to authorise proposals such as the one made in Glasgow – although I accept that that proposal would require widespread consultation in Glasgow.

Perhaps unusually, I agree with Neil Findlay: there is always a need for new and bold thinking on the issue, and we should try to come together to do that. Where there is an evidence base, we should be prepared and have the courage to do things that may be controversial and unpopular in some areas. I want the Scottish Government to be fully part of that and to lead on those issues.

23 March We lost out in the Penicuik by-election. The SNP won with Tories second, Labour 55 votes behind them. We must get these by-elections sorted out. I spoke to Simon and Richard about the party doing a proper organisational review in Scotland. Now is the time to do this.

Owen Smith was sacked from the Shadow Cabinet for writing an article in *The Guardian* calling for Labour to support membership of the single market and a second referendum. He knew what he was doing.

25 March In the media anti-semitism is being weaponised. The newspapers are claiming that Corbyn, one of the foremost anti-racist campaigners of the last 30 years, is a racist. Nothing could be further from the truth. In the '80s, the same newspapers were attacking Jeremy for supporting so called 'looney left' policies that defended minority communities.

26 March TV news is being dominated by anti-semitism, with rival groups demonstrating outside the House of Commons. Corbyn's long-standing critics, MPs like John Woodcock, Ian Austin and Liz Kendall, are stirring it. There is no doubt the party has handled accusations of anti-semitism badly but this is just the latest stick to beat Corbyn.

Spoke to Ian Lavery MP, the party chair. He said the recent parliamentary Labour Party meeting was awful.

28 March The campaign against Corbyn is raging. The Labour right wing is working hand-in-glove with the Murdoch press and *Daily Mail*, the paper that supported the blackshirts.

Went to Easter mass with Archbishop Cushley. Apparently it was the first time mass has been celebrated in the parliament, so a wee bit of history was made.

Kezia Dugdale came to the Shadow Cabinet to present a proposal for a bill to ensure a Fatal Accident Inquiry would be held into the death of any young person 21 or under who is 'looked after'. A very good idea.

3 April I went over to Broadwood Stadium with Elaine Smith and Anas Sarwar to meet Norrie Innes, the Clyde FC team manager, to discuss their signing of the player David Goodwillie, who was found guilty in a civil court of raping my constituent. Innes seemed like someone trying his best at a club with no cash but he really didn't get it that football players are role models and what they do matters. We had very robust exchanges with him.

4 April Met the team at Labour Party HQ for a campaign brainstorming session. This has to be the kickstart to shake up the party organisation and our campaigning approach and capacity. We have a huge amount to do and party officers are not on the same page.

5 April Heard today that the GPs at Stoneyburn Health Centre have all resigned and the practice will close if they don't get replacements. The SNP have failed to address the GP crisis. I posted this information on Facebook and was immediately attacked by cybernats who claimed it wasn't an issue people were concerned about.

7 April Went with my mum to look at a smaller house. Her existing home is far too big and needs a lot of work done but she is very reluctant to move. She has lived there since 1974. We will have to see what her thoughts are in the next few days.

9 April A big chemical weapons attack has taken place in Syria. Scenes of children and citizens choking in the rancid air are too hard to watch. Trump is banging the drums of war. Unbelievably, the TV news is asking Tony Blair for his views about what to do. Jeremy Corbyn said very clearly that 'only a political solution brought about through dialogue will end the carnage'. Of course he is correct but the Labour right are attacking him.

A poll out today suggests Labour could win 13 Scottish seats if there was a General Election.

10 April I posted cheques off today to charities and organisations who will benefit from the money raised from my book *Socialism and Hope*.

Went to Newton Mearns to meet Elaine Holmes and Olive McIlroy from the Scottish Mesh Survivors Group, Patrick McGuire of Thompson's solicitors and Marion Scott from the *Sunday Post*, to discuss developments with the mesh campaign.

My Aunty Ellen has been taken to hospital today, she is 89 years old and my mum's last remaining sibling.

11 April I wrote to Shona Robison about the closure of the GP services at Stoneyburn, asking her to come to the village to discuss the future of services with the local community.

15 April Drove to Aviemore for the STUC annual conference. On the first really decent day of the year Scotland was at its spectacular best.

Spoke to Dave Watson of UNISON regarding his retirement. He will be a huge loss to the trade union movement. Dave is a workhorse, a very bright guy with good politics.

16 April Satnam Ner, an engineer from Prospect, gave the President's address. He is the first black STUC President.

I went in for Nicola Sturgeon's speech. As usual in front of this audience she made all the right noises, though much of what she said wouldn't stand up to scrutiny. I heard that prior to the vote UNITE members were going to protest with specially made tee-shirts highlighting the removal of the UNITE Convenor at West Dunbartonshire council but Grahame Smith the STUC General Secretary told them they shouldn't do it as this would embarrass the First Minister.

18 April To the Labour Group meeting, where Jeremy Corbyn was attacked for his approach on Syria.

19 April A raucous FMQ session today. The SNP were attacking the Tories for their involvement with Cambridge Analytica, who have been harvesting people's Facebook data, then it was revealed that the SNP met with Cambridge Analytica too.

Richard Leonard led on the crisis at NHS Tayside, which is Health Secretary Shona Robison's home patch. His questions were well put, culminating in a call for her to resign. It was his best performance to date.

I spoke in the afternoon debate on drug consumption rooms. The SNP are desperate to focus on this narrow but nonetheless important issue because it diverts attention away from their own failure and onto Westminster.

23 April I met the local Police Area Commander, Liz Macleod. The two big issues she raised were the shortage of staff and the number of mental health related cases the police are having to deal with.

24 April At committee we discussed the Prescription Bill. Mike Dailly from the Govan Law Centre gave evidence. He does excellent work on housing and consumer protection. The deliberations were around debt. Scotland pursues debts for Council Tax and reserved benefits for up to 20 years, in England it is five. The SNP want to retain the 20 years. I questioned Mike on this and he agreed it should be the same as England. I will put down an amendment to this effect.

Mike Russell gave a statement about Brexit, as crunch time is getting nearer in the House of Commons. I heard from contacts in the Welsh government that Russell thought he had a deal with the Tories but Sturgeon blocked it. In the chamber the body language between Russell and Sturgeon was bad, they couldn't look at each other. I mocked them and they tried to laugh it off but it was not at all convincing. I then asked if the Welsh had a deal (which they have), Russell dodged the question, looking very uncomfortable. We have worked with them all along as this is what they claimed they wanted, now at the last minute we are cut off with zero information.

25 April Emails released today show Sturgeon misled parliament about the SNP's involvement with Cambridge Analytica.

At Stage Three of the Social Security Bill, I raised with Jeane Freeman the SNP's desire to retain a 20-year liability period for reserved social security debts, exactly what we have been discussing with Mike Dailly. With typical arrogance, she attacked me saying I hadn't a clue what I was talking about. Clearly she was the one who was totally unaware of the content of her government's own Prescriptions Bill.

Former BBC sports reporter Charlie Mann was appointed head of communications for Labour today.

26 April At FMQs Richard Leonard and Willie Rennie called on the health secretary Shona Robison to resign over her handling of the NHS.

I was called and raised the closure of the Stoneyburn GP service:

Neil Findlay (Lothian) (Lab)

At the Breich Valley medical practice in my region, all the general practitioners have resigned and there are zero applicants to take over from them. Patients from Stoneyburn will no longer have a GP in their local health centre. If they do not have a car, they will be forced to travel on the bus – at a cost of £4.50 a time – to another health centre that is already under pressure. Across Lothian, 40 per cent of GPs have closed their waiting lists, training places go unfilled and the system would collapse without locums. The Cabinet Secretary for Health and Sport has overseen a disaster in general practice in our communities. For the sake of patients in places like Stoneyburn, will the First Minister ask her to stand aside and bring in someone who will get a grip of that disaster?

The First Minister (Nicola Sturgeon)

While the Opposition might want to continue to play politics with us, we will continue to focus on the hard work of supporting our national health service and delivering for patients. The health secretary is taking a range of actions to boost recruitment in general practice. We are also working to build the multidisciplinary teams that support GPs. Of course, the new GP contract will go a considerable way towards addressing some of the concerns that they have been expressing. Neil Findlay mentioned training places: I do not have the exact figures in front of me but, if memory serves me correctly, the fill rate for training places for this year is higher than it was last year, which suggests that those actions are starting to have effect.

There are challenges facing health services all over the United Kingdom and, indeed, all over Europe and the world. However, we will continue to focus on providing the investment and taking the action that allows us to address such challenges and to ensure that patients continue to have record high levels of satisfaction with the services on which they depend.

We then had an address to the parliament from the President of Malawi who spoke very warmly about the relationship between Scotland and his country.

Scottish Tory leader Ruth Davidson is having a baby following successful IVF treatment, good luck to her and her partner.

Kim Jong Un and Trump held talks and visited the Korean peace line. Lots of symbolic handshakes and photos.

28 April I spoke at the International Workers' Memorial Day commemoration at Bathgate. There was a good attendance. I spoke about workers' struggles at home and abroad and how these should inspire us to work for improved rights at work.

My good friend and mentor Jim Swan was there; he is a trade union stalwart in his 80s and is going through chemotherapy but is doing well.

30 April I took part in a conference call with Richard Leonard and his team to discuss our position on clause 11 of the Brexit bill which is about devolving powers coming back from Brussels. Richard and I don't want to be on the same page as the Tories, calling for the devolution of these powers to Scotland is the right thing to do.

1 May Anabelle Ewing, the Minister was at the Delegated Powers committee to discuss the Prescriptions Bill. She tried to deflect away from the fact that Scotland's debt recovery system will be significantly worse for debtors if this bill passes.

Mike Russell was also there to discuss the Continuity Bill – he is still claiming he is trying to get a deal.

Spent all day toing and froing on details of the Brexit Bill.

Went to Stoneyburn Community Centre for a public meeting on the proposal to move GP patients to Fauldhouse. Three hundred people attended. There is a national crisis with a shortage of 857 doctors. Residents raised excellent points about poor public transport, the plight of older people and the poor health of the community. The meeting went well with people express their opposition.

2 May STV and *The Evening News* picked up on the meeting last night.

Met with Simon Fletcher to discuss how I want to see things moving on in terms of campaigning. We are making slow progress; the party machine is hostile to change.

Spoke in the Health debate. Shona Robison appeared oblivious to the deep-seated problems of delayed discharge, social care, waiting times, GPs and drugs.

To the Labour Group meeting for a discussion on Syria and Brexit. The atmosphere was sombre and serious, we had a very good and intelligent discussion. Johann Lamont appealed to everyone not to use Syria as a proxy for other debates, which was a very good point to make. I led the discussion on Brexit and the laws being repatriated from Brussels and urged us to support a principled position similar to Donald Dewar's on devolution, that anything not reserved is therefore devolved. There was almost unanimous support for this position. Kezia Dugdale spoke and argued for federalism and the devolution of employment rights and immigration. Well, how times have changed.

3 May Met USDAW to help with a recruitment campaign at Lidl. They are an anti-union company. We took Andrew Whitaker, Political Editor at the *Sunday Herald* with us, to get a decent union story in the paper. Andy has just been recruited to work as John McDonnell's Press Officer.

At the Health Committee, Secretary of State David Mundell and Chloe Smith MP came along to discuss Brexit and Health. SNP MSP Tom Arthur tried to cause a rammy by shouting at Mundell, then afterwards went up and slapped him on the back, all smiles, and said jokingly, 'Well David... you know this is all just a game ho, ho, ho...'. Sadly it is all just a game to some.

To FMQs where Richard Leonard told the story of a couple who contacted him about the failings of a mental health unit in Dundee. A relative was sent away three times before taking his own life. Horrific story.

4 May The fallout from the English local elections are in full swing and the commentary is astonishing. Labour won over 1,000 seats more than the Tories, took its highest share of the vote in London since 1971, won Plymouth and came within 141 votes of winning Wandsworth – yet the Labour right are claiming it was a terrible result. They rolled out Alistair Campbell, David Blunkett, Ian Austin and Ian Murray to claim it was an 'unmitigated disaster' and effectively called for a coup against Corbyn. They really hate him. They believe they have the divine right to run the party and are never wrong. They have short memories. In Scotland their outriders are stoking up sheer hatred, there is no other word for it.

5 May There was a big Independence rally in Glasgow today. The SNP leadership are running a mile from these events. I wonder when the 'Yes' movement will wake up to this.

Noel Dolan, Sturgeon's former Chief of Staff, and Kevin Pringle, Salmond's former spin doctor both called for the SNP to support a second EU referendum on any Brexit deal. Alex Neil and Jim Sillars are opposed.

7 May Went to London with Richard Leonard to meet Keir Starmer, Welsh MPs and Peers and their advisers to discuss Brexit, we had a very good and respectful discussion.

The SNP are likely to go for EU withdrawal bill approval minus Clause 11. This is a position we will support. It means a different position from Labour in Wales but they have a different devolution settlement.

8 May Met with Mike Russell, Adam Tomkins, Patrick Harvie, Tavish Scott and Mike Russell's adviser. The bottom line is that little has changed. The Scottish Government will propose an LCM (Legislative Consent Motion) minus Clause 11.

Into the chamber for a Labour debate on mental health services in Dundee. The government was forced to announce an independent inquiry. This is very good news and would never have happened had not Richard Leonard raised it.

10 May To the Shadow Cabinet where my call to join with the SNP, Liberals and Greens on the EU Withdrawal Bill LCM was supported.

Met with 25 MPs from a Swiss canton for a very good discussion about Brexit, federalism, socialism, Corbyn, Scotland and the future. One of them asked to come campaigning with us on Saturday in Edinburgh.

11 May To Labour Party HQ in Glasgow for a discussion with the Scotland working group. Jeremy Corbyn, Ian Lavery, Karie Murphy all up for the meeting. I pushed hard for financial support to allow us to campaign effectively and raised our failure to come up with a positive and radical policy of further devolution. I told Jeremy in no uncertain terms this had to be moved on and quickly. Later he made an announcement about maintaining ship-building jobs. He also met UNITE members in the hospitality and construction sectors.

13 May We had a very good turnout at the Almond Valley Labour Party meeting. It looks like Rhea Wolfson will be the only candidate seeking nomination for the coming election.

14 May Met with Richard's team to discuss long-term planning. Richard made a very telling point when he said the thing he dreads most is not First Minister's Question time but the weekly Labour Group meeting. No wonder, it is bloody dreadful, dominated by the most negative people you will ever come across. He spends more time fighting his own side's negativity and the undermining of his leadership than anything else.

On the way home I got off at Bathgate station and as I started to walk up the steps to the bridge realised I had left my bag on the train with my work computer, £300 of cash (a charity donation from my book) and sensitive papers in it. I immediately contacted the Scotrail staff, then Central Station lost luggage to alert them but it was closed. I called Helensburgh station where the train terminates but there was no answer so I left a message in hope rather than expectation. I went home gutted. Then at 9.30pm a woman from Scotrail at Helensburgh phoned to tell me she had my bag with all the stuff untouched. I could have jumped through the ceiling with delight. I got the name and contact details of the ticket examiner who found it and sent him a card and a reward.

15 May Today's debate was on Brexit and its impact on devolution. It was extraordinary with Mike Russell rewriting history trying to recast the SNP as the great champions of devolution when the reality is they exist to rip it up and refused to take part in the original constitutional convention. Russell was full of bluster. I set out how Labour delivered devolution, will defend it at every opportunity and how we want to strengthen it. I pointed out the SNP's double standards and hypocrisy and how the Tories have completely failed to deal with further devolution appropriately. I repeated Richard Leonard's call for cross-party talks to try and thrash out a workable deal. Tavish Scott for the Liberals came on board with a very good speech. Patrick Harvie was at his sanctimonious worst, dismissing my call for talks. Speeches from Ash Denham and Christine McKelvie were terrible. Daniel Johnson spoke well as did Alex Neil, head and shoulders above his colleagues. Jackson Carlaw made a decent contribution. In the end all parties except the Tories rejected the legislative consent motion.

This was a difficult issue for Labour but I think I got us into the right place.

16 May In the afternoon I took part in a Talk Radio programme with the dreadful Julia Hartley-Brewer and Tory Eurosceptic MP Bernard Jenkin. Lots of accusations from them about me taking a nationalist viewpoint and bending to SNP pressure. All crap and I told them so.

17 May *The Herald* carried a column from Alan Roden, attacking Scottish Labour for... well, everything. He is doing this whilst employed by Kezia Dugdale, Anas Sarwar and Catherine Stihler MEP. Richard Leonard will have to end this nonsense.

Went over to the PCS union Scottish Government group annual meeting to give my report in my capacity as parliamentary group chair.

18 May Another planning session with party staff and MSPs, progress being made but a lot more to do, especially on fundraising.

It was reported today that Anas Sarwar's friend Asim Khan, who is trying to get selected to stand at the election in Glasgow South, is taking the Labour Party to court over the freeze date for selections. This will cost around £10,000. The *Daily Record* are calling it 'Labour's race row'.

19 May Today is the wedding of Prince Harry and Megan Markle. I couldn't bear to watch it.

20 May Ex Labour adviser Paul Sinclair is spouting rubbish in the papers claiming party leaders have been cutting a deal behind the scenes with the SNP to keep the Tories out – he is simply making it up.

Nicola Sturgeon said she would not oppose a second referendum on Brexit. Earlier this week Ian Blackford opposed such a move. Somehow, I don't think she would accept such a position if Scotland left the UK and there was a demand by the losing side for another referendum.

21 May Jackson Carlaw, Alex Neil and myself have been nominated for a *Holyrood Magazine* award for our work on the Mesh campaign.

It would have been my dad's 78th birthday today. Fourteen years since he passed away. I miss him greatly.

22 May At the Delegated Powers Committee we discussed its annual report. Stuart McMillan MSP who says some words every week that don't amount to a row of beans gave his contribution, which amounted to not liking a picture in the report. God, what am I doing on this woeful committee?

I got a call from UNITE advising there would be a vote at today's meeting of Labour's NEC (National Executive Committee) for Vice Chair. It is between Wendy Nichols, a UNISON right-winger who wanted to keep Corbyn off the second leadership ballot and Andi Fox from TSSA, who is on the left. UNITE have heard Richard Leonard will be voting for Nichols. What is he thinking? I texted him but he did not reply. When the vote came, he indeed voted for Nichols, who won by one vote. I find this inexplicable. The right wing are delighted and the left, who supported Richard, very angry.

Later I heard the party lost the Glasgow South court case. Anas Sarwar immediately put the story on social media. What a shit day.

In an appearance at the Economy Committee, the Cabinet Secretary for the economy Keith Brown was asked what currency would be used in an independent Scotland, to which he replied: 'I am not an economics expert.' He is getting slaughtered for this.

23 May Still seething about Richard's NEC vote.

24 May Tomorrow the SNP's new Independence blueprint 'The Sustainable Growth Commission Report' will be published. It is rumoured to be a free market, neoliberal programme for Scotland. The fact that it is going out on a bank holiday with no press launch tells you everything. They are trying to strangle it at birth.

25 May The SNP's Growth Commission Report is a recipe for more austerity, with sterlingisation, tight fiscal rules, interest rates set by another country (England), no Scottish central bank, no official currency union and weak employment rights. No trade unions were involved in its development, yet the CBI, Institute of Directors and Chamber of Commerce were. It sets six tests on the currency and speaks of pooling and sharing of resources (Gordon Brown's favourite phrase) and says Scotland is more integrated with the UK than any other country that has left a union. The deficit will be cut from 6 per cent to 3 per cent under EU rules, which would mean huge austerity, especially with the end of the Barnett formula and falling oil revenues. It calls for the doubling of immigration and tax cuts for the wealthiest and a £1 billion of public sector 'efficiency'. How could an independent Scotland join the EU without its own monetary policy outside the Euro and without its own central bank? The report is certainly not the vision of many on the left of the 'Yes' movement. The response from Commonweal, Robin McAlpine, Jonathon Shafi and others has been ferocious.

27 May Newspapers are full of the Growth Commission. Ian Macwhirter in *The Herald* has savaged it, right-wing commentators are praising it. SNP MSPs and MPs are completely silent – they haven't been told what to think or say yet.

29 May Lesley Laird was confirmed Deputy Leader of the Scottish Labour Party. She has done well after being thrown in at the deep end as Shadow Secretary of State for Scotland. Lesley is no left-winger but has been loyal and committed since being elected and saw off Jackie Baillie without even a contest.

Big developments in Italy today where the President rejected a democratically elected Eurosceptic candidate for Prime Minister following the election. We now see a temporary PM put in place who is much more acceptable to the EU. Irrespective of the rejected candidates' views, it is not for the EU to interfere in the election of a member state. This is dangerous.

There are more ructions amongst Independence supporters following publication of the Growth Commission Report.

I was advised that the UK party is preparing for an expected autumn/winter election. There is huge speculation at Westminster about this.

I heard over the weekend that Mesh campaigner Michele McDougall has died of cancer.

31 May At FMQs Ruth Davidson got slaughtered. She tried to go on the Growth Commission but left herself wide open for Sturgeon to list all the positive policies the government is implementing. She keeps getting painted as some kind of Tory superstar and was in the papers recently as one of the country's 25 most influential women, I just don't buy the hype.

1 June Wendy Milne confirmed she will seek selection in Linlithgow. I have no doubt the press will attack her as she stood for the Scottish Socialist Party previously and was expelled from the Labour Party in the '90s for being a member of Militant. Wendy is a very good person and will be an excellent candidate.

Met again with Janice McSeveney whose son died of cot death in the '90s. The little boy had his brain and some organs removed without the consent of the parents. After years of asking what happened to the hospital slides and NHS Lothian's repeated denial that they have them, the Crown Office has said the slides do exist but that the brain was disposed of. What an appalling thing to happen. NHS Lothian's dealings with families over this has been completely callous.

The high street cosmetics company Lush has launched a campaign in their shops highlighting the Spycops scandal. They are getting pelters from the right-wing press. I posted a comment supporting the company, so the trolls are piling in on me.

4 June Went to Glasgow City Halls for the announcement of Lesley Laird's election as Deputy Leader of Scottish Labour.

5 June Went to Warriston Crematorium for the funeral of Michele McDougall. Her family and friends are convinced that mesh contributed to her death – she had six mesh implants and developed cancer in her vagina.

When I returned from the funeral, I was advised that Justice Secretary Michael Matheson will make a statement on 'the impact of policing on communities during the Miners' strike'. I am really hopeful this is a positive announcement. This is an issue that means a lot to me, I have poured my heart and soul into the campaign.

I met with Aileen Campbell, the Public Health Minister, to discuss the failing drugs policy. I took with me my constituent Jamie Hardie, a recovering heroin addict who is now clean after nearly dying. He works as an addictions support worker. We put to the Minister that with mental health provision woeful and drugs deaths soaring, we need a completely different approach, similar to Portugal. I also raised the progressive and effective actions of police and crime commissioners in England who are going much further than the Scottish Government. I am not convinced the Minister understands the urgency of the situation.

To Carers of West Lothian to meet 12 young carers, hearing the impact of caring on schooling, friendships and social lives. They give each other support, love and care. Around ten of them have been referred to mental health services for anxiety, depression and self-harm. They all mentioned the lack of mental health support in schools.

6 June I met with the CBI to discuss Brexit. The main issues raised were procurement, skills, staffing, tariffs and customs.

Over the last two days I have been working with UK colleagues and Professor Jim Gallacher to try and find a way through the UK/Scottish Government conflict over devolution and Brexit. Jim has helped us draft amendments to say that the UK government can only legislate without the consent of the Scottish

Parliament if the subject matter relates to international obligations. This respects devolution. I have been seeking support from the other parties with Willie Rennie and Adam Tomkins appearing positive – as does Mike Russell, but he cannot sign it off without Sturgeon's say so.

7 June What a day – I met with Mike Russell to discuss the EU Withdrawal Bill. I presented the amendments we have been working on and urged him to come together with us to support them. He was previously positive and supportive, but not now. He claimed the SNP Westminster Group would have the final say. He also said the SNP is going to run a summer campaign on the single market and customs union. I asked if he meant 'a' customs union or 'the' customs union. He couldn't answer.

This afternoon we got a copy of Matheson's statement on the policing of the miners' strike in Scotland. He announced an independent review to be led by John Scott QC. It is not a public inquiry, but still fantastic news. After the statement I went over and shook Matheson's hand. I then went out to celebrate with campaigners and did a lot of media interviews along with former miners. Afterwards Jeremy Corbyn tweeted a supportive message, which got a lot of social media coverage. This is a huge step forward.

8 June I spent the morning with Alex Rowley in North Queensferry to meet former Prime Minister Gordon Brown. I must admit I like these meetings and the debates we have. We discussed the economy, politics and the Labour Party, the rise of the Tories and the SNP Growth Commission. We come from the same point of view that we have to have a credible position that links social justice and equality to the constitution. Brown believes further powers combined with the pooling and sharing of resources is the strongest argument. He is trying to push Richard Leonard into making a big speech on this. We agreed to keep in touch.

Poll out today has Labour down 5 per cent from the election.

10 June Went to the Scotland v England one-day cricket match at The Grange with my brother John, brother-in-law Jim and pal Alan Brown. What a game it was, Scotland racked up a tremendous 371. England started their innings well and looked as though they were in control until they had a batting collapse and a final LBW decision saw Scotland defeat the world one day champions. The scenes of celebration were amazing.

12 June I pushed hard for Delegated Powers and Law Reform Committee to support a proposal for council tax and reserved benefits debt to be prescribed (effectively written off) after a five-year period, the SNP want this to be 20 years. In England it is six, so with the SNP proposal people will have these debts hanging over them for 14 years more years than those in Tory England.

I was absent from the Labour Group meeting but found out later that there was an all-out attack on Richard Leonard by Jackie Baillie, Anas Sarwar, Neil Bibby,

Lewis MacDonald and others. They claimed the polling was the worst ever and pointed to the situation with the Aberdeen councillors (suspended for doing a deal with the Tories), Islamophobia, Brexit, etc. Apparently, it was awful. The reality is too many members of the group leak and brief the press and snipe at every opportunity. They believe their view of the world is the only legitimate one and if only Sarwar had won the leadership, we would be marching to victory. I called a meeting of Richard's team. We must end this once and for all or they will grind us down.

All day I was on calls about the EU Withdrawal Bill going through the House of Commons. As the debate was about to start, Theresa May suffered a ministerial resignation and was forced into making a number of concessions. The timings for the multitude of Lords' amendments was just six hours with only 15 minutes for the devolution-related ones. There was no time for the Labour and SNP amendments to be heard so Labour abstained to ensure we got the least bad option, the SNP voted against. Had the SNP position prevailed it would have taken us back to the original Clause 11, which would have given the Tories all powers over devolution, in contrast to the deal the Welsh government negotiated. What a disingenuous approach – but of course they are grandstanding and claiming their vote against was the right thing to do when in fact it was the worst.

13 June Met with Richard Leonard's team. We discussed the need to get the gloves off and take his internal critics head-on. I am completely up for this, but I am not sure Richard is.

A damning report came out today exposing the extent of the Scottish Government's deliberate manipulation of the Freedom of Information system. It described a dual system discriminating against requests from MSPs, researchers and journalists, with special advisers politically screening requests. The Minister responsible, Joe FitzPatrick, made a statement to parliament about the report. He took a hammering from MSPs.

Afterwards, we had a debate on mental health. In the vote the government knew they were going to be defeated, so voted in support of all the opposition amendments then opposed the final amended motion.

We also debated the SNP's Growth Commission. Derek Mackay led by defending the Commission's findings. I had a go at the Commission's neoliberal agenda, return to austerity, low taxation and disregard for the views of the large section of the 'Yes' movement who are on the left. I also raised the influence of lobbyists Charlotte Street Partners, who employ the Commission's Chairman, Andrew Wilson. I enjoyed getting back to debating meaty issues.

At PMQs, in a premeditated staged move, Ian Blackford led a walk out of his MPs over Brexit. Yesterday he was claiming the SNP were the only ones 'standing up for Scotland', now they are 'walking out for Scotland'.

14 June The SNP are milking the Commons walkout for all its worth, claiming 5,000 have joined the party in the following 24 hours.

Prior to FMQs, Presiding Officer Ken Macintosh asked us to welcome the Speaker of the Ukrainian parliament Andriy Parubiy, who was in the public gallery. MSPs applauded him and he acknowledged this with a wave. Afterwards, I got a call from *Morning Star* correspondent Conrad Landin to advise that Parubiy was in fact from a party that only a decade ago was neo nazi and that he was the leader of their youth wing. At decision time, I raised a point of order advising the chamber that the parliament had applauded someone with a neo nazi past and that maybe from now on MSPs should be given a note of who was attending parliament each week so that they could make an informed choice whether or not to applaud visiting guests.

15 June The World Cup started today with Russia defeating Saudi Arabia 5-0.

A number of newspapers carried coverage of my exchange with the Presiding Officer about Andriy Parubiy. I have written to him calling for a revised protocol for dealing with international visitors. I later received a letter from the Ukrainian Embassy criticising me for raising the issue and speaking out in the media. The letter was published on Twitter before it was sent to me. It looks like I am being dragged into a propaganda war. I emailed the Embassy back, asking:

1) Was Mr Parubiy previously a member of the Social National Party?

2) If the Social National Party followed social nationalism and based its ideology on Hitler's Nazis?

3) If the party used Nazi iconography?

4) If the party was only open to ethnic Ukrainians?

5) If the EU called it a racist party?

Let's see if they reply.

16 June Today, the Scottish executive of the Labour Party referred the Aberdeen councillors to the party's NEC for defying party rules on coalitions. Right away Jenny Marra MSP was on twitter criticising the move.

18 June Met Richard Leonard's advisers. We had a full and frank discussion about how to take on our opponents in the group. We also have to replace senior people at party HQ and revolutionise the way the organisation operates. We have to raise Richard's profile and drive a positive and transformational policy agenda.

19 June At the Labour Group, Richard raised the issue of the Aberdeen councillors who were suspended by the then leader Kezia Dugdale for striking a coalition agreement with the Tories. Jackie Baillie, Anas Sarwar and Neil Bibby attacked the SEC and the parliamentary groups' representatives on the executive, Mary Fee and Monica Lennon. They are now calling for a special evening meeting to discuss the situation. The reality is the SEC were following a conference decision that allowed local Labour Groups to negotiate deals with other parties but that these had to be ratified by the SEC. The Aberdeen councillors ignored this procedure and went into an agreement with the Tories without approval. Kezia Dugdale then went on Twitter attacking the decision that she herself made.

I know I shouldn't get bothered by this, but I do, these people are some of the most self-entitled, arrogant people I have ever come across. I cannot believe I am in the same party as them.

Mike Russell gave a Brexit statement which was a lot of waffle and hyperbole. What we are seeing is Scottish and British nationalism clashing with no real desire to see things resolved as it suits both the SNP and Tories to see the debate polarised. We can get Trump and Kim Jong Un to meet but we can't get the Scottish and UK government to sort out common fertiliser standards.

Later in the afternoon all MSPs got an email from the Presiding officer saying that the parliament's procedures would change and that now members will get details of who the international guests visiting parliament are. They have clearly been embarrassed by the Parubiy case. This is a little victory, I am pleased with the result.

David Leask from *The Herald* ran a story about my comments about Parubiy, saying the incident had reverberated around Eastern Europe and Russia. Really?

20 June I had a tense meeting with Mike Russell and made it clear I was pissed-off by his antics last week stoking up the cybernats over the EU vote that he knew was the worst possible option. He defended his position but he knew that it was wrong. He will now put down a debate without motion so we can discuss the latest developments.

The government's record on Freedom of Information was the subject of today's debate. I thought we had all the opposition parties on board with our amendment calling for an independent review of both FOI and government record-keeping, but when the vote came the Liberals had done a sneaky deal with the SNP.

21 June After FMQs I met with Richard Leonard and Mark Drakeford, the Welsh Minister for Brexit, to discuss our joint approach. Mark gave a good insight into developments. He is standing for election to succeed Carwyn Jones when he steps down. I really liked him.

This evening I went to the *Holyrood Magazine* political awards. It was a beautiful night and glorious setting in the Botanic Gardens. Jackson Carlaw, Alex Neil and I won the 'Political Hero' award for the work we have done on Mesh. It's great to see the campaign being recognised.

23 June Over to Govan to speak at an event on the spycops scandal. We heard from Donna McLean who was duped into a long-term relationship with an undercover police officer who was monitoring her activities as a socialist and trade unionist. He left her emotionally devastated and violated. The only people on the mainland of the UK to have no access to a public inquiry are Scots. This is because the UK government refuses to give Scottish victims access to the inquiry and the Scottish Government refuses to run a parallel one.

24 June Rhea Wolfson was endorsed unanimously as our candidate for Livingston for the forthcoming General Election.

26 June Nicola Sturgeon reshuffled her Cabinet today. Michael Matheson was demoted to Transport, newly elected SNP Deputy leader Keith Brown was sacked, Jeane Freeman was promoted to Health, Humza Yousaf to Justice, Aileen Campbell to Communities and Fiona Hyslop stayed at culture. Mike Russell has returned to the Cabinet. This is a fairly major reshuffle and there are some very unhappy people around. They took the cover of the reshuffle to bury bad news – they shelved their key Education Bill. This is a humiliation for John Swinney and for Sturgeon, who claims education is her number one priority.

Joined my pal and former researcher Tommy Kane to celebrate him graduating with a PhD, a fantastic achievement. Tommy started his adult life working on a market stall, then in a tyre factory, now he has a doctorate. It shows the power of education and his dedication. John McDonnell and his wife came along as they are in Glasgow for their son's graduation tomorrow.

28 June Last day of the parliamentary term – yippee!

The government finished its reshuffle with junior ministers appointed including Ivan McKee, Kate Forbes, Mhari Gougeon, Gillian Martin and Christina McKelvie. Later it emerged that Martin had previously written an offensive blog insulting Muslims, the disabled, gay people and Jews. The appointment of ministers is usually a time for light-hearted banter in the chamber but Richard Leonard was going to propose an amendment to remove Gillian Martin's name from the motion on appointments. Just before the debate Nicola Sturgeon sacked Martin. What a mess.

At the specially convened Labour Group meeting we had an undignified shouting match about the suspended Aberdeen councillors. It was pathetic.

29 June Attended the Scotland Joint Working Group with Jeremy Corbyn and Ian Lavery. Then to Howden Park Centre for an NHS 70th birthday rally. There was a major accident on the M8 that caused Jeremy to be delayed by an hour.

The meeting went very well with me, Rhea Wolfson and Jeremy speaking. There were lots of people there.

2 July Met John Scott QC to discuss the Miners Policing Review he is chairing. We had a good discussion on his remit and built up a good rapport.

3 July Figures out show 859 Scots died of drug-related deaths in the last year, an appalling record 2½ times the deaths of anywhere else in the UK and one of the worst death rates in Europe. The regions of England operate under the same legislation yet they do not have anywhere near the level of deaths we have.

Labour's NEC referred the case of the nine Aberdeen councillors to the party's National Constitutional Committee.

5 July Terrible news this morning, a six-year-old girl has been murdered by a 16-year-old boy on the Isle of Bute.

Visited the Edinburgh Beer Festival to act as a judge. It was very interesting. Ian Murray MP was there. Thankfully I was at another table.

6 July Theresa May took her Cabinet to Chequers for a Brexit session. They all had their mobile phones removed so they wouldn't leak information – sounds like the Holyrood Labour Group! After a day of arguments, a position setting out an unworkable soft Brexit close to the EU was press released in an attempt to show unity. Jeremy Corbyn went on TV saying it would unravel in days.

7 July Out campaigning in Livingston. Martin Hyman joined us. He is a remarkable man who fled from Jersey with his family when the Nazis were about to invade. Martin was an international long-distance runner who took part in the 1960 Olympics. At one point he was number three in the world and defeated the great Abebe Bikila in a road race. He eventually settled in Livingston and taught at Inveralmond High School. What a character, I really enjoyed talking to him and hearing his life story.

9 July Today, David Davis resigned as Theresa May's Brexit Secretary, then Boris Johnson resigned as Foreign Secretary, stating in his resignation letter that May's red lines had been replaced by white flags. Then a number of others resigned. May was forced to go to the House of Commons to defend herself. She will be gone soon. The media are in a frenzy. I cannot believe people are taken in by Boris Johnson. He is an horrendous individual, a complete fraud.

Brilliant news that after 12 days stuck in a cave, a group of young boys from Thailand and their teacher were safely rescued.

10 July The UK government review of mesh has recommended a suite of excellent recommendations that go far beyond what Scotland has done.

Two Vice Chairs of the Tory Party have resigned. The coup against Theresa May goes on.

11 July England lost to Croatia in extra time in the World Cup semi-final.

14 July Off on holiday touring in Spain.

The main issue that happened back in the UK was Boris Johnson's self-indulgent resignation speech. He will now haunt Theresa May from the back benches. As Labour went 5 per cent ahead in the polls, the party's right wing, egged on by the media, brought back the issue of anti-semitism. It is doing real damage.

4 August Former Labour MP Tom Harris announced he was leaving the Labour Party today. I have to say not a single tear will be shed about that, good riddance.

7 August Boris Johnson said women who wear a burka look like 'pillar boxes or bank robbers'.

9 August Visited the MS therapy center in Leith to pass on a cheque from my book sales.

13 August My mum's last remaining sibling, Ellen, died today; she was 89.

Hostile media are now trying to claim that Jeremy Corbyn attended a memorial service and laid a wreath in memory of terrorists. He has publicly denied it, but the truth does not appear to matter to the haters.

14 August A terror attack on Westminster today with a car driving into passengers.

15 August I texted Jeremy Corbyn today to give him support and solidarity as he faces fierce attacks from the media and Labour right-wingers.

I met with West Lothian Council officers to discuss the dreadful condition of a block of flats in Blackburn, one of the first sold under 'right to buy'. I have been raising this for three years. The roof of the communal staircase has now collapsed under the weight of pigeon shit. Private landlords rent out the properties and trying to get them to pay for repairs would be a torturous process. The block needs to be demolished.

16 August Met Richard Leonard's team to discuss polling. We are on 24 per cent for the Scottish Parliament and 26 per cent for Westminster. We are on 47 per cent for Westminster among young people, ahead of the SNP; but only on 20 per cent for older people. The SNP are doing well overall, less so on public services. We have to exploit this by raising the profile of our policies on the NHS, housing, education etc. *But* we have to have a credible alternative on the constitution.

Went to see Graham Spiers in conversation with Rory Bremner. Bremner hates Brexit, ripped Boris Johnson apart and said that Corbyn wasn't intelligent enough to run the country because he hadn't gone to university. Elitist bollocks.

17 August Attended my Aunty Ellen's funeral.

18 August To the Fringe for 'In Conversation with Richard Leonard' with Susan Morrison. Richard was candid and relaxed.

19 August I wrote to the Lord Advocate, Chief Constable and Jeane Freeman calling for charges to be brought against mesh manufacturers after the *Sunday Post* revealed that they had ignored warnings not to implant Marlex plastic into humans but did so, injuring hundreds of women.

20 August Met NHS Lothian officials to raise concerns about waiting times manipulation, the closure of St John's children's ward, mental health and drugs service provision.

I heard today that Kezia Dugdale's defamation case with the dreadful 'Wings over Scotland' website owner is going ahead. She wants the Labour Party to financially underwrite it.

Jeremy Corbyn is in Scotland for a few days.

Over to the Quaker Meeting House to do an event at the Fringe with former First Minister Henry McLeish.

At the Edinburgh International Book Festival Yanis Varoufakis interviewed Jeremy Corbyn. I have to say Jeremy was a bit flat and repetitive. I think the personal attacks on him are taking their toll.

21 August The Petitions Committee report into mesh implants was published. It was very good. Petitioners Elaine Holmes and Olive McIlroy did TV and radio, they were excellent. The Chief Medical Officer, Catherine Calderwood, claimed mesh was more effective than using natural tissue! She also claimed that England had come into line with Scotland, which again was completely misleading. She is a big part of the problem.

The Labour Party community organisers held an economics event in Glasgow with over 400 people in attendance.

22 August I met with two young people who are victims of trafficking from Vietnam. Their story was heartbreaking. They are here with no family and speak no English. They are clearly terrified. They are being accommodated in a children's home and have very limited access to education and other support services.

23/24 August Spent the next two days in the Western Isles with Richard Leonard, Rhoda Grant and local candidate Alison McCuorquodale. The flight over was spectacular. We met with air-traffic controllers on Benbecula, a community trust on Uist and South Harris, Council leaders, the local housing partnership, ferry campaigners, visited McLeod's black pudding factory and held a very well attended Labour Party meeting with over 50 people there. It was an excellent two days spent listening to islanders about housing, jobs, austerity,

Brexit, problems with the ferry service, the social care crisis and Council finance. I would love to return to these islands for holiday. Alison was very impressive and is well known across the islands. She is up against Angus Brendan MacNeil of the SNP.

24 August The *Daily Record* splashed a huge story that Scotland's former First Minister Alex Salmond is being investigated for an alleged series of sexual assaults. The investigations are being carried out under a code of conduct that was introduced retrospectively after the events in question took place in 2013. He is challenging the process in the High Court. The media has gone mad. He conducted a press conference and set out his defence claiming, 'I'm no saint.' The cybernats are claiming this is all a conspiracy by unionists.

25 August The *Daily Record* has followed up yesterday's story with more lurid allegations.

26 August Sturgeon is under pressure to expel Salmond from the SNP.

There are rumours today that right-wing members of the Parliamentary Labour Party are going to leave just prior to the Party conference. Mike Gapes is being named as one of them.

27 August A leaked memo has shown that The People's Vote campaign will be pushing hard at Labour conference for support for a second EU referendum.

28 August Nicola Sturgeon's former Chief of Staff Noel Dolan is calling for Lesley Evans, Scotland's top civil servant, to be sacked if Salmond wins his legal challenge.

In the *New Statesman* the Chief Rabbi, Jonathan Sacks, called Jeremy Corbyn an antisemite and claimed his concerns about Zionism are on par with Enoch Powell's Rivers of Blood speech.

29 August I heard today that Jackie Baillie is going to put a motion on antisemitism to the Labour Group on the day the NEC meets.

Alex Salmond resigned from the SNP, releasing a video appeal to crowdfund his legal case. Amazingly, people are donating.

30 August By 10am, Salmond had raised £20,000.

Over to Stirling University for the Labour Group development day. Judith, the facilitator, drew out some of the negative behaviours that have blighted our work since Richard became leader. She covered team working, confidentiality, mutual respect, openness and transparency. There was a simmering undercurrent of bitter negativity from the usual suspects.

31 August I gave a presentation on our latest polling to the group. We had a wide-ranging discussion. Jackie Baillie, Neil Bibby and Anas Sarwar were very unhappy but couldn't offer any alternative strategy.

Last night Frank Field MP resigned the Labour whip. He was going to be deselected by his constituency party because of his vote supporting the Conservatives on Brexit. He claims it is all about antisemitism.

1 September I spoke at a UNITE meeting in Glasgow along with Jeanette Findlay of the UCU (University and College Union). Given the many different strands of socialist thinking in the room it was only a matter of time before things kicked off. Jeanette spoke about the UCUs campaign of industrial action over pensions. Les Huckfield a former Labour MP, now a nationalist, was there. With a permanent scowl, he called Jeanette many things, including an 'apologist'. Jeanette came back with a tremendously, calm riposte saying: 'I suggest you go and take two fucks to yourself.' No messing, Huckfield's political sectarianism was despatched in those few words. The meeting reminded me of the final lines of Jim Monaghan's poem, 'The United Left' which says: 'There is nothing more divisive than a call for left wing unity.' Indeed.

2 September Into Edinburgh for the annual MSPs versus the journalists cricket match. A solid victory for the MSPs, courtesy of a couple of ringers from the local club. I scored a magnificent seven runs.

3 September Over to Addiewell Prison to do a visit with the organisation Families Outside Prison. I met with staff members and prisoners. One man told me of the progress he had made on an education course about parenting. He said it gave him a real insight into the world through a child's eyes. One of the common issues raised by both workers and prisoners was understaffing. I raised this with the Governor when I met him.

All nine of the left slate were elected to Labour's NEC. In Scotland the entire Campaign for Socialism slate was elected to the Policy Forum with Caitlin Kane who works in my office topping the poll. A tremendous result.

4 September First day back after recess. The call for evidence on the miners' strike policing review is out today. I will get the message out to all concerned.

At the Labour Group, Jackie Baillie produced a motion out of the blue on antisemitism. Elaine Smith proposed a sensible delay until next week so we can consider the motion on the basis of what the NEC decides to do following its meeting today. We then had a vote with myself, Pauline McNeil, Elaine Smith and Claudia Beamish the only ones supporting a delay. Within half an hour of the meeting, former *Sun* journalist Kevin Schofield was tweeting the details of our discussion. It seems we cannot have a private discussion without it being leaked. They would be as well inviting the media into meetings to save time.

The Scottish Government announced its programme for government with around 11 bills, including the creation of the Scottish National Investment

Bank, a South of Scotland Enterprise Agency and a bill on organ donation. Nothing transformative.

6 September The *Scotsman* today ran a story about 75-year-old Mrs Eileen Baxter who died a week ago. On her death certificate it was stated that one of the underlying causes of death was a pelvic mesh implant. To my knowledge, this is the first case that that has identified mesh as a contributory cause of death on a patient's death certificate.

At FMQs I asked the First Minister about the case. Sturgeon gave a reasonable reply. However, on social media the cybernats started abusing me, saying I did not know which issues were reserved and which were devolved. Philippa Whitford MP joined in, claiming that only Westminster had the power to ban mesh implants, which is nonsense. The Scottish Government could end mesh implants tomorrow by using procurement powers to end the purchase of these devices.

7 September The Tories won the Fife by-election with Labour on just 12 per cent of the first preference votes. This is a dreadful result and reinforces my belief that until we have a credible constitutional offer we will continue to lag miles behind.

8 September Chuka Umunna MP called Labour Party members dogs and said the party was institutionally racist. This is a real insult to the tens of thousands of Labour members who have fought racism all of their lives.

9 September The *Sunday Times* has exposed Boris Johnson's infidelity and published a story about a file that the Tories have on his love life. He responded with an extraordinary comment saying the Prime Minister's Brexit stance was like 'a suicide vest.'

10 September Had a conference call with Royal Bank of Scotland to try and get to the bottom of a complex debt case for a constituent, hopefully we made some progress on it.

To Livingston to speak to Crown Office reps regarding my constituent whose child died young and who was told the medical slides they took at the time do not exist when in fact they do. They were very helpful.

12 September Jeane Freeman gave a statement on mesh implants. She has taken some welcome action to halt the implantation of transvaginal mesh but not hernia or abdominal mesh. There will be a new high alert system, reporting mechanism and audit. All of this could have been done four years ago, saving hundreds of women from being implanted with this poison.

13 September Charlie Mann, the Labour Director of Communications, resigned today. He is a decent guy but he wasn't a political animal. I texted him my best wishes.

The Labour Party is refusing to pay Kezia Dugdale's legal fees for her impending court case against 'Wings over Scotland'. She has publicly attacked Corbyn, uses her spin doctor Alan Roden and her *Daily Record* column to denounce the party. I was under the impression the £70,000 she got from her five minutes in the jungle was for the court case, obviously not.

15 September To Coatbridge for the by-election. We have put in a really good show here and have a real chance of winning.

16 September To Auchengeich Miners Welfare for the annual memorial service to commemorate those who lost their lives in the mining tragedy.

17 September Met Keir Starmer and Richard Leonard to discuss Brexit and the forthcoming Labour conference; 150 motions have been submitted on Brexit. Keir's belief is that it is only a matter of time before Theresa May is taken out. He discussed the difficulties Labour faces over a second referendum. I have to say he was very well informed and on top of his brief. It is clear he will be a candidate for the Labour leadership at some point.

We then met with the CBI and 40 businesses from different sectors to discuss Brexit.

Over to Labour Party headquarters for a meeting with general election candidates, MPs, MSPs and party officials. I asked Keir to emphasise to them the privilege of being a parliamentary candidate and the need for them to get working on their campaigns.

19 September Went to a Brexit briefing this morning with political scientist John Curtice. His polling shows public opinion has not shifted very much; people are remaining loyal to their Leave/Remain positions. The voters blame the politicians for the situation, not themselves. During the follow-up questions he said he thought there would be a general election soon.

Jackie Baillie went on TV to attack the Labour Party decision not to fund Kezia Dugdale's legal expenses. At Shadow Cabinet she suggested the Scottish Labour Party should pay up or that MSPs should donate to the fund. Well, I'm sure the bold Jackie would be the first to delve into her purse if it was me who was asking for funding – aye, right!

The reality is that this issue is being used as another stick to beat Richard with and he is too weak to take them on. I really have had enough. Life's too short to be dealing with this crap every day.

20 September I went with Mark Baxter and his sister Audrey (the family of the woman who had mesh identified as a contributory factor in her death) to see Jeane Freeman. We asked for an inquiry into the role of mesh in Eileen's passing, the suspension of the use of abdominal mesh and a full audit of how many people have had this type of implant. Freeman agreed to consider the issues and come back to us. Mark and Audrey were excellent.

After months of reflection, I spoke to Lesley Brennan and told her that I am going to resign from the Shadow Cabinet after the party conference. We cannot go on like this with people in the Shadow team constantly undermining everything. In Westminster, Corbyn tried to have a big tent, inclusive approach but those political adversaries he brought in used it as an opportunity to attack him at every turn and the same is happening here.

21 September Went to West Calder Chapel for Leo Thomson's funeral. There was a big turnout for this huge local character. Leo was a regular visitor to my office. We discussed socialism, fishing, the latest books he had read and a mutual loathing of the Tory party. He worked as a carer and a was very skilled artist and taxidermist. He was also a field sports enthusiast and poacher – he called it 'proletarian confiscation'.

The European Union has demolished Theresa May's plan, Donald Tusk saying the Chequers proposals were unworkable. May issued a statement saying she will fight on.

22 September Train to Liverpool for the party conference. The city is absolutely rammed, the conference is going to be huge.

24 September Met with Ian Lavery MP, the Chair of the Labour Party, for a discussion on building capacity for the election campaign.

Spoke to Keir Starmer today, who confirmed there was a five-hour meeting with delegates to try and agree a motion on Brexit. They eventually came to a unified position leaving all options on the table including the possibility of another referendum.

John McDonnell gave his Shadow Chancellor's speech setting out a plan for employees to gain a stake in the companies they work with, the nationalisation of water, post and rail and a range of other radical announcements. It was full of substance and reassurance that the next Labour government will not water down the radicalism.

Went to Scottish night with Lesley Laird, Ian Lavery, Richard Leonard and Jeremy Corbyn and lo and behold who turned up but none other than Alan Roden who does nothing but attack Jeremy, Richard and the Labour Party at every opportunity.

23 September Over to the conference for Starmer's speech. He proposed we leave all options open and added that supporting Remain in a future referendum should not be ruled out. I am not sure this was agreed beforehand.

Len McCluskey said a Remain option couldn't and shouldn't be on the ballot paper. I agree.

We then had a speech from Emily Thornberry who was excellent with references to the Spanish Civil War, the Internationale, Palestine and Yemen. Her speech was fantastic.

There was a debate on Palestine with a huge show of strength from Palestinian support groups. Masses of flags were waved throughout the debate. It was quite a spectacle.

24 September I spoke at the Orgreave Truth and Justice Campaign fringe meeting about the miners' strike policing review in Scotland.

26 September To the conference centre for a meeting with Richard Leonard. He is constantly firefighting and defending attacks from the New Labourites and their supporters. They are doing everything possible to bring him down. I have been urging him to take them on. He has to sack Jackie Baillie and Anas Sarwar and stamp down on the attacks, briefings, leaks and repeated undermining of him.

Just before his speech we had a cup of tea with Jeremy Corbyn. He was as relaxed and laid-back as ever, letting everything just wash over him. John McDonnell was cheery and upbeat and in good spirits.

In the hall they played 'You'll Never Walk Alone' and conference delegates almost lifted the roof off.

I am always a bit nervous when Jeremy speaks as he is not a natural orator, but this was easily one of his best and most confident performances. He took head-on the controversies of Brexit and antisemitism and was very clear on the economy, housing, poverty and international affairs. The 'Red Flag' was sung with gusto at the end.

Home absolutely shattered.

27 September After FMQs I went into the chamber for a statement from Jeane Freeman on St John's hospital. She didn't say very much, other than they are still trying to recruit staff and that it might take three to five years to do so. We are no further forward.

28 September Met the West Lothian College new principal Jackie Galbraith. I really liked her; we had a good chat about all things related to the college. Having been a student there three times, I am really keen to support the work they do.

30 September The newspaper headlines are all about Boris Johnson moving in for the kill on Theresa May.

Speculation today is that Richard Leonard is going to do a reshuffle, that Kezia Dugdale will resign from the Labour Party and there may be Shadow Cabinet resignations. We may be entering a phase of all-out civil war. Ian Murray told the media that Richard Leonard is Corbyn's nodding dog.

1 October Jennie Formby wrote to all MSPs setting out very clearly why the Labour Party will not fund Kezia Dugdale's legal expenses. Good on her.

Met with Richard and his team. There was a wide-ranging discussion on the need to deal with senior Shadow Cabinet members who are leading the attacks, the need for a new press officer and a reshuffle. We went round the houses several times without making a decision. I tried to bring it to a conclusion by asking Richard if he agreed that we had to remove Jackie Baillie and Anas Sarwar. You could have knocked me down with a feather when he said, 'No, not really'. I could take no more, picked up my stuff and walked out. What is the point of investing my time in this?

Went to Coatbridge to do some campaigning in the pouring rain, a grim day.

2 October Private WhatsApp exchanges between Labour MSPs have been leaked. I have no doubt today's meeting will be leaked too. Elaine Smith opened up with a brilliant and measured contribution raising issues around the leaking of private conversations, meetings and failure to respect each other. Jackie Baillie said people should not be leaking information (the irony meter exploded with that comment). Anas Sarwar spoke about people leaking and briefing the press. I called this out because, in my opinion, it is a person on his payroll who does all the negative briefing. Johann Lamont said this wasn't about Richard but the reality is all weekend this is exactly how it has been portrayed by those who attack him. I laid into them about the repeated attacks on the leader, the poisonous atmosphere within the group and the undermining of efforts to turn things around. On cue as we left the room, the press pack was waiting outside. If this is not the start of a revolution in the group and the removal of some of the key critics both within the Shadow Cabinet and party headquarters, then I can't stay involved.

Into the chamber for a motion of condolence following the death of former Presiding Officer Alex Fergusson.

Met with NHS Lothian officers to discuss the case of my constituent whose child died in infancy and where the NHS have covered up how they had dealt with the child's remains. We managed to get a number of concessions from them about the handling of the case and a commitment to repatriate any slides they have to the family for burial. They said the family could come and collect the slides. I said, 'Absolutely no chance,' and that an undertaker should respectfully deal with the child's remains in the normal way. This was accepted. I am pleased we have got some real progress for the family and that they have been proved right about what happened to their son. Helping bring some comfort to this family really picked me up. This is what makes the job worthwhile.

Boris Johnson made a ludicrous speech about Brexit, openly mocking the Prime

Minister. He was also photographed in a field of wheat, mocking May. It is only a matter of time before he challenges her.

3 October I watched Theresa May's conference speech today, she came on like a robot to Abba's 'Dancing Queen', which was excruciating. The speech was slightly better than last year's fiasco but still woeful.

Richard Leonard will reshuffle the Shadow Cabinet tomorrow.

4 October Lots of comings and goings in preparation for the reshuffle. Richard wants me to be the party Business Manager but continue with Brexit and party engagement. I told him I didn't want to do the Business Manager's role but reluctantly I agreed to do it.

The press were already speculating that Sarwar and Baillie would be sacked. And thankfully, they were. Immediately, the Labour right-wingers were out spouting the line that these were our most talented and effective MSPs and it was a disgrace they had been sacked. Their social media cheerleaders are attacking anyone associated with Richard.

The reality is that those who were sacked have been at the heart of all the negativity since Richard was elected.

5 October Went to North Queensferry with Pauline Bryan, Tommy Kane, and Alex Rowley to meet Gordon Brown. We had a wide ranging and frank discussion about further devolution and the political situation in the country and the party.

7 October The SNP conference starts today. Nicola Sturgeon was on the *Andrew Marr Show*, getting grilled on her domestic agenda. She said SNP MPs would now support and vote for a second EU referendum. I wonder if she would agree to a second referendum in the event of independence, if those who lost demand one. Somehow, I don't think so.

Shadow Chancellor John McDonnell has announced that Labour will scrap Universal Credit.

8 October I got a letter from Jeane Freeman advising me that 1,000 children have had to be treated at the Sick Kids hospital in Edinburgh, when they should have gone to St John's in Livingston. This is unacceptable.

October 9 Nicola Sturgeon gave her conference speech on a day when it was revealed two homeless people a day die on Scotland's streets. She spoke to her fan base about independence, ignoring the growing education attainment gap, NHS waiting times, homelessness, the drugs death crisis and social care. Astonishingly, the *Daily Record* editorial said she is a steady captain of the ship!

18 October The past week has been dominated by Brexit. The Tories are fighting like ferrets in a sack. Theresa May is looking weaker by the day. The

EU are trying to be helpful but she cannot get out of the bind she is in with her Brexiteers and the DUP.

George Galloway is claiming that he has heard the Tories have done a deal with the SNP to get Brexit through in return for another independence referendum. If it were true, it would be dynamite, but it's Galloway so it'll be nonsense.

Glasgow City Council today announced that the Wintergarden and People's Palace are to close indefinitely as they cannot afford to pay for renovation and repair. This is a national scandal.

19 October I emailed Jackie Baillie and Anas Sarwar about committee changes. Baillie is refusing to come off the Economy Committee and Sarwar does not want to go on the Environment Committee. I will speak to both next week.

20 October The People's Vote campaign held a march in London with about half a million people attending. It was rather astonishing to see Alistair Campbell there talking about how the government must listen to the huge numbers of people who had turned up; the same Alistair Campbell who, when he was Tony Blair's spin doctor, completely dismissed the million-strong march against the war in Iraq.

21 October This week will be the big showdown between Theresa May and her MPs, 46 of whom have called for a leadership contest. She is due to go before the 1922 committee this week. The *Sunday Times* is calling this a kangaroo court and says she is 'entering the killing zone'.

3 October I met with Jackie Baillie, who is pretending she is not upset by her sacking in reality is furious. She is refusing to come off the Economy Committee and will continue to play games. Sarwar was much easier to deal with and we had a straightforward conversation about what role he wants to play.

Lots of coverage on TV tonight about the dispute involving bin men in Glasgow. The SNP Council wants to use anti-trade union laws to break the dispute.

24 October Over to Monklands for the by-election where we delivered direct mail to homes before a photo shoot outside the hospital with Richard Leonard and a group of activists and candidate Geraldine Woods. In parliament we led a debate on the future of the hospital. The North Lanarkshire SNP MPs were on the back foot trying to blame the NHS to cover their embarrassment.

In a debate on inequality, Tory MSP Michelle Ballantyne said those who claimed benefits should not have more than two children – but apparently it's okay for her to have had six children. She got slaughtered in the debate. It later emerged that she had claimed tax credits and child benefit for her own children. The press are all over the story.

25 October The Michelle Ballantyne story is big news there is pressure on the

Tories to sack her.

Today is the by-election in Coatbridge. God we need a win to boost morale.

Met the Information Commissioner to discuss the government's dreadful handling of Freedom of Information requests. I showed him evidence of the government having three months to register ministerial meetings but then advising that they destroy the same records within three months – this is therefore not subject to FOI. He was unaware of this; his face was a picture when I pointed it out. He agreed to investigate.

At 11 o'clock I got a text from Elaine Smith to say we won in Coatbridge and increased the vote by 12 per cent. What a relief.

26 October Professor Alison Britton's report into conducting independent reviews was published. It is a damning critique of the way that the Scottish Government sets these up. It made over 40 recommendations for change, a terrific piece of work.

Tory leader Ruth Davidson had a baby today, called Finn.

28th October I spoke at the launch of Wendy Milne's campaign in Falkirk East. She is up against the SNP's Martin Day. I was a councillor at the same time as him and on numerous occasions he fell asleep at meetings.

Got a flight down to London for a series of meetings on Brexit, miners' justice and mesh.

29 October To the House of Commons to take part in a round table meeting on constitutional reform with the Electoral Reform Society.

Jeremy Corbyn's office arranged for me to go into the 'underbuilding' of the Commons to watch the budget. This is two rows of the green benches at the very back of the chamber opposite the speaker. I had an MPs eye view of proceedings. Just as things were getting under way, I was joined by Alex Neil who was also in London for meetings. One thing that struck me is how small the chamber is, how close both sides are to each other and how cramped the place is. Without doubt it creates more theatre and atmosphere than Holyrood, but it is a museum.

30 October Back to Edinburgh to meet Jennie Formby and Richard Leonard to discuss party organisation and campaigning. Jenny was very impressive in a no-nonsense way.

We were expecting a big row at the Labour Group about Kezia Dugdale's legal expenses. Jackie Baillie was the mouthpiece but Jenny handled her well. She showed real authority swatting away Jackie.

31 October The atmosphere at the Shadow Cabinet meeting was so much better without Jackie Baillie and Anas Sarwar there.

In the chamber we had a tied vote on the failure of the government's early years education provision. The Presiding Officer used his casting vote in favour of the government.

1 November I called on Jeane Freeman to undertake a new independent review of mesh following Professor Alison Britton's report and for her and Nicola Sturgeon to meet mesh survivors. Neither of them has done so, despite this being Scotland's greatest health scandal.

4 November The *Sunday Times* is claiming that May has a deal which will include a customs union. The Brexiteers will not accept it.

5 November Alan Roden has an article in *The Herald* attacking the Labour Party, John McDonnell and Richard Leonard. He works for four elected Labour politicians, yet he does this.

Michelin announced the loss of 850 jobs in Dundee, a disaster for the city.

6 November Went to a showing of *Nae Pasaran* in parliament. What a wonderfully inspiring film of the story of Shop Stewards at the East Kilbride Rolls Royce plant who refused to service jet engines destined for use by the fascist government in Chile.

7 November We had another Brexit debate this time on the impact on scientific research. The Lib Dems added an amendment calling for an 'unequivocal commitment to a public vote'. There was no way we could vote for it as it is not party policy. We agreed to leave all options open and not tie ourselves to any position. I spoke to Ian Gray, who doesn't like the position but accepted we would abstain. I then spoke several times to Daniel Johnson who advised he would break the whip to support the Liberal amendment. Kezia Dugdale said she would, too. Jackie Baillie and Mark Griffin were not happy with the position but accepted it. When the vote came, we had two rebels. There were also one or two in the SNP Group.

8 November I substituted for Clare Baker at the Culture committee today where senior BBC people were giving evidence. It was an opportunity for a bit of fun. They had provided a paper with details of the new 'Scotland channel'. I asked, will this 'new channel be on each night from 7pm to 12pm? If so that's five hours a night. 50 per cent of shows will be repeats. One hour of the remaining 2.5 hours will be news with four other hourly news updates of five minutes each, leaving 1 hour 10 minutes a night for original programmes. How much is this costing? The answer was £32 million a year.' I could see the colour drain from the guy's face as I spoke.

Afterwards we had a members' led by debate by Monica Lennon on a care home closure in Lanarkshire. For the first time in my eight years in parliament the government failed to put up the relevant minister to reply. It should have been Christina McKelvie or Clare Haughey who are both Lanarkshire MSPs but they bottled it so Graham Dey their Business Manager was sent to respond.

Today, we had Stage Three of the Prescriptions Bill. I again moved amendments supported by Money Advice Scotland and the Govan Law Centre, to reduce the period debts on council tax and reserved benefits can be pursued from 20 years to five. It turns out that the Minister Ash Denham following Stage Two had written to Esther McVey of all people to ask for support in rebutting our amendments.

I attended a meeting in Bathgate organised by a local group supporting drug users. They had speakers who are going through treatment and Karyn McCluskey from the Violence Reduction Unit. The meeting was excellent and I was thrilled to hear Steven McKnight, the son of a friend of mine (Wullie, now deceased) speaking. Steven has gone through a lot but is now clean and working on a bike project that helps people who have gone through what he has. Fantastic stuff. Every meeting I do on the subject of drugs convinces me more that we need decriminalisation.

9 November Boris Johnson's brother resigned today over Brexit.

12 November Lots of utter nonsense in the media about the size of Corbyn's poppy and the coat he wore at the Cenotaph. They really are scraping the barrel now.

SNP down 9 per cent in the constituency poll and 10 per cent in the regional poll for the Scottish Parliament elections. We are at 23 per cent and 25 per cent. Progress is slow but going in the right direction.

13 November Theresa May said she had a Brexit deal to take to the Cabinet. The DUP have already rejected it, Johnson has said it is unacceptable and Labour will only support it if it meets the six tests. This is crunch time. Even if she can get agreement in the Cabinet she will have to get it through parliament, the European Parliament and member states. The agreement is 500 pages long with a customs agreement to address the Northern Ireland border issue.

All of the opposition parties at Westminster (except the Greens) wrote to the government demanding the right to amend Brexit legislation. The Greens want another referendum.

14 October Labour called for the Scottish Government to enact the break clause in the Scotrail contract to end the privatisation shambles but when the vote came the SNP and Tories voted together to defeat our call.

May's cabinet met for five hours trying to reach an agreement on Brexit. Speculation swirled around all day. At 7.15pm she came out to speak and said very little but the Brexiteers, the Remainers and the DUP have all rejected the deal. Resignations will come.

15 November Early this morning a junior Tory minister resigned, then Dominic Raab. Over the next few hours more junior ministers stood down as did Esther McVey. May then made a statement and took three hours of questions in the Commons, where all sides laid into her.

Jacob Rees-Mogg gave a press conference to say he and a number of others had submitted letters calling for a leadership contest.

In the afternoon I responded to a statement from Mike Russell on Brexit and called for a General Election, although I have serious reservations about our prospects.

We are entering the final play in a 40-year-long civil war in the Tory Party. The EU has dogged every Tory Prime Minister since we joined the EEC in the early '70s.

19 November Went to Livingston Fire Station to meet firefighters and management. The management had tried to get heavy with the firefighters who contacted me and tried to stop the visit. The Chair of the Fire Board, Councillor Pat Watters, was there on his last day before retiring. Watters spoke at me for 45 minutes without stopping and then dismissed every concern raised.

The DUP voted against Tory government on the budget bill. Rees-Mogg and the his right-wing colleagues seem to have failed in their coup.

Sturgeon was in London for talks with opposition leaders. We briefed Corbyn's team that the only agenda item should be Brexit.

21 November Met with Labour researchers and press officers. They are a very good group of bright young people who put up with a lot from egotistical MSPs. I gave them my full support and assured them if they have any issues they should come to me. I was aghast to learn that some of them had been working for months without a contract. That will stop immediately.

22 November To the Scottish Politician of the Year awards at Prestonfield house. Pleased to see the mental health campaigners from Dundee won the public campaign award. Jeane Freeman won the Politician of the Year award, which was quite extraordinary as the NHS and social care are both in a real mess.

24 November Boris Johnson addressed the DUP conference – God help us.

25 November May released a letter calling for unity. She is responsible for creating an extremely hostile environment for migrants, has introduced the bedroom tax, benefit sanctions and cuts to disabled people's rights and the rape clause, all of which seek to divide people. And now she calls for unity!

26 November Visited the new West Lothian foodbank warehouse in Livingston.

They advised me of a big increase in demand because of the introduction of Universal Credit.

A group of journalists from across the world released a report on medical implants. *Panorama* followed up on the issue with a series of shocking revelations. This should get a lot of coverage.

In the Commons, May gave a statement and was attacked from all sides. Corbyn called her approach an act of self-harm. Looks like between 80 to 90 Tories will vote against her proposal. There will be a 'meaningful vote' on 11 December.

27 November Nicola Sturgeon gave a press conference to present the government's report into Brexit, which she claimed will cost each Scot £1,600 per year. She also said Brexit makes the case for independence even greater but wouldn't call a referendum because of the uncertainty. So, the argument now is that leaving the EU will make us poorer but leaving the UK will make us richer and leaving the EU is full of uncertainty but leaving the UK brings certainty? Hmmm...

Went down to Fauldhouse miners' welfare club for the public hearing held by the independent review into the policing of the miners' strike. John Scott QC and his panel took evidence from former miners, their families and an ex-police officer. The testimonies were powerful, people spoke about the impact on their lives, relationships, blacklisting, dealings with the courts and loss of redundancy money. I really hope these contributions bring about a pardon for those involved.

Theresa May says she is going to go around the country selling her Brexit deal. Good luck with that.

28 November I met with Mike Russell to discuss next week's Brexit debate. We agreed to work together to try to unite the parliament and leave the Tories isolated. He showed me a draft motion for a straight rejection of May's deal with no mention of The People's Vote. I made some minor amendments to it. Willie Rennie wanted The People's Vote mentioned and Patrick Harvie wanted a reference to revoking Article 50.

After decision time, we met again and agreed to go with the original wording; it gives everyone the opportunity during the debate to put their own position but maintain a unified position on the motion. We agreed to put out a joint press release and that we would have equal speaking time in the debate a good position.

I spoke in the Tory debate on drug and alcohol strategy. The Tories are trying to give the impression that they are now more understanding and humane on drugs policy but they still in favour a law and order approach. SNP members latched onto the issue of drug consumption rooms to present this as a constitutional issue where Westminster is blocking progress. The reality is there is so much more we could be doing in Scotland with the powers we have. In my speech I set out how the war on drugs has failed, how the trillion pounds spent on it has made things worse, how people cannot get help for addiction or mental ill health and again I called for radical reform along similar lines to the Portuguese model.

29 November At FMQs Richard got stuck into Sturgeon about the SNP council in Falkirk sending out letters to parents advising them of cuts to education services and possible teacher redundancies. Sturgeon was on the back foot, as education is supposed to be her priority. I was able to ask her a question about the issues raised in the *Panorama* programme on mesh.

Neil Findlay (Lothian) (Lab)

This week, *Panorama* exposed serious failings in the regulation and testing of medical devices and implants. This is a global issue and dozens of countries are affected. It is clear that the system in the United Kingdom, the European Union and across the world is not fit for purpose. As a positive step, will the Scottish Government now introduce a register of all implants?

The First Minister (Nicola Sturgeon)

We are happy to give consideration to anything that lies within our power. As the member is aware, the regulation of these devices is a reserved matter. Responsibility lies with the Medicines and Healthcare products Regulatory Agency, and we have written to it on more than one occasion asking for it to take action.

However, as we have done with mesh implants, we will continue to look at what we can do within our powers. I will ask the health secretary to look into the specific suggestion and write to the member in due course.

This afternoon, I substituted for Clare Baker at a joint meeting between the External Affairs Committee and the Finance and Economy Committee with David Liddington, the UK Minister for the Cabinet Office. I asked him about the politics of the coming vote and the Hobson's choice between No deal or May's deal. I likened the situation to handing your car into the garage and getting it back without the wheel nuts on. Brian Taylor from the BBC called me later to say he would use the clip for the news.

During a debate in the House of Commons, Labour MP Lloyd Russell-Moyle announced that he was HIV positive. He was surrounded by colleagues including Jeremy Corbyn and was given a standing ovation when he finished.

30 November St Andrew's Day and my mum's birthday.

I watched tonight's BBC documentary on the Foreign Office. Boris Johnson featured heavily and came across as an absolute tosser. At one point he was left a briefing to read during a flight to Paris but said he was 'bored' and couldn't be bothered reading it. A very revealing documentary.

I am hearing that next week there will be a head-to-head TV debate between May and Corbyn. Personally, I think Corbyn should avoid this and let the Tories stew in their own festering cesspit.

1 December Went to Stirling for the first meeting of the National Policy Forum. Lesley Laird was put forward to chair it and was challenged by Jackie Baillie. Lesley won by five votes. The media were being briefed from inside the room. The sniping continued all day with claims that Lesley's election was evidence of Labour being controlled by London and Scotland being a branch office. It really is pathetic nonsense.

I got a call from academic David Miller who briefed me on an organisation called the 'Integrity Initiative' which is based in a run-down building in Auchtermuchty. It is registered as a Scottish Charity and is funded by the US state department to pump out anti-Russian and other propaganda. This will be a big story when it breaks.

3 December The Attorney General Geoffrey Cox had to go before the Commons to explain why he was defying a parliamentary vote which called for the full legal advice on Brexit to be published. The Speaker will rule on this tomorrow. Cox could be held in contempt of parliament, which would be remarkable.

4 December The Presiding Officer is digging his heels in on the government wanting to give up some of their speaking time to the opposition in the Brexit debate on our joint motion. I have no idea why he is making such a big issue of this. I made my point along with the others but he is being intransigent.

This afternoon the House of Commons took the astonishing step of holding the government in contempt for failing to release the legal advice on Brexit. Within an hour, May suffered three defeats. The coverage is brutal.

5 December Mike Russell opened for the SNP in the Brexit debate with Adam Tomkins for the Tories. Tomkins has looked thoroughly miserable throughout the whole Brexit process because he doesn't believe a word of what May or Johnson says on the issue, but he is forced to parrot their lines. He was in denial about yesterday's shambles at Westminster and had so little confidence in his argument that he would not take a single intervention.

I was fired up for the debate and opened with: 'So much for the great constitutional lawyer afraid to take an intervention from a bricklayer [me], a used car salesman [Gil Paterson] and a Liberal Democrat. How timid is he?'

Tomkins hated being mocked. All through he and his colleagues had their heads down, trying their best to hide behind their phones and computers, but they could not hide their humiliation.

Just before the debate, the UK government issued their legal advice and it was devastating.

6 December John McDonnell was supposed to be up today to speak at the Scottish parliamentary journalists' lunch but couldn't come as he is embroiled in the Brexit mayhem at Westminster, so Richard Leonard took his place. He spoke pretty well but was grilled with tough questions. Jackie Baillie sat grinning like a Cheshire cat as one journalist asked why Richard had sacked her.

7 December John McDonnell came up today for a meeting with the Labour affiliated unions. He took us through the situation at Westminster, the work they are doing on policy development and planning. It was very good.

8 December Went to a great night to celebrate Loganlea Miner's welfare's 60th anniversary. I was asked to speak and thanked the club for the brilliant work it does. We had a night of music and comedy with a great bunch of people.

9 December The *Sunday Mail* ran a story I gave them on the 'Integrity initiative' and the 'Institute of Statecraft'. It got the front page with a headline 'Black Ops Targets Corbyn' and revealed the Foreign Office funded 'infowar on Labour.' The Tories are up to their necks funding this very shady organisation, which amongst other things shares briefings and stories trying to link Labour with Russia. It is outrageous. I phoned John McDonnell and gave him all the information and sent him the 18-page briefing I got from Spinwatch. Later, Emily Thornberry put out a statement and it became a big social media story. The *Sunday Mail* gave it brilliant coverage.

10 December The 'Institute of Statecraft' story has really taken off. There is now a Foreign office inquiry. David Leask from *The Herald* took to social media to criticise the *Sunday Mail*, whose Editor fired right back and put him in his place. Leask was named in the documents as a supportive journalist. This squares with his involvement in the Andriy Parubiy story from earlier this year. How very interesting.

11 December Today was supposed to be the big Brexit vote. David Mundell was at Peterhead fish market wearing a bloody baseball cap telling the fishermen the vote would be today. Rudd, Gove and others were assuring everyone it was going ahead. The vote was then pulled and all hell broke loose. There was uproar in the Commons with MPs shouting at each other. A Labour MP grabbed the mace and was suspended. Fifty Labour MPs led by the ever-helpful Ian Murray have written to Corbyn calling for a vote of no confidence in May and then a 'People's Vote'. This would be tactically inept as it would unite the Tories in her defence. You only get one crack at a confidence vote and have to time it for when you can win. Later, there was a three-hour debate on the failure of the vote to proceed. May is toast.

May has set off to fly around Europe seeking the support of EU leaders to give her a better deal, this despite saying the deal was non-negotiable.

Later in the day, Tory MPs started sending letters of no confidence to the 1922 committee. The writing is on the wall.

A press conference with representatives of different parties took place, including Ian Blackford of the SNP and Tory Anna Soubry who sat side by side calling for a vote of no confidence in May. Soubry then inexplicably said she would vote against such a vote if it came forward, work that one out? The reality is the SNP want a confidence vote that will be lost since the DUP won't support it, then for the pressure to be so great that it will force Labour to support a second EU referendum. If called, Scotland would vote to remain and they hope England to leave, paving the way for another independence referendum.

We should only be calling a confidence vote when the DUP are on board and there are numbers to win the vote.

12 December The threshold has been reached for a Tory leadership election. May has cancelled all her meetings and said she would fight on. It's Thatcher all over again. She will be gone in a day or two, the Tory Party don't piss about when they scent blood. The vote is tonight between 6 and 8pm.

The Scottish Government budget was today with Derek Mackay delivering his scintillating oratory. He has apparently been for public speaking lessons.

Just before the budget, the media ran a story leaked by the usual suspects in the Labour Group slating our budget strategy and failure to provide a costed alternative. Very helpful, as usual.

After the statement I asked a question about the failure to even mention the drugs deaths crisis. MacKay ignored our calls to end the cuts, make payments to prevent families being punished by the two-child cap and to freeze train fares.

At 9pm it was announced that May had survived by 200 votes to 117, but over half of her MPs wanted rid of her.

13 December Rees-Mogg and others are calling for May to go. She has said she will not lead the Tories into the next election, as if that is going to placate them.

The Supreme Court struck down some of the Scottish Government's Continuity Bill. When it was passed, only Section 17 was deemed outside the competency of the Scottish Parliament but when the EUWB became UK law, other sections fell outside of the parliament's competency. Mike Russell made a statement on developments, and I agreed we would work with them to try resolve these matters.

At FMQs I raised the issue of the 'Integrity Initiative' and called for an investigation by OSCR (later in the week a review of its activities was announced).

Neil Findlay (Lothian) (Lab)

The Office of the Scottish Charity Regulator states that an organisation cannot continue to be a charity if 'it is set up to be or advance a political party' or 'its governing document allows it to use its assets… for non charitable purposes'.

Does the First Minister believe that the Institute for Statecraft, based in Fife, should continue to be registered as a charity with OSCR, given the revelations this week that it has been engaged in partisan political activity?

The First Minister (Nicola Sturgeon)

I was concerned about the revelations published in the *Mail on Sunday* involving alleged actions of the Foreign Office. It is not for me to investigate their veracity or otherwise, but it was certainly, on the face of it, a concerning report, and I hope that there will be a full investigation and full answers to the questions that people will rightly and understandably have.

On the question whether an organisation is a charity as far as OSCR is concerned, I absolutely understand the sentiment behind Neil Findlay's question and why he is asking me it, but I know that he will appreciate that OSCR takes these decisions independently – and rightly so. I am sure that OSCR keeps the charitable status of a range of organisations under review if concerns are raised about them. If, as he clearly and understandably does, Mr Findlay has concerns about this issue, I encourage him to raise those concerns directly with OSCR.

17 December The media is full of Brexit with intense pressure on May but also on Corbyn who is being targeted by remainers to support a second referendum.

The *Sunday Mail* did another big spread on the 'Integrity Initiative' highlighting the UK government's involvement with this organisation.

Yesterday, Jeremy Corbyn was in Edinburgh meeting people who have experienced homelessness and groups who fight poverty. It seemed to go very well, there was a good attendance.

17 December Theresa May said there would be no meaningful vote until 14 January.

18 December I spoke to Karie Murphy to push for urgent investment in staffing and party reorganisation to prepare us for the election. We need this asap.

I went into the chamber for Mike Russell's statement on preparations for a 'no deal' Brexit. The Tories are seriously considering this as a scenario, especially if May is replaced by Johnson. There would be chaos at ports and airports, with food supply, security, trade, crime, etc. It really is very worrying. The Scottish Tories hate the thought of this but disgracefully say nothing.

Afterwards Humza Yousaf made a statement on Professor Alison Britton's review into how to conduct independent reviews. The government has sat on this for six months and failed to say whether they would accept all 49 recommendations.

20 December Got a phone call from a pal, John Jack, to advise his employer Kaiam have not paid their staff this month. They employ a couple of hundred people in Livingston. I hope to God this is not them about to go under days before Christmas.

21 December Kaiam has told 300 staff that they won't be paid this month and there will be redundancies after Christmas. People are devastated. I put in calls to the council, the government and Scottish Enterprise and we held a multi-agency meeting at 3pm. It transpired the Chief Executive of the company was in Scotland a few days ago and said nothing to staff before heading back to the US. The company has received £550,000 of financial support from Scottish Enterprise. The council is going to do advice sessions next week for staff. People in the community are volunteering to set up a fund to help which is great.

22 December The media is full of Kaiam stories. They are going into administration and seeking a buyer. I did a phone round to shops and organisations to see if they would donate to the community fund.

23 December Great response from trade unions and companies to the Kaiam fund with generous donations coming in.

24 December Livingston FC hosted a meeting with KPMG who have been appointed to wind up the Kaiam. It was very grim. People were numb. No wages, no job, no Christmas, bleak future, some were in tears. There is real anger at the conduct of the CEO Bardia Pezeshki, The community has raised £12,000 in just a few days.

25 December Christmas day with family and friends – food, music and bad dancing, it was brilliant.

26 December I put out a press release calling for a parliamentary inquiry into the award of government grants to companies who take money then disappear leaving chaos. I followed it up with a letter to the Economy Committee.

27 December What a relief, it looks like the banks have paid the Kaiam workers' wages after all. I don't know how but people have been paid. Thank the lord.

I spoke to Peter Swindon of the *Sunday Post*. He has had a number of exchanges with Bardia Pezeshki who said he told Scottish Enterprise on 15 November that Kaiam was in trouble. This is a big story as the Scottish Government would have known at least a month ago and did nothing to alert workers there was a problem, instead allowing this bombshell to be dropped just before Christmas. In the meantime, Fiona Hyslop, a government minister, has been busy taking selfies showing her helping with the fundraising effort.

30 December The *Sunday Post* ran Peter Swindon's story on Kaiam. Scottish Enterprise told the Scottish Government on 22 November that the business was in trouble and they did nothing allowing the workforce to learn of the closure a few days before Christmas. I posted the story on social media and said this was now a political scandal; immediately the trolls started attacking me. I later found that Alex Neil MSP and Neil Gray MP had said the government should have intervened earlier to alert the workforce of a company closure in their area but when I pointed this out, I was told they were entitled to raise this but I, on the other hand, was just attacking the SNP.

2019

UK AND SCOTTISH politics continued to be dominated by Brexit. If Theresa May's troubles were bad in 2018, then they got a whole lot worse in 2019. A series of votes in the House of Commons culminated in the biggest defeat for any government in modern times. The pressure was unsustainable, resulting in her standing down as Prime Minister following disastrous European election results and the failure to get her Brexit plan through parliament.

In the contest that followed, the Conservative Party elected serial liar Boris Johnson to lead the country. What could possibly go wrong?

Brexit was also the source of major divisions in the Labour Party. Holding seats in the 'leave' voting Midlands and north of England, and in 'remain' voting London and other English cities, the party's deliberately ambiguous position tried to balance these competing pressures. In Scotland this resulted in the party losing all its MEPs and slumping to its worst ever share of the vote.

These results fuelled the ongoing civil war in the party with the attacks on leaders Jeremy Corbyn and Richard Leonard growing more visceral and more destructive. Something had to give and when Johnson called an election late in 2019 the writing was on the wall.

1 January Up to Mum's house for New Year dinner with all the family.

2 January Kezia Dugdale has had an article published criticising Theresa May and Jeremy Corby for poor leadership. Irony is dead.

3 January Lots of coverage of the 2.8 per cent increases in rail fares. Children, who used to go free, will now be charged £1.

4 January The newspapers covered my call for the independent review of the policing of the miners' strike to offer a pardon to those convicted.

6 January Theresa May was on *Andrew Marr* today, she was terrible. I cannot see her lasting much longer.

A poll has Labour down 5 per cent.

The next ten days will be crucial. The meaningful vote is on 15 January. There are all sorts of parliamentary manoeuvres going on.

I am back at work tomorrow after a good break. This year will be political dynamite. Brexit will dominate everything, the country is completely divided, there are huge schisms in the Tory Party and the Labour Party and if Chuka Umunna and others think they can succeed where the SDP failed they are living in cloud cuckoo land. In Scotland the nationalists will exploit the situation and continue their drive towards independence. Labour must continue the rebuilding work and Richard Leonard must face off the right-wing of the party, who believe hard unionism and a return to New Labour are the recipe for success. We must select a panel of progressive socialists who will breathe life into the party and transform the parliamentary group after the Scottish elections. This is essential if we are going to fight off those who seek to take the party backwards.

7 January Theresa May's whips are using every trick in the book to cajole, threaten and bribe MPs into supporting her. Knighthoods, drinks parties, entertainment at Number Ten for MPs wives.

Sturgeon said today that she will publish her timeline for a second independence referendum soon. When have we heard that before?

8 January Alex Salmond won his judicial review case against the Scottish Government's handling of the sexual harassment claims against him. He won on the basis that a senior civil servant carrying out the investigation had prior knowledge of the case, having met two of the women complainants. He has been awarded several hundred thousand pounds.

At the Labour Group meeting people seemed a bit more cooperative and less confrontational. Doubt it will last.

The Economy Committee has agreed to carry out an inquiry into regional selective assistance grants following the Kaiam debacle. This is a good result.

In the chamber, Nicola Sturgeon gave an extraordinary statement on the Salmond court case. She said that while the investigation was under way, she had met Salmond, not once but three times, twice at her home and once at the SNP conference. Then she had two further telephone calls. None of this was registered in ministerial diaries and no minutes were taken, despite her being the head of the government that was investigating his behaviour. We had the usual patsy questions from the SNP side but Rhoda Grant and Jackson Carlaw got to the nub of the issue, questioning the propriety of the three meetings and two phone calls. This will run and run.

Theresa May lost a crucial vote on the Finance Bill. This makes a no deal Brexit much more difficult to achieve.

9 January After days of trying, I managed to catch up with Keir Starmer. He believes there will be a confidence motion and if that fails May has 21 days to make a statement to parliament before an explanatory motion is laid, which will attract lots of amendments including one for a 'public vote'. Labour will then have to decide whether it supports this, which will create a split either way. If Labour whips instruct their MPs to oppose a 'People's Vote' motion there will be a big rebellion; if they instruct their MPs to support the motion there will also be a big rebellion.

Later, the Speaker accepted a vote on an amendment to make Theresa May return within three days of a defeat, with a new plan. This leaves very little time and stops her running down the clock. I have never seen the House of Commons in such uproar and that's saying something.

The newspapers today are full of stories of the SNP's civil war breaking out over the Alex Salmond case.

10 January Allies of Salmond, including Kenny MacAskill and Alex Neil, are calling for an inquiry into the case with claims that people at the top of the SNP are trying to destroy him.

At FMQS, Jackson Carlaw and Richard Leonard raised the Salmond case and Sturgeon's meetings with him. Richard asked if Sturgeon had breached the ministerial code. Willie Rennie asked about the Scottish Government misrepresenting an academic's use on primary one testing and Patrick Harvie raised budget cuts affecting children with autism. It was probably the worst session I have seen Sturgeon have. I was called to ask a question on the Kaiam situation and raised the Minister Jamie Hepburn's failure to alert the workforce or even lift the phone to the company to try and prevent the crisis that emerged.

11 January I met with a local contractor who lost £30,000 and had to pay off staff because Kaiam placed an order with him before going bust. He is rightly angry that contractors have been hung out to dry.

12 January I spoke to Patrick Harvie about our proposal to establish a committee to investigate the Salmond case. As usual, he is on the fence.

13 January I got a phone call from Graeme Day at 1pm advising me that Nicola Sturgeon would be referring herself to the special panel to establish whether she breached the ministerial code over Salmond. She did this because the situation was getting out of control.

I launched my Members' Bill on double jobbing by MSPs. The bill seeks to restrict the amount of time spent and money earned by MSPs second, third or fourth jobs.

14 January Tomorrow is the Brexit 'meaningful vote', May is trying to rally her troops. The Tories are trying to spin that a defeat of around 70 would be a success.

It is being reported that Liz Lloyd, Nicola Sturgeon's Chief of Staff ,met Salmond before Sturgeon did. The Salmond team are claiming that there is a plot to prevent him from returning to politics.

Hospital parking chaos at St John's Hospital dominated my surgery tonight.

15 January The parliamentary bureau unanimously accepted our proposal for a committee to investigate the issues relating to the complaints against Alex Salmond. The SNP support it and clearly think this is an opportunity to throw Salmond well and truly under a bus.

The *Daily Record* revealed that when Salmond and Sturgeon met at her house, Salmond had both his lawyer and former adviser Geoff Aberdein with him. Where exactly was Nicola Sturgeon's husband Peter Murrell at this time? He is the Chief Executive of the SNP after all.

There is now a police inquiry, a civil service inquiry, an inquiry into whether the ministerial code was broken and a parliamentary inquiry.

At 7:45pm Theresa May went down to the biggest defeat of any government in modern history losing by 230 votes. Immediately, Jeremy Corbyn put down a confidence motion. Despite all the criticism and backbiting from the Labour right, the Blairites and the Corbyn haters, Labour has just delivered the biggest defeat of a sitting PM in modern times.

16 January At Westminster, Corbyn moved the confidence motion exposing the Prime Minister's incompetence and the government's abject failure over Brexit. During the debate it emerged that she had bought off the DUP with a one-billion-pound bribe. Gove summed up for the Tories with a speech that was a leadership pitch. In the vote May won by 19 votes including that of the odious Labour turncoat John Woodcock.

At the Labour Group meeting, all MSPs said they were for a second referendum on the EU with the exception of Elaine Smith, Lewis MacDonald and me. No one knows what the question would be or the consequences for Labour Leave voters or for another independence referendum.

Today is my daughter Chloe's 23rd birthday. We had a lovely family dinner at home.

17 January The media coverage today is extraordinary – it was the Tories who brought about the referendum, refused to speak to any party for two years, refused to try and build consensus, lost three Brexit secretaries, were held in contempt of parliament and suffered the biggest parliamentary defeat in modern history and yet the media are blaming Corbyn and Labour for the Brexit fiasco.

At FMQs the Salmond case was brought up again. The committee of inquiry is to have an SNP chair. This is not a good look.

Seafield Community Council hosted a meeting tonight about a major housing development. It was telling that no SNP MP, MSP or councillor was in attendance. The proposed housing scheme is in an area of 'special landscape control' and outside of the development plan. It is a speculative development, there is understandable opposition to it.

18 January I met with a senior executive of MacDonald hotels, they have just announced 50 job losses. I appealed for them to redeploy as many staff as possible and allow those who want to leave to go first. I also said I would write to the government about the situation.

I heard tonight that Ian Murray fancies himself as a possible leader of a breakaway party.

21 January Two constituents with acute mental health problems came into the office today. People who desperately need help and just cannot get it.

Theresa May made a statement which said nothing new. Labour put down an amendment on the need for a customs union and for the six tests to be met but also said there could be a public vote on any renegotiated deal. This is a change aimed at keeping the party together.

23 January The newspapers are full of the story about the new Queen Elizabeth Hospital, where a child has died because of a disease picked up from pigeon droppings in the roof space.

I heard today that Barclay Care have won the contract to take over the Breich Valley Medical Practice but will not provide a GP service at Stoneyburn. This is unacceptable and would mean the village will not have a GP practice for the first time since the creation of the NHS.

24 January Alex Salmond was arrested and charged with two counts of attempted rape, several counts of sexual assault, indecent assault and breach of the peace. This is an astonishing development.

25 January The newspaper front pages are ablaze with the Salmond story. Salmond is a huge political figure. Had all of this occurred prior to the 2014 referendum the modern political history of Scotland would have been very different. The victims appear to be being treated as an afterthought.

27 January I flew to London for a series of meetings. Afterwards, I met my sister Anna and her husband Jim. She has just finished up working after 34 years as a stewardess with British Airways. I am pleased she is finished as I was always worried about her flying but she has enjoyed her career, visiting a huge number of countries.

28 January Went to meet the campaign group Unlock Democracy to secure their support for my double jobbing bill. They are very keen to help. Today's *Daily Record* ran a brilliant piece supporting the bill.

Went to the House of Commons for the all-party group on mesh with Alex Neil and Jackson Carlaw. It was a very good meeting. We agreed to cooperate with the group.

29 January NHS Lothian are reinstating some services at St John's children's ward. This is good news but there is a long way to go before it is back to its previous level of service.

Met with Gordon Brown at the UNITE union office in Edinburgh. We spoke about Brexit, Blair, Corbyn (he did not criticise him) and where we go from here. He didn't think another party was likely.

30 January Alex Rowley, our local government spokesperson, has apparently been trying to cut a deal with Derek Mackay that would have seen Labour support the Scottish Government's budget in return for an end to cuts. Alex did this with the best of intentions but the reality is he flew solo and never referred it to the Shadow Cabinet. It has been leaked to the papers. I spent all morning trying to deal with group members who are putting the boot into Alex.

At lunchtime I hosted a memorial event and wreath laying ceremony 20 years after Michael McGahey, the former miners' leader, died. Friends, family and old colleagues attended. One interesting story that came out is that Mick's ashes are scattered in the foundations of the Scottish Parliament. This was apparently arranged by Donald Dewar.

31 January At the last minute I was called in to take part in the budget debate and bashed out a speech which I tried to send to my staff team to check some detail but instead sent it to Derek Mackay who was leading the debate for the government. In his speech Mackay did his big reveal and rightly took the piss, milking my stupidity for all it was worth, as I would have done had it been him.

I joined in the banter mocking my dreadful IT skills.

The Green Party bailed out the government in return for a consultation on a tourist tax and a roundtable meeting on Council Tax reform. There will be £200 million of council cuts and job losses thanks to Patrick Harvie.

The trolls had a collective orgasm on Twitter about my email balls up.

2 February In for another meeting of the Scotland Joint Working Group with Jeremy Corbyn.

3 February The *Sunday Herald* ran a story today about Scottish Labour membership falling by 20 per cent. This has clearly been leaked from officials, as only they have the information, it is appalling. The Sunday papers are also saying that Chris Leslie, Angela Smith, Mike Gapes and Chuka Umunna are going to set up a new party. I hope they don't let the door hit them on the arse on the way out.

4 February An email sent this morning to the Scottish Executive of the Labour Party and MSPs about the leaking of membership figures was immediately leaked to the media.

I attended the Labour Group development day and gave a presentation on polling and strategy. I got through a lot of items we have been working on. I hope it showed our detractors how much work is going on in preparation for the election.

For some time now I have been contemplating whether I will stand at the next election. All of this internal crap from people I can't stand is driving me to the conclusion that I won't, but I will continue to reflect on this over the coming weeks. I will discuss it with Fiona and Chloe and my close pals, but I am heartily sick of it all.

5 February At the parliamentary bureau there was a discussion on setting up the Salmond inquiry committee. The SNP are proposing Linda Fabiani to chair the committee. I objected in the strongest possible terms, not because it is Linda but because it will drag a Deputy Presiding Officer into what will inevitably become a heavily politicised committee.

I spoke in the World Cancer Day debate. I was very emotional, reflecting on the treatment both Fiona and my Da received when diagnosed with the disease.

6 February At decision time there was a motion to set up the committee to investigate the handling of the complaints against Salmond. I moved opposition to appointment of an SNP chairperson, but this was defeated. The inquiry will now be chaired by Salmond's long-standing friend and former colleague Linda Fabiani MSP. Not good.

I got agreement from Mike Russell, Patrick Harvie and Willie Rennie for a letter to the Prime Minister calling for her to rule out 'No deal'. The letter will go tomorrow.

Donald Tusk, President of the European Council, said today 'there is a special place in hell for those who pushed for Brexit with no idea how to deliver it'. This will send the Tories tonto.

7 February I have been trying for months to get the Scottish Labour Party officers to take fundraising seriously, we cannot continue to rely on UK party handouts. The Scottish party secretary has shown zero interest but I have insisted this issue is addressed and we had a productive meeting with the UK party's new head of fundraising. I will have to keep the pressure on the staff to deliver.

I spent this morning getting people to sign up to the letter to May ruling out a 'no deal'. Then at 12 noon I got a call from Graeme Day saying the government were withdrawing the SNP signatories because Corbyn has written to May setting out five steps she needs to take to secure Labour support. Apparently, Russell, who is in London, claims that the letter would show Corbyn's support for a deal. What a load of bollocks. May will never agree to what Corbyn proposes and the only thing we are doing with the letter is showing unity. The reality is that Russell has been told by his MPs not to sign it. I had an angry exchange with him, since he is now reneging on the agreement we had. I have dealt with him in a very straight and cooperative way for months but when I ask him for one bit of cooperation, he does this.

8 February Attended sexual harassment awareness training at the Scottish Parliament today. It is being rolled out for everyone who works in the building. It was good that MSPs and staff from across the parliament were there so we could hear everyone's contributions.

10 February *Mail on Sunday* today had 15 pages of excerpts from a book on Jeremy Corbyn with revelations such as 'he doesn't buy Heinz beans' and 'he went on a camping holiday camping instead of a luxury hotel'. Desperate stuff.

10 to 17 February In Lanzarote with Fiona – really nice break.

18 February MPs Chuka Umunna, Chris Leslie, Anne Coffey, Angela Smith, Gavin Shuker, Luciana Berger and Mike Gapes have all left the Labour Party citing antisemitism and Brexit. They have been doing all they can to undermine everything the Corbyn project has tried to do. They are vitriolic in their hatred. One thing is clear, this is not the SDP mark II: Gapes is no David Owen, and Smith is no Shirley Williams. Interestingly, Ian Murray put out a statement saying that he would not leave, for now. He has bottled it at the last minute. Almost immediately, Angela Smith made a racist comment in an interview and was forced to apologise. They appear to be being funded by big business to split Labour and keep the Tories in power. Apparently, their view is we have to stay in the EU to change it – but you have to leave the Labour Party to change it.

None of them will resign and stand in a by-election, as they would lose.

19 February At the Labour Group meeting I was expecting the worst after the split in the party. Richard opened up and took it head-on. Pauline McNeil, Claudia Beamish and I spoke, having a go at the splitters. Elaine Smith was brilliant and recalled how she was abused, ignored and picked on for years because she refused to support the Iraq war, council housing transfers, etc. She said people had short memories. The usual critics were very quiet.

In her newspaper column, Kezia Dugdale talks of 'a braying mob' hounding out MPs who have views similar to her on Brexit. It's her version of 'Holy Willie's Prayer', condemning everyone else and seeing no failings in her own position. Presumably, she sees the 'braying mob' as people on the left, like me, who supported her when candidacy when she stood against Ken McIntosh. Of course, that's long forgotten.

20 February There was a lot of speculation this morning that three Tories were about to join the Umunna gang. Lo and behold, just before FMQs, MPs Anna Soubry, Heidi Allen and Sarah Wollaston joined them, going into the Commons chamber to take selfies. At a press conference, Soubry said the Cameron coalition was great and the public spending and welfare cuts were the right thing to do.

I did a TV interview along with Maurice Golden of the Tories and the SNP's Keith Brown and attacked Soubry's record voting for cuts that impacted worst on the poorest and Labour's extensive history of work on equalities.

Derek Hatton was readmitted to the Labour Party today. Not a wise decision.

Later I spoke to Gareth Williams, Mark Drakeford's excellent Special Adviser, we have been looking at trying to do a joint letter and joint session of the two parliaments on Brexit.

21 February I met with Jackie Baillie and we had a very tense argument about leaks, attacks on Richard, briefings to the press and much more. She was not a happy bunny but I am glad to have raised these issues with her.

I met with Lynn McMath to discuss the Head of Comms job; I hope she will consider it.

In the final budget debate Derek Mackay was trying his best to use the techniques he was taught on the taxpayer-funded £1,000 public speaking course he has been on. Sounds like he has been practising in front of the mirror with a hairbrush.

Dealt with a worrying case about a child who has been removed from school by a parent and 'radically home schooled'. What this appears to mean is not educated at all. The authorities seem unable or unwilling to act. I will have a look into the issues it throws up.

Holyrood Magazine has an interview with Tony Blair in which he claims that moving to the left caused Scottish Labour to end up in third place at the last Scottish election and that Ruth Davidson was now the centre ground. What utter garbage, it was his protégé Jim Murphy that took us to one MP and Kezia Dugdale who took us to third place.

25 February Jeremy Corbyn told the PLP that if Labour's Brexit plan was not accepted then Labour would advocate a public vote. This is in line with the policy agreed at conference: 1) to call for an election 2) to push Labour's five tests 3) to remove the threat of no deal 4) and if stalemate, public vote. This is a very risky move. I was immediately called by the BBC for an interview and made a little bit of broadcasting history as I was the very first guest on the new BBC Scotland channel's flagship news show *The Nine*. It was quite exciting to see behind the scenes of a new and important TV programme.

26 February I thought that with a change of emphasis on Brexit policy the Labour Group would be more content. Not a bit of it. They just keep on moaning.

After the meeting, Richard Leonard and I did interviews with the media who appeared to be shocked that we preferred Labour's plan to the Tory shambles.

Did a *Holyrood Magazine* roundtable discussion with Alex Neil, Jackson Carlaw and John Finnie about men and gender issues, with a bit of focus on the mesh campaign. It was enjoyable and thought-provoking.

27 February Last night Chris Williamson MP spoke at a meeting about antisemitism and said Labour was too defensive on the issue. He has been suspended by the party.

Labour's Brexit plan was defeated in the Commons.

28 February Social Security Secretary Shirley-Anne Somerville made a statement saying the Scottish Government would not be taking control of devolved social security benefits until 2024. They constantly demand more powers and said they could set up a new state in 18 months but introducing 11 benefits will take five years.

3 March The *Sunday Mail* carried a blistering attack by the GMB Scotland Secretary Gary Smith on Richard Leonard. I suspect this might be about Gary's ambition to become the General Secretary of the union.

4 March God, I feel awful today. The madness that has infected the party, the media and country over Brexit, antisemitism, independence, the attacks on each other and anyone associated with Corbyn or Leonard, the left or trade unions who support the project are wearing me down. I am always up for a fight against our opponents but when those on our own side lead never-ending attacks it really is wearing. Comrades, indeed!

5 March I am getting nearer to a decision about whether to stand for election in 2021. I have been thinking about it for months and don't know if I can stomach another two minutes of all this crap never mind another five years.

Met with Mary McLaughlin, a university lecturer from Ireland. She came over for the mesh debate and wants to tell the world about the positive changes in her life following surgery by Dr Veronikis. She has got her mobility back, is pain free and back at work. We held a well-attended press conference.

In the chamber we had a Brexit debate held at the same time as the Welsh Assembly. There followed four hours of dull, clichéd, predictable speeches repeating the same old arguments read from the same old party briefings. God it was grim. The Tories took a pasting.

Afterwards, I held led a members debate on mesh. Forty women and their families were in the gallery for it. I set out the case for US specialist Dr Veronikis to come here to help mesh victims. Jeane Freeman's response was really poor. Some of the women and I then had a long and emotionally charged meeting with Freeman and the Chief Medical Officer, Catherine Calderwood. They really do not want to do anything but were forced to give a commitment to look at the proposals we put to them.

6 March Well, it's my 50 birthday today and I am shocked at how bad I feel about it. Outwardly I am all smiles as people wish me well but inside I feel dreadful. Birthdays never bother me but this one most definitely has had a profound impact. The realisation of how I am aging and that no matter what way I look at it I am now heading into my years of decline is a shock. I have never felt like this before. If this is my midlife crisis then I don't like it. I am going to make some serious decisions about my future in the next few weeks.

The Scottish Government were defeated on their failing early years strategy.

Home for dinner with all the family.

With the Labour Party conference this weekend coming, Kezia Dugdale sent an email out to party members falsely claiming Richard Leonard had changed the words of MEPs David Martin and Catherine Stihler in the conference magazine. Not true, but why would that matter? It is all designed to cause disruption and division on the eve of conference.

7 March Joined a meeting with the Palestinian Ambassador. He was very impressive and spoke of a deliberate strategy by some to conflate antisemitism with actions of the Israeli government in attempt to close down debate.

8 March Up to the Caird Hall for the opening of the conference.

In the afternoon, Jeremy Corbyn spoke in his quiet, conversational way. He set out Labour's proud role fighting racism and inequality, attacked the Tory

Brexit shambles and called for unity to win power. There were no fireworks, it was serious and what was required.

9 March Mark Drakeford, the First Minister of Wales, addressed the conference. He was excellent and comes across as a very decent man.

Met Karie Murphy to discuss threats being made to topple Jeremy and Richard.

Richard Leonard gave his speech to the conference; he needed a good one and delivered. It was clear, passionate, radical with good policy announcements on the devolution of employment law, land reform, a wealth tax and free bus travel. It shut his critics up, for five minutes at least.

Went to see John McDonnell in conversation with Graham Spiers. He was funny, confident and candid. I had a long chat with him afterwards.

10 March There has been a lot of back-and-forth discussion over the weekend to avoid a big split on Brexit. The Scottish Executive agreed a statement that goes before conference today and if passed takes priority over any motion. I spoke in favour of the statement and called for a united approach. We had a good, civilised debate that avoided the bloodbath the media were predicting. Ian Murray and Kezia Dugdale didn't take part or even stay for the debate. So much for their big intervention. The conference supported the Executive statement, a good result. All round, the conference went well without any real problems. The atmosphere was good and our internal opponents were quiet for a change.

11 March Theresa May is in Strasbourg trying to get a last-minute deal.

12 March I met with Richard's team to discuss how we now press on after the conference. I stressed the need for a clear strategy that we can all sign up to in order to take us forward.

At the Labour Group I put forward a plan for increasing our donations to the group funds. Grumbles from Jackie Baillie, of course.

After decision time I had a one-to-one with Anas Sarwar to raise with him his employee Alan Roden's columns in the newspapers attacking everything Labour does. Sarwar claimed this was nothing to do with him and whatever Roden does when he is not working for him is his own business. He said Richard had no strategy and no credibility and that apparently I am the real boss making all the decisions (this was a line written in a column by Chris Deering in the *New Statesman*). It is nonsense and I told him that. It is clear he still wants to be leader and thinks he is the man to turn Labour's fortunes around. I suppose that a private school education stokes that level self-belief and entitlement. I challenged him about being Deputy Labour Leader during the Better Together debacle. He said it was nothing to do with him and tried to claim he didn't support Jim Murphy either. I suspect he may be rewriting history.

I was a guest on BBC's *Debate Night* along with Jamie Greene MSP, lawyer Aamer Anwar, Alex Cole-Hamilton MSP, a representative from Amnesty Scotland and Jeane Freeman MSP. It was less confrontational than *Question Time* and quite enjoyable.

Before going on the show, we watched the chaos in the Commons, where Tory Ministers were voting against their own side. They rejected a 'no deal' option and May lost the meaningful vote by 150 votes; her days are numbered.

14 March MPs voted to extend Article 50.

David Steel was suspended by the Lib Dems today over the historic abuse cases involving former MP Cyril Smith.

15 March A white supremacist murdered 50 worshipers at a mosque in New Zealand and posted it all on Facebook. What a world we live in.

16 March Tonight was my 50th birthday bash with around 130 family, friends and colleagues. We had terrific music and food with everyone dancing and joining in the mayhem from the first song to the last. Loved it, very late to bed.

18 March The Commons Speaker threw a spanner in the works by ruling Theresa May couldn't bring her Brexit deal back for a third time. It looks like only an election will sort this but I am very worried about Labour's prospects.

Over the weekend, Paul Sweeney MP said the deselection of some of the Labour MPs who have deliberately and consistently attacked and undermined the party could be a period of 'natural cleansing'. He is now being accused of antisemitism. I despair.

19 March The right-wing media are attacking Commons Speaker John Bercow, claiming he is trying to stop Brexit. They are railing against Corbyn for removing MPs Mike Gapes and Ian Austin from their places on the Foreign Affairs Select Committee. Why would they not be removed – they are no longer Labour MPs.

20 March At PMQs Theresa May blamed MPs for blocking her deal, which went down very badly. Later she called cross-party talks and invited Chuka Umunna. When Corbyn turned up and saw who was there he walked out. I understand why but it left him wide open to attack.

21 March May is at the EU summit, she has eight days to rescue a deal. Corbyn was in Brussels speaking to EU leaders.

23 March The 'People's Vote' campaign organised a march and rally in London with Nicola Sturgeon sharing a platform with, among others, Alistair Campbell, Tom Watson and Michael Heseltine. It was Better Together on steroids! A million people attended the event. Jonathon Shafi and others are rightly calling Nicola Sturgeon out for posing for photos with Alistair Campbell, a key player in the Iraq war debacle that left millions dead, but hey, what's a few dead Iraqis when there's a selfie at stake?

I hate the idea of another EU vote.

25 March Kezia Dugdale's defamation case against Stuart Campbell, the Wings over Scotland blogger, has started. I hope she is successful as he is poisonous. It has been reported that at one point her lawyer asked about a term used in one of his articles: 'What is a wank hole?' To which he replied, 'A hole you wank into!' Rumpole of the Bailey, eat your heart out.

26 March Spent all morning on Brexit and the Green party motion on Article 50. We are now in a position where if there is not going to be another referendum and end up in a position of having to accept 'no deal' or revoke Article 50, we should have a free vote. I took this to the Labour Group where we had a measured discussion; the Group came to the same conclusion.

I hosted an event on the Spycops scandal. Paul Heron from the London Public Interest Law Unit was there with Tilly Gifford who was spied upon in the run up to the G8 summit. Nick McKerrell spoke about his work with Pollok Free State and his subsequent blacklisting. Nick dropped a bombshell when he said the notorious spycop Carlo Neri had operated in Scotland. This should breathe new life into our campaign for a Scottish public inquiry.

In the debate on Brexit, I set out our position on why we would support revoke in the event it was a choice between 'no deal' and revoke. This is not a position I like but it is where we are. In the end the Green party motion was amended by us and the SNP with only the Liberals voting against.

I heard today that Jon Trickett, Ian Lavery, Rebecca Long-Bailey and Richard Burgon all threatened to resign from the Shadow Cabinet if Labour support a second referendum.

Later, May announced she would resign if she got her deal through. On cue, the slugs crawled out from under their stones with Boris Johnson and Michael Gove saying that the deal they both hate might be worthy of support after all.

There was a real 'revolution' in the Commons tonight when for the first time ever they actually voted using pen and paper.

28 March None of the proposals voted on in the Commons last night secured a majority. Kenneth Clarke's amendment to create a customs union was defeated by seven votes with the SNP abstaining; had they not done so it would have passed. They were supported in their abstention by Chuka Umunna and his chums. On the vote for a second referendum Angus McNeil and Pete Wishart broke the SNP whip and voted against.

29 March The Westminster Brexit nonsense goes on. May is talking about bringing back her deal. Johnson et al are jockeying for position.

31 March Went with my brothers-in-law Martin and Louis to the Celtic v Rangers match today. It was the first Celtic match I have been at in about 12 years. It was a glorious day but the match itself was poor. I used to love football but the corporatisation and influence of the money men who now control the game of the working class has been to the detriment of the fans and the game.

1 April To Glasgow for a meeting with the Red Paper Collective for a discussion with Sean Griffin who has been recruited to do an extensive piece of work on the constitution. Sean is a constitutional lawyer by profession and was very impressive. I hope he will lay the ground for a credible Labour position. We have been calling for this since 2011.

More House of Commons votes tonight, none of the three positions secured a majority with the customs union option losing by three votes.

2 April Went into parliament to meet Graeme Day, the SNP business manager. The Govenrment is proposing the recall of parliament next week if there is no Brexit deal.

The Tory cabinet met for eight hours. Afterwards, May made a statement that amounted to bugger all.

Attended a show at Whitburn Academy. It was one of the most powerful and brilliant events I have attended in any school. It used music and theatre to discuss anxiety, depression, eating disorders, suicide, bereavement, illness and addiction. Staff, pupils and parents contributed.

3 April I cannot stop thinking about the brilliance of last night's event. I wrote to the school headteacher with my congratulations and submitted a parliamentary motion and questions on the issues raised. I will also arrange for the group to come into parliament.

More Tory Ministers resigned.

Looks like the European elections will go ahead.

I was cheered up today by a brilliant social media tweet by Lossiemouth Football Club that said: 'Game temporarily suspended tonight due to referee spewing in the centre circle.' Then, 'That's him yakked up his tea... game back under way.' Ah, the beautiful game.

At his meeting with May, Corbyn proposed a customs union, single market alignment and a confirmatory vote on the deal.

5 April Went into the Labour Bath Street HQ for more work with Brian Roy, the Labour Party Scottish Secretary, Richard Leonard and others. We are still miles away from being ready to fight an election.

7 April Sunday papers full of speculation about who will take over from Theresa

May. They also exposed the SNPs Ian Blackford's earnings from his various directorships, including one that pays £3,000 a quarter for eight hours work. Not bad for the 'humble crofter'.

8 April I read an interview by Kenny Farquharson with Pauline Bryan, who is a close ally of Jeremy Corbyn and has just been appointed to the Lords. She spoke about the importance of having a credible Labour position on the constitution. In response, the obnoxious Lord George Foulkes tweeted that Pauline was 'out of her depth'. I messaged him to ask if he had been drinking when he tweeted it.

Tory MPs have written to May accusing her of a sellout on Brexit.

Blackford's earnings are still in the news. Each time stories like this come up my Members' Bill consultation on ending double jobbing gets more support: there are now 500 responses.

9 April Keir Starmer and Rebecca Long-Bailey continued talks with the government on Brexit.

10 April I took a call from the Presiding Officer, who is in Skye on holiday. Parliament may be recalled because of Brexit.

12 April The Leith by-election was even worse than expected. We polled a dismal 15 per cent of the vote. Leith was the constituency with the biggest Remain vote in Scotland.

13 April Nigel Farage launched his Brexit Party saying he would put the fear of death into the established parties.

14 April With Labour ahead in the polls, the *Sunday Times* ran reheated stories on antisemitism and the secretly recorded conversation between Jeremy Corbyn and Margaret Hodge. We are ahead in the polls and this is what our own MPs are up to.

15 April Up to the STUC Congress in Dundee.

I was advised today that NHS Lothian cannot recruit GPs and are closing the out of hours GP service nine nights out of 23 because of this.

Two days ago, I launched a local online petition about the need for improved parking at St John's – 2,500 local people have already signed.

Nicola Sturgeon said she would not delete any emails or texts about the Salmond case. How very gracious of her.

Kezia Dugdale won her defamation case against Wings over Scotland.

A poll out today has the Brexit Party polling neck-and-neck with the Tories and Labour. In Scotland we are on 15 per cent, just ahead of the Greens. This is woeful and the only surprise is it's not worse.

18 April Kezia Dugdale's court case victory all over the papers.

We got a presentation from the pollsters Survation. What came across was the need to target working-class SNP voters with a strong, clear offer that will improve their lives. We need to talk positively about Labour's credible alternative, not just attack the government. This confirms what I have thought all along and shows the strategy of the previous leadership to chase a small number of unionist voters who are now loyal to the Tories is flawed. I am not convinced the Shadow Cabinet will agree.

23 April Back to parliament after recess with speculation that Sturgeon will announce Indyref2 tomorrow. Kezia Dugdale said it will happen. Reading Ministers and SNP MSPs body language, I wouldn't say we are on the brink of a big moment.

Spoke to Karie Murphy, who is back at work after a breast cancer operation. Thankfully she doesn't need chemo or radiotherapy. I told her we must change the Euro election material to make it relevant in Scotland.

I have been asked by the campaign group Justice For Colombia to go as an observer of the peace process. I would love to go and help but with the Euro elections coming I might not be able to.

24 April I did a Radio 5 interview on Brexit, Independence, and Trump's state visit. I said Trump was 'repulsive and offensive' and the last thing a divided UK needs at this moment. Nicky Campbell joked about me 'sitting on the fence' with my comments.

Into the chamber for Sturgeon's statement on Brexit and Indyref2. The atmosphere was flat and her backbenchers were muted. She said she wants to bring in a referendum bill and use it if Brexit proceeds. She talked about holding Citizens' assemblies and would hold cross-party talks about more powers for the parliament. It clearly was not about another referendum and all about party management ahead of her conference.

25 April Spoke to several journalists who all think that Sturgeon's statement yesterday is going nowhere fast and is all about heading off opponents at the SNP conference. There are some who think the Salmond case may be the end of her. Derek Mackay thinks he is the leader in waiting.

Richard had a good attack line at FMQS, saying: 'Sturgeon can bring in legislation for a referendum in six months but can't bring in support for the poor for three years.'

Met with David Martin and Richard to discuss the European elections and take on board his advice for the campaign, we all know this is going to be very difficult.

Made a short video to encourage people to take part in my Members' Bill consultation.

26 April Still arguing with party HQ about the EU elections materials, it is ridiculous. I told them we cannot put out the leaflet they are using in England and Wales, it does not work for us here as the photos and some of the references are not relevant. I also demanded that Richard's photo go on the front but they want Jeremy on it. We eventually got the text changed but they won't budge on the photo. I heard Mark Drakeford and Sadiq Khan have been making the same points.

Went to a strategy meeting in Glasgow. As I was leaving, I got a WhatsApp message from Jackie Baillie with the EU election leaflet on it, asking why we are not taking the opportunity to promote Richard, as if she cares about promoting him. This will give her another chance to attack us and stir up others. I was furious about this being leaked to her and asked a party official if he knew who did it. I got a short answer: 'I have no idea.' It will be all over papers tomorrow.

27 April Well, knock me down with a feather, the Euro election leaflet row is all over social media and the papers.

At the SNP conference Sturgeon was defeated on one of the key elements of the Growth Commission, the currency plan to use the pound.

28 April The *Sunday Times* ran a story saying that Kezia Dugdale is going to leave parliament in the summer. She must have a new job. She will have Alan Roden spinning a sob story on the way out. If she stands down, Sarah Boyack will return.

29 April The papers are covering Kezia Dugdale leaving parliament with the *Daily Record* saying how terrible it is, how badly she has been treated and what a loss she will be. I have to say I am struggling to buy this. I saw at close hand her inability to accept constructive criticism, her loathing of the left and Corbyn, how she was an ultra-unionist of Better Together who is now revelling in speculation that she may join the SNP. Apparently, she is going to work with the John Smith Centre for Public service.

30 April Up to Dundee to help Jim Malone. They are running a brilliant by-election campaign.

After a lot of hard thinking and discussion with my family and close pals I have made up my mind and will not stand at the next election. I will tell my staff team first before making any announcement. It won't come as too much of a surprise to them as I have mentioned the possibility of it before.

When Fiona was diagnosed with cancer a few years back it made me reappraise my life. It was only then that I seriously took time to think about it and the realisation that we are only here once and there is a world to see and many more things in what remains of my life, to experience. Life genuinely is too short to be worrying about the latest gripe from some of the self-entitled egomaniacs who have been central to the Scottish party's decline over 20 years. They will do anything and everything to undermine what we have been trying to do and our efforts to build an alternative. When I compare their petty, spoilt brat behaviour to the outstanding commitment and campaigning of Jim Malone and his team in Dundee, it shows who the real socialists are. I am feeling a sense of relief and contentment and know I have made the right decision.

1 May In the afternoon, the European election leaflets were delivered to Labour HQ and within an hour were leaked to Paul Hutcheon at the *Daily Record*. I hit the roof and called for an immediate investigation into the leak and a report back to me by 5pm tomorrow. In the last week we had repeated briefings, leaks, hypocrisy, and duplicity from disgruntled party staff and MSPs.

Gavin Williamson, the Tory Defence Secretary, was sacked for leaking information from a National Security Council meeting.

At the parliamentary bureau, the Chief Executive and Presiding Officer introduced a discussion on 'Operation Unicorn'. I initially had no idea what this was about but it turned out to be a briefing about how the political class and parliament will close down for ten days in the event of the Queen's death. It's all been worked out with X happening on Day 1 and Y on Day 2 and Z on Day 3, etc. It is completely over the top. Ken McIntosh said, 'The palace doesn't want any fuss.' Apart from ten days when the country will close down, of course.

2 May The local elections in England and Dundee Council by-election is today.

It is being reported that some of the Scottish Government evidence relating to the Alex Salmond case has been destroyed or deleted. Shocked I am not. There is speculation that Nicola Sturgeon is being lined up for a UN job. Not sure if I buy this.

3 May Gutted to hear Jim Malone lost in Dundee but increased the Labour vote by 11 per cent, a great effort.

In the English elections the Tories lost 1,000 seats, Labour down 70, Independents and Greens up with the Lib Dems gaining 800 seats. The knives will be out for Corbyn and those who have stoked negative headlines and division will run a mile from accepting any blame. What is clear is that the European elections will be even worse and at this stage there is little we can do to prevent it. The constitutional division that has inflicted huge damage in Scotland is about to hit England like tsunami. Labour cannot win in these circumstances as we are trying to appease both Leave and Remain voters by saying... maybe.

Heard from some of the Mesh campaign women who have been fast-tracked by the so-called 'National Centre of Excellence' for partial removals. The surgeons don't have the skills or knowledge to do removals safely and patients are coming out with greater injury and disability.

4 May Full results from the English elections show the Tories down 1,330 seats; Labour down 84; Liberals up 704; Greens up 194; others up 660. The usual suspects are attacking the Labour Party, Corbyn and anyone associated with him.

Big independence rally in Glasgow today. Around 50,000 there.

5 May Sunday papers full of attacks on Labour. Ian Murray has called those running Scottish Labour 'thugs and incompetents'. I texted him and asked him to be honest and make it clear who he was talking about. I never got a reply.

7 May I spoke to Andrew Fisher, Head of Policy in Corbyn's team. He said the Tories are conceding ground on workers' rights and environmental and consumer protection, and want to offer a temporary customs union until an election; then whoever wins can take things forward on their terms, but any new Tory leader could unravel it all at any point. So, despite all the negotiations between Labour and the Tories, no deal will be agreed and even if it were, it would never get through parliament.

To the Labour Group where Jackie Baillie, Neil Bibby, Anas Sarwar and others went on the attack about Brexit, the opinion polls and the EU elections. Not one of them mentioned Ian Murray's outrageous comments. The reality of all of this is that their conduct is driven by one thing and that is the forthcoming list selections, where party members will determine who will top Labour's regional list. This will determine whether some of these people will have a job come 2021. They want Richard Leonard gone so they can impose a system that will ensure they are all elected again. What we need is a system that brings in new candidates, with new ideas and new energy, not the same, tired old faces.

During the discussion I blew a gasket and hit out at all those who are leaking stories, undermining our efforts and attacking the leader and the party. Not a single person responded to my comments, because they knew I was telling the truth. Kezia Dugdale said we shouldn't be canvassing, because it would provoke Labour voters opposed to Brexit to vote for other parties. She used her friends as examples. I'm not sure they are likely to be typical voters.

8 May Shock, horror, *The Scotsman* is carrying full details of yesterday's Labour Group meeting. More leaks.

I heard that at last night's Labour dinner to mark the 20th anniversary of the Scottish Parliament, former First Minister Jack McConnell gave a speech and made a reference to Jackie Baillie being 'as loyal as ever'. I can only assume everyone fell about laughing.

Went to a talk on leadership with Shelley Kerr, the Scotland women's football team manager. She was very impressive. I reminded her of the time she scored two goals against my school team when I was the goalie and she was the star of the Parkhead Primary School team.

In the chamber, we debated our motion on air passenger duty. The government was forced into a complete u-turn on their call to scrap it.

9 May I heard today that Brian Roy, Labour General Secretary, has made a complaint about me calling for an inquiry into the leak of the European election leaflet. Why wouldn't I ask for this to be investigated?

At FMQs I asked about mesh victim Clare Daisley – this was the exchange with the First Minister:

Neil Findlay (Lothian) (Lab)

This week, I have been contacted by constituents who are victims of mesh but do not want to be named. They have raised with me the issue of women being directed to the so-called centres of excellence in Edinburgh and Glasgow for treatment, where many have received partial mesh removal that has produced very poor and debilitating results. The belief is that clinicians at those centres do not have the required skill set to carry out full mesh removal using the latest techniques.

One woman who is not a constituent of mine who has broken her anonymity is Claire Daisley, who will lose her bowel and bladder if she does not get a full mesh removal procedure within the next two months. Will the First Minister personally intervene in Claire's case to ensure that she gets the treatment that she deserves? Will she halt partial mesh removal at the Edinburgh and Glasgow centres until a full appraisal has been carried out?

The First Minister (Nicola Sturgeon)

I thank Neil Findlay for raising what we all agree is an important issue. Obviously, I will not clinically intervene in any individual's case, but I undertake to have the Cabinet Secretary for Health and Sport look into the case that has been brought to the parliament's attention to make sure that everything possible is being done for the individual concerned.

More generally, as Neil Findlay knows – he might have facilitated the meeting; he certainly attended it – the Health Secretary met a group of affected women. As a result of that, a group of medical directors and senior clinical managers are looking at a range of options to improve care and support. Among a range of issues, the group is considering the course of care for women who suffer complications. It met for the first time in early April, it will meet for a second time tomorrow and it aims to make recommendations to health board chief executives by the autumn. It will fully take into account the views that patients are expressing.

I absolutely understand why some women will want to retain anonymity and privacy, but if Neil Findlay is aware of any women who want to speak confidentially to the Health Secretary or health officials, we would be happy and, indeed, keen to facilitate that on the assurance that we will protect their privacy and anonymity.

Every tiny advance in the mesh scandal is like pulling teeth. The government and the media establishment are having to be forced to act at every turn.

10 May In my role as Business Manager I emailed all Labour MSPs about the leaking of private discussions at Group meetings and all Lothians members about Ian Murray's disgraceful comments. No doubt both of my emails will immediately be sent to the media.

We had a dreadful result in the by-election at Haddington, down 12 per cent. In the middle of all the Brexit chaos the Tories won.

At my surgery I met a prison officer who was badly affected by the drug 'spice', which he inhaled in a prisoner's cell. It sent him mad, punching the wall and smashing a chair, all out of character. I agreed to write to the government and ask parliamentary questions about the prevalence of this drug in prisons.

Got a good result today, a constituent who had to wait years from treatment to her knee and was in so much pain she was on the brink of having to give up her job that her family paid for her to be treated in Romania. After our intervention she will now get the costs refunded by the NHS. It shouldn't come to this but she is pain free and still working, so, a good result for her.

12 May Had another chat with my wife Fiona and daughter Chloe about my future. I want to get back into the real world. I will never give up campaigning and pursuing the issues I believe in, but this will now be from outside of parliament. I will wait until after the hammering we will take at European elections before going public.

13 May A poll out today has Farage's Brexit Party on 34.

Dealt with an astonishing case at my surgery. An older woman was sexually assaulted by a man who she works with in the NHS. He was put on the sex offenders register but not sacked; he went on to assault another woman and was again redeployed.

I received lots of supportive replies from party members to my email about Ian Murray's comments. Only two were critical.

14 May To the parliamentary bureau where we moved on to 'Operation Forth Bridge', the parliament's plans for when the Duke of Edinburgh dies. Every day's a school day, as they say.

To the Labour Group for another joyous meeting and this week's complaints: the Euro election leaflet, Jeremy Corbyn, the People's Vote, Monica Lennon speaking out on drugs policy, etc. Relentless.

Spoke at the Law Society hustings on Brexit. Quite enjoyed it, in a masochistic sort of way.

I heard tonight Ian Murray has made a complaint to the Labour Party about me bullying him – yet it was he who labelled us left-wingers as 'thugs and incompetents'.

15 May I spoke to members of Richard's team about my plans for the future. They offered support and suggested I take a few weeks off but there is no way I will do that. I have hardly ever been off work in my life and am not starting now.

After the Euro elections there will be an all-out attack on Jeremy and Richard.

We had an evening group meeting tonight. There is a total rejection by the ultra-unionists of the polling evidence that we presented which shows we have a far better chance of winning support back from working class Yes voters than from former Labour voters who have gone to the Tories. They want to adopt a 'Scotland says No' approach like Poundshop Ian Paisleys.

16– 20 May Went to Tiree for my 50th birthday weekend with my pal Damian Byrne who is also 50, and 30 of our family and friends. A brilliant weekend of madness and laughs in a magical place.

21 May Picked up election day materials from Labour Party HQ. We will need 11 per cent to win a seat on Thursday, it will be touch and go.

My dad would have been 80 today so, went to the cemetery today to lay flowers.

22 May Last bit of leafleting before polling day tomorrow then a candidate call to thank them all for their efforts.

23 May Polling day was steady. No sign of any opposition members or candidates. Very low key.

Lots of speculation May will announce her departure after the polls close.

Tory minister Andrea Leadsom resigned in opposition to May's commitment to a second referendum if the withdrawal bill is agreed.

24 May Met prison officers to discuss spice in jails. It is a huge problem.

May made an announcement outside Downing Street to say she will stand down on 7 June. She gave an absurd speech, before breaking down when she mentioned her 'love of her country'. There were no tears for those who queue at food banks, or have been victims of her hostile immigration environment, or for the Windrush people. Only tears for herself. Within half an hour, the vultures had declared themselves as candidates.

Got information from a constituent that Edinburgh City Council are banning homeless people from parks at night. The SNP cut budgets, can't provide housing and now ban the people who are the victims of these cuts from the city's public spaces.

25 May MPs Rory Stewart, Jeremy Hunt and Andrea Leadsom have joined the Tory leadership contest.

26 May The *Sunday Post* ran the story of the Edinburgh parks ban on homeless people. The council have done a U turn on the ban. Great result.

Went to the Euro election count at West Lothian College. I then had to go to Glasgow to do media with Mike Russell, Jackson Carlaw, Christine Richard and Ross Greer. It was dire, we lost both seats. There is now no Scottish Labour MEP. We polled 9 per cent, yes, 9 per cent in Scotland, 15 per cent in England and were third in Wales.

27 May There are big repercussions following the results. Corbyn getting pelters, Thornberry and McDonnell calling for another referendum under any circumstances.

On the conference call with the team I advised them I was standing down not just from the front bench but from the parliament and would go at the next election. On social media there is a campaign under way to get rid of Richard and Jeremy.

28 May Got a call from a few close comrades asking me to stay put. Ian Murray and his sidekick Martin Whitefield have articles and quotes in the papers calling for Richard Leonard, Lesley Laird and me to go. There may be a confidence motion tabled at the Labour Group today. I took calls from John McDonnell, Ian Lavery and Jeremy Corbyn asking me not to stand down. I had good comradely chats with them all, they are very good friends, but I have made up my mind. I published my resignation letter to Richard and his reply on social media. I did interviews with TV, radio and newspapers and received hundreds of phone calls, texts and emails from family, friends, party members, constituents and colleagues from across the political spectrum asking me to stay on and wishing me well. It was very humbling. I didn't go to the Labour Group meeting, I couldn't face it. Later Daniel Johnson resigned from the front bench over Brexit policy.

I went on *The Nine* Scottish news programme and gave a full and frank account of what has been going on in the Scottish Labour Group and the party over the last few years and the outrageous conduct of some of those in senior positions.

I got supportive texts from MSPs Mary Fee, Elaine Smith and Claudia Beamish and friendly texts from Johann Lamont and Claire Baker. Jenny Marra texted to say she didn't think the group meetings were too bad, that's because she never attends. No contact from the rest. I feel heart sorry for the staff who work for the group and leader having to put up with the crap being thrown at them.

Later Richard announced Scottish Labour would support a second referendum under any circumstances. If this is the policy, we should push for a confirmatory vote in any future independence referendum.

Alistair Campbell was expelled from the Labour Party today for voting Lib Dem. He was one of many crying crocodile tears at the loss of Labour MEPs but failed to understand that voting for someone else might just have contributed to their demise.

Still getting hundreds of messages and emails from people including, MSPs Tavish Scott, Murdo Fraser and Ruth Davidson and former MSPs Jim Eadie and Chic Brodie, the mesh women, Orgreave campaigners and blacklisted workers are amongst the latest to get in touch.

I heard Jim Murphy and Blair McDougall turned up at Eastwood CLP to vote in a confidence motion against Richard. First time they have shown face in years.

Reflecting on the last 48 hours, I am more convinced than ever I have done the right thing. Our country is horribly divided and polarised, the Labour Party is in one almighty mess and the right wing will not rest until they are back in.

I wrote to Nicola Sturgeon asking her to meet with the Mesh campaigners, she has never met them in seven years.

Sturgeon published a draft referendum bill today.

30 May David Clegg at the *Daily Record* wrote an article about 'the failure of the hard left takeover of Labour'.

Rory Stewart MP, one of the Tory candidates for leader, said in the past he smoked opium at a wedding in Iran. At the weddings I go to you might get a half of whisky or vodka, not a chase at the dragon. How the other half live.

31 May I got a phone call today from Gordon Brown. He left a message thanking me for my contribution over the years and asking if I can call him for a chat. I will leave it to next week before I do.

I heard today that at the Labour Group meeting the leakers had planned a vote of 'no confidence' in Richard but didn't have the numbers to win the vote. Then apparently, Colin Smyth was to resign but shat it, so it turned into 'carry on coup'. You can make your own mind up who is Sid James, Joan Sims and Charles Hawtrey.

Later, Anas Sarwar issued a statement to all Glasgow members – leaked to the media, of course. His leadership campaign has started.

This got me reflecting on the claim by Kezia Dugdale and her chums that a left conspiracy forced her out, when in fact it was those who she thought were her allies who were plotting her demise.

Got a phone call from Johann Lamont's former spin doctor, Paul Sinclair. He and I have little in common politically but he urged me to stay on and said I had too much to offer. He also said he had been dropped from writing a column for the *Daily Mail* for someone more left-wing – Ruth Davidson. He's not far wrong on that front.

1 June Alan Roden wrote an article in *The Herald* which attacked me and claimed Labour could have won more seats in 2017 if it wasn't for Jeremy Corbyn. Delusional guff. The additional six seats Labour won in Scotland were because of Corbyn. Anyone who thinks this was down to Dugdale needs to lie down in a darkened room.

2 June Richard Leonard did an interview with *The Herald*. He mentioned the failings of the European elections campaign, addressed issues of racism and Ian Murray's intervention. Some of what he said was fantasy such as 'there is no reason why we can't win the elections in 2021.' Sorry, but we need to survive first, comrade.

The papers are full of speculation about the list selections, saying Richard will remove his critics this way. The Labour Group is paranoid about this.

3 June Trump arrived in the UK and immediately insulted Sadiq Khan, the Mayor of London, saying the NHS should be opened to competition from US firms and praising Johnson, before going to a banquet with the Queen – which Jeremy Corbyn rightly boycotted.

4 June After last week's events I was welcomed back by MSPs Claudia Beamish, Monica Lennon, Alex Rowley, Pauline McNeil and Rhoda Grant; other group members didn't even look in my direction. Spoke to a few of the press pack, who were friendly, as were kitchen, security and postal staff.

6 June I met with Michael Clancy of the Law Society for a catch-up. We had a long chat about life, politics and the future. I have really enjoyed working with him.

In response to a government-inspired question from Alex Neil, Jeane Freeman set out the plan for a new Scottish Mesh Centre. At the end of the written answer, it said women could apply to have treatment abroad and this would be considered. This is important as it could open access to Dr Veronikis's expertise, but let's see if it is genuine or more spin.

7 June Great news, Lisa Forbes won the Peterborough by-election for Labour defeating the Brexit Party. There was no support or congratulations from the leakers in the Scottish Parliamentary Labour Group, they will be gutted we won.

Theresa May resigned as Prime Minister. She will stay on until a new Tory leader is elected. She has been useless, held to ransom by the far right of her party, scared of the voters, lacking in empathy with zero vision – good riddance but I really fear what might come next.

8 June The newspapers are running a story about Michael Gove having taken cocaine in his 30s. The issue is not his drug taking, it is his hypocrisy.

9 June Gove is taking a pasting in the papers. We now have Gove – cocaine, Johnson – cocaine, Stewart – opium, Raab – cannabis, Leadsom – cannabis, all of them pushing 'a war on drugs' policy line.

Marion Scott in the *Sunday Post* has splashed a story about Jeane Freeman and Catherine Calderwood having set up a group to plan the return of mesh implants. The group was established before we met these two in March, yet they never said a word and all the time planning the return of this horrific product.

10 June The Tory leadership election kicked off. Johnson is refusing interviews. His minders are trying to stop him from losing by making gaffs.

My mum got a clean bill of health today from the hospital where she had been for tests, great news.

The Tories voted to abandon free TV licenses for the over 75s.

11 June I heard that at the coming Labour Group AGM Jackie Baillie is to challenge Mary Fee for the position of Labour Group chair. Mary's husband is terminally ill, she needs support, solidarity and care, not to be turfed out of her position.

John Swinney said today he is ploughing on with Primary One testing, despite a parliamentary defeat on the issue. What is the point of parliament if defeats are ignored.

12 June Up at 4am for flight to London for a series of meetings. Then over to the RMT headquarters for the Cuba garden party.

Spoke to Ian Lavery MP, who told me about the appalling behaviour of the PLP. Sounds familiar.

13 June First round of voting in the Tory leadership race, Johnson topped the ballot with Hunt and Gove next, Harper out.

14 June I am getting an increasing number of people coming to my office saying that they have come to me as they know the local SNP MSPs will not represent them as it will mean they have to go against or criticise their party.

It's extraordinary how some voters just seem to accept this.

16 June The *Sunday Post* ran a front-page story calling for Jeane Freeman to resign and had another three pages inside detailing how she and the Chief Medical Officer have misled mesh women with quotes from some of them who are very angry indeed.

The *Post* also ran a story I have worked with them on, about new psychoactive substances in prisons; my parliamentary questions revealed that 1,600 prisoners and 90 officers have required medical attention for the effects.

17 June I went to a meeting with NHS Lothian with my constituent who was sexually assaulted at work and the assailant kept his job. The senior managers who were there were astonished at the case. How they didn't know about it is quite incredible.

18 June At the Labour Group AGM there was a full attendance for Jackie Baillie's challenge to Mary Fee for the position of chair. By 13 votes to 10 they kicked Mary out like a dog in the night. An act of self-harm.

Dominic Raab is the latest to leave the Tory leadership election race.

19 June Thinking about yesterday's dreadful Labour Group meeting, the right is taking control of different levers of the party. They will give Richard the summer then crank up the pressure in the hope he resigns, or they will move against him. The reality is there are two Labour parties – one is socialist, grassroots-based, working-class, grounded in the trade union movement, critical of the EU and in favour of much more powers for the Scottish Parliament with a belief Better Together was a disaster. The other is economically liberal, socially woke, middle-class, Pro EU and hard-line unionist with a hatred of the SNP and belief Better Together was a triumph. These two sides coexist very uncomfortably in times of relative calm and break into open warfare at other times. Something will have to give.

19 June A reply to a planted question by an SNP MSP said that Dr Veronikis is coming to Scotland at the invitation of the Scottish Government. However, I know there is no agreement and he is pulling his hair out in frustration.

I sat in the chamber throughout the amendments on the Planning Bill. The SNP and Tories having done a deal and voted together to defeat amendments on regulating short-term lets and third-party rights of appeal, despite SNP MSP Sandra White bringing in a bill on this while in opposition.

Rory Stewart was kicked out of the Tory leadership.

20 June I asked Jeane Freeman a question about the plans to bring back mesh implants. She denies it but we know that this is their plan.

21 June Amazing footage emerged of a Tory MP at a dinner grabbing a protester by the throat and marching her out. If that had been a Labour MP there would have been wall-to-wall coverage.

Michael Gove was kicked out of the Tory leadership contest; it is now between Boris Johnson and Jeremy Hunt,which is the equivalent of a choice between shooting yourself through the head or through the heart.

22 June The newspapers are covering a domestic incident at Boris Johnson's house where the police had to be called. Can you imagine the outcry if this had happened at Jeremy Corbyn's house.

23 June A Panelbase poll out today suggests that support for independence will rise if Johnson is Prime Minister.

24 June I wrote an article for the *Daily Record* today on the drug deaths crisis and the need for massive reform.

Boris Johnson was interviewed on the BBC. Asked the question about Brexit and he replies 'magic beans', asked about the backstop and he replies 'unicorns', asked about a 'no deal' he replies 'Lord Lucan'.

Got a call from Gordon Brown asking to meet next week.

25 June Woke up to a text to advise that my pal Tommy Kane's mum has died. She has been ill with cancer and the family hoped she would be able to get home but it wasn't to be.

Boris Johnson has released a photo of him and his partner holding hands sitting on a bench in a field in Sussex just to show how much in love they are and that the barney at his home involving the police was a minor tiff. He has appointed Iain Duncan Smith to 'inject some energy into the campaign.' Ian Duncan Smith, a man who barely has a pulse!

I spoke in the debate on the community impact of aircraft noise and referred to the proposal to extend the flight path across the west of Edinburgh airport. This has been an ongoing campaign for a number of years.

On the way home I listened to a radio interview with Boris Johnson. He was asked about what he did in his spare time and spouted some gibberish about making model buses out of cardboard crates.

26 June Did an interview for STV on my Members' Bill on MSPs double jobbing. The big media story today is the horrific images of a Mexican man and his daughter face-down dead, having drowned trying to cross the Rio Grande. It is so upsetting but the media do not want to accept that this is also happening every single day in the Mediterranean as people are kept out by the EU.

Lib Dem MSP Tavish Scott announced he is leaving parliament for a job with Scottish Rugby. I will be sad to see him go as he is a personal friend.

Went into the chamber for a statement on mesh by Jeane Freeman. Apparently, the government is still speaking about bringing Dr Veronikis to Scotland but this has been going on since November with no progress. Freeman denied they were discussing the return of mesh implants. This is contradicted by the minutes I have of a planning meeting of senior NHS people. I quoted this and said she had lied to parliament and was unaware of what her Chief Medical Officer was doing on her behalf. Ken Macintosh, the Presiding Officer, told me to withdraw my comments. I said that I respected him but I also respect the women who made the call for her to resign two weeks ago and with an apology to the Presiding Officer refused to withdraw my comments. He then told me to leave the chamber, I left but was not suspended as is the norm.

There was a Labour Group drinks reception tonight but I avoided it like the plague.

Received lots of emails and texts from mesh women supporting me for calling out the Freeman.

Kezia Dugdale gave an interview to the media today saying Corbyn would agree to an independence referendum in return for the SNP supporting a minority Labour government. She just makes this stuff up, there is absolutely zero truth in it.

28 June Got an email from the Presiding Officer ticking me off for calling out Freeman. No suspension or loss of a day's pay. A small victory.

29 June Went into the parliament for events for the 20th anniversary of Holyrood. The Queen and Prince Charles were in attendance for all the pomp. Fiona and my mum came with me and we had a pleasant day. My mum enjoyed listening to music and poetry. No sign of Alex Salmond.

The Times has a story about civil servants briefing the media that Jeremy Corbyn is too physically and mentally frail to become Prime Minister. The establishment is going for him. Corbyn is a fit, calm, relaxed and strong individual.

1 July At 11.30 am two security officers came to check out my office before Gordon Brown visited. It must be a complete pain to have to have these people trailing round with you everywhere. Gordon and I spoke for over 90 minutes about the economy, constitution, Boris Johnson, the Labour Party and much more. We agreed to keep in touch.

Paul Wheelhouse, Minister for Energy, Connectivity and the Islands, has extended one of the main fracking licenses in Scotland. We were previously told that fracking was banned.

2 July Visited Shotts Prison where I visited the halls and workshops, and met staff to discuss morale, sickness absence, stress and the impact of new psychoactive substances. This is a big issue but the service doesn't seem to have any idea of how to cope with it.

I watched the second episode of Alan Little's BBC documentary, *Children of the Devolution*. The most telling comment was from Professor James Mitchell who said, 'the reality is that the Scottish Parliament has helped the middle classes most because they are the ones who vote.'

3 July Went over to Addiewell for Helen Kane's funeral. We walked behind the hearse to the Miners' Welfare then to Livingston crematorium for a lovely service where Tommy gave a moving eulogy full of dignity and decency, highlighting his mum's contribution during the miners' strike and work with the club's women's section. Afterwards, we went to the club for a catch-up with friends and members of the family and had a drink and sing-song, just as she would have wanted.

4 July Today was a very significant day. The *Daily Record* had a front page splash calling for the decriminalisation of drugs to address Scotland's crisis. This is a big breakthrough. I spoke to the Political Editor about this a year ago and encouraged him to go to the Editor with a proposal to support decriminalisation. My rationale for this was that the drug deaths crisis is impacting on the families of *Record* readers. I urged them to do this to try to change the debate in Scotland. I am absolutely over the moon that they have followed through and submitted a parliamentary motion congratulating them on this bold move.

The Scottish Government announced another four-month delay to the opening of the new Sick Kids hospital. This is an NPD project, PFI by another name, and is already six years late.

5 July I wrote an article for *Scottish Field* based on my experience of learning about fishing, shooting, snaring, and all things country sports when I was growing up. I recalled the skills and knowledge being passed on by my pal Jimmy and his da, who was a miner. I really enjoyed writing the article.

Jeane Freeman has stepped in and made a decision not to open the new Sick Kids hospital until it is complete, which runs contrary to what NHS Lothian said a few days ago. I called for an immediate inquiry into this shambolic project.

6 July The weather was beautiful this morning, a relief as it was Fiona's 50th birthday party in our garden. It was a lovely day with around 60 friends and family there. We had a singer, a DJ and a piper. We had a ball and didn't get to bed until 3am.

7 July *Ooft* – six-hour clear-up after the party.

8 July Fiona's 50th birthday. I know it's a cliché but I really cannot believe it. We met when we were 16 and now we are both 50. Bloody hell.

This morning I was on BBC's *Good Morning Scotland* with Ayesha Hazarika to discuss alleged splits within Jeremy Corbyn's office. She loves all of this stuff. I asked her why she never comments on the progressive policies that would transform the lives of so many people? No answer.

The *Daily Record* published my drugs article today in which I called for Scotland to follow the Portuguese model by decriminalising drugs, expanding treatment services and taking a public health approach. We desperately need to change direction.

9 July *Scottish Field* sent a photographer to do a photoshoot of me and Jimmy to accompany the article. We had great fun posing with fishing rods and shotguns.

Public Health Minister Joe Fitzpatrick appeared before the Scottish Affairs Select Committee calling for the devolution of the misuse of drugs act and declaring Scotland's drug deaths a national crisis, a bit bloody late. The reality is we have been operating under the same legislation as England and Wales yet our drug deaths are three times as bad. Calling for the devolution of powers is a smokescreen for abject failure.

Labour's position on a second EU referendum changed today after the Shadow Cabinet and National Executive Committee met. The party now supports a second referendum and will campaign for Remain. This is madness, Labour MPs represent many Leave voting areas.

10 July *Panorama* focused on antisemitism within the Labour Party. It was a real hatchet job.

12 July Deputy Leader of The Labour Party, Tom Watson, published an extraordinary letter attacking Jenny Formby, the Labour Party General Secretary, who is currently undergoing chemotherapy. I sent Watson a message saying: 'Dear Tom as someone who voted for you in the deputy leader contest, can I advise you to please stop making a complete tit of yourself. This is sent in the spirit of comradeship and solidarity.' I got no reply.

13 July Train to Durham with Fiona for the gala. We met lots of people we knew and took up our usual spot outside the County Hotel. The music was fantastic, everything from hymns to Abba played by the dozens of brass bands that pass by. All of the union banners were on show in a true celebration of working-class culture and heritage. We met up with a big group from Scotland before going down to the park where we heard speeches from Laura Pidcock, Len McCluskey, Jeremy Corbyn and others. I love the gala and will keep coming back.

16 July Figures released today show 1,186 Scots died of a drug-related death, the worst rate in the developed world. The SNP have been in power since 2007 and have overseen a catastrophe on our streets. Nicola Sturgeon has been Health Secretary or First Minister as this unfolded. She bears personal responsibility for the policies and budget cuts. Joe Fitzpatrick went on TV to blame the Westminster government. Both he and former Health Secretary, Shona Robison represent Dundee which is the drug death capital of Europe and they were the ministers who slashed the budgets of alcohol and drug partnerships. Will they take responsibility? Will they hell?

17 July Alex Neil MSP of the SNP, Alex Cole-Hamilton of the Liberal Dems and John Finnie of the Greens and I launched a petition on Scotland's drug deaths crisis. I approached Adam Tomkins and Oliver Mundell from the Tories to see if they would sign and both said they were supportive but didn't sign, no doubt fearing repercussions from their whips.

50 Labour members of the House of Lords took out an advert in *The Guardian* claiming that Jeremy Corbyn had 'failed the test of leadership'. A test set by them, of course. Presumably, taking out a full newspaper advert to attack your own party is showing leadership. It was signed by such 'heroes' as Peter Mandelson, Helen Liddell, George Foulkes and Meta Ramsay.

18 July The House of Commons voted by a big majority to prevent any Tory government closing down parliament to get Brexit through.

Last night Jeremy Corbyn sacked the Deputy Leader of Labour in the Lords for saying Corbyn's conduct was 'like the last days of Hitler'.

19 July This is Andrew Maguire's last day before leaving my office to take up a new role in Housing. I will be very sad to see him go, as he has been an excellent member of staff who works very well with constituents and was good fun to have around.

The battle lines are now being drawn in the Labour Party. It's all very depressing.

21 July The *Sunday Post* is running a story about mesh victim Claire Daisley, who, if she does not receive expert treatment in the US from Dr Veronikis, will lose her bladder and bowel. Dr Veronikis has agreed to do a pro bono operation for Claire if accommodation and flights are paid. We will get her the money somehow. She cannot be allowed to go through more suffering.

22 July The Chancellor Phillip Hammond said he will resign if Boris Johnson is elected Prime Minister today.

Met with John Scott QC to talk over his independent review of the policing of the miners' strike. He has done a very thorough job of the review. However, he said he may not make any recommendations and that my call for a pardon would go beyond his remit. I expressed my extreme dissatisfaction with this and said he must recommend a pardon for all those convicted. This is the whole point of the review and he can't duck out of it. I said I would send him my proposal on how a scheme of pardon would work.

To the Edinburgh Royal Infirmary with Mark Baxter and his family to meet the clinical team who dealt with his late mum who had mesh identified on her death certificate. This was a very difficult meeting for the family; we saw the medical establishment closing ranks but we will not give up on the fight for justice.

Jo Swinson MP was elected leader of the Liberal Democrats.

23 July Another Tory minister resigned just before Boris Johnson was declared the new Leader of the Conservative Party and Prime Minister. He then gave a vacuous speech. Ruth Davidson, David Mundell, Jackson Carlaw and others are now saying how jolly good he is.

Rhea Wolfson resigned as our parliamentary candidate. The left in my constituency worked to get her elected to Labour's NEC, supported her candidacy and backed her campaign and now she has bailed out, leaving us with no candidate and an election looming.

Theresa May did her last Prime Minister's Questions with all the Tories who had just stabbed her in the back proclaiming what a great person she is.

We then had Johnson going to see the Queen and all the rest of the flummery that goes with a change of regime. His Cabinet puts in place all the Eton and Oxford right-wingers, Rees-Mogg, Patel, Raab and the like. The signs are we will have an autumn election. Dominic Cummings has been appointed as head of strategy.

25 July Johnson sacked David Mundell as Scottish Secretary, replacing him with Alistair Jack, who I have barely heard of. He also appointed the horrendous Esther McVey and Gavin Williamson.

26 July The Caley Railworks in Glasgow closed today after 160 years building trains. The trade unions organised a march with a pipe band leading the workers out for the final time. Not a word from Sturgeon, the local MSP and Trade Minister Ivan McKee, or the SNP trade union group. What a waste of industrial talent, 150 jobs gone.

I have decided to call for the recall of the Scottish Parliament in light of the drugs deaths crisis. Someone dies every seven hours. Does this not constitute an emergency?

27 July Spoke to journalists about running a story on the recall of parliament over the drugs crisis. It would give the call a push if they did.

2 August The Tories lost the Brecon and Radnor by-election today to the Liberal Democrats following the sitting Tory MP being recalled due to fiddling his expenses.

3 August Went to Stoneyburn Centenary Gala Day with my mum. She was a past gala queen. The weather was nice and there were lots of families out for day.

4 August The ongoing delay of the new Sick Kids Hospital is dominating the news. Six years late, it is costing £1.4 million a month in fees and has not treated a single patient.

It is reported that the Green Party's membership has fallen 28 per cent and only 12.5 per cent of them took part in their recent leadership election.

5 August Wonderful news today, Claire Daisley is to fly to the US this week to be operated on by Dr Veronikis. She has had to crowdfund to pay for it.

I joined two police officers for a shift at Livingston Police station. Over the course of the day, we were called out to deal with eight cases, including a stabbing. Two were about child welfare, one an alcohol-related incident another a sexual offence, the rest mental health. The officers said they repeatedly find themselves picking up the pieces of a broken mental health system. They are understaffed and spread too thin. They want mental health workers based in police stations. I am very pleased I went out with them.

6 August The exam results are out today with a 2 per cent fall in Higher results. And education is supposed to be Sturgeon's top priority.

Later, social media went wild reporting John McDonnell's comments at an Edinburgh Festival event where he said that a Labour government would not block an independence referendum if there was a nationalist majority in Scotland. This is commonsense but Ian Murray and Jackie Baillie are going nuts. I gave supporting comments on McDonnell's statement and was immediately attacked. They think hard unionism will win Labour votes. It is fantasy, Richard Leonard is boxed in by this lot and said today that Labour would block any such move, it is undemocratic and incoherent.

7 August Well, well what day. The kickback from John McDonnell's comments is raging. Ian Murray was on the radio claiming McDonnell and Corbyn are destroying the Labour Party. The Scottish media are lapping it up, laying into Richard Leonard. I put out supporting statements saying McDonnell and I oppose another referendum, and while I would vote against independence, I will argue for a confirmative vote in any independence deal negotiated but I defend the right of any Scottish Government elected on a clear manifesto commitment to an independence referendum to enter into negotiations with the Westminster government on it. I really don't know why this is controversial. Ian Murray then appeared on *The Nine* and couldn't give any sort of logical answer to the question 'Why is it OK to have another EU referendum but not another Scottish one?'

Later I got an email from Jackie Baillie saying the Labour Group Executive had drafted a statement on today's events. I sent her my position and said I want to see any statement before it goes. I am not signing up to any of their mince.

8 August Went out for a shift with BT Openreach to see the broadband installation process. It was very interesting.

Jackie Baillie emailed Labour MSPs to get agreement to put the statement out supposedly supporting Richard Leonard's position and condemning John McDonnell. Alex Rowley, Elaine Smith and a few others didn't want it to go out and said so, and I told her not to put my name to it, but she put it out anyway and said it was the Labour Group position. I immediately put out a statement saying it was not my position.

9 August The newspapers are full of stories of 'Labour's civil war'. It will get worse today as Brian Roy, the Party's General Secretary, has resigned. He was a Jim Murphy appointment and a close ally of Baillie and Sarwar. He was never onboard with Richard or any of what Jeremy tried to do and the Party HQ in Scotland worked against the direction we wanted to go in.

I was called by the BBC and several newspapers but refused to give any quote. The Labour Group awayday on Monday will be a treat. Richard is a decent man but is being strangled by those who never wanted him in the first place and have worked to undermine him from day one.

Went over to Bannockburn to meet Dennis Canavan about the miners' policing review. He was recuperating from a triple bypass. I took him through my proposal for a pardon. He was very keen on it. I like Dennis and enjoyed our chat.

10 August Alan Roden has an article in *The Herald* today full of revisionist guff, recalling the 'glory days' of Kezia Dugdale's leadership where her approach – *and not Corbyn's* – won us seven seats in Scotland. Fantasy.

11 August The papers were full of stories about the latest crisis in Scottish Labour with one suggesting Richard won't even turn up to the MSP awayday tomorrow. Paul Hutcheon's column in the *Sunday Herald* was brutal.

12 August I did not attend the Labour Group meeting but was advised that all the folk who have been attacking Richard were pledging their loyalty and supporting his anti-independence stance.

13 August I read media reports of the group meeting (leaked of course) and laughed at the following in one paper: 'One member of the group commented that the atmosphere was better than expected, which was probably because Corbyn ally Neil Findlay was not in attendance.' Probably true. I put a message on the Labour Group WhatsApp group saying 'thank you' to the 'comrade' who leaked this to the ever helpful media.

14 August–1 September Fiona and I spent three weeks visiting San Francisco, Las Vegas, Chicago and New York for our 50th birthday celebration.

At the end of August, Boris Johnson went to the Queen to seek permission to shut down parliament in order to get his Brexit plan through. All his nonsense about reasserting British parliamentary democracy has turned to dust. Can you imagine the response if a Corbyn government tried to do that? The security services, media and establishment would swoop into action and there would be a 'very British coup'. Remember, the Tories claimed there would be a run on the £ if a Labour government was elected well, the pound is at parity with the dollar.

While I was away, Ruth Davidson resigned as the leader of the Scottish Tories. This has taken Scottish politics by surprise. She is claiming she is going because of her opposition to Johnson's Brexit but also because she wants to be there for her young son.

2 September The Tory Chief Whip warned that Tory rebels in the House of Commons face being deselected. This will have zero impact on the likes of Kenneth Clarke and Dominic Grieve.

Johnson made a statement outside Downing Street to say he didn't want an election, then his Press Officer briefed the media that there would be one if the House of Commons voted to prevent his deal passing. The stakes are huge.

3 September Sarah Boyack has returned to parliament, replacing Kezia Dugdale; and the new Lib Dem MSP for Shetland, Beatrice Wishart, was also sworn in. At Westminster, Johnson's threat of deselection has stiffened the resolve of his Tory critics. As he got up to speak one his MPs, Phillip Lee, crossed the floor to join the Liberal Democrats.

A group of Scottish politicians have taken a case to the Court of Session challenging Johnson's proroguing of parliament. The verdict is due tomorrow.

After a day of rancour, bile and speculation, the Tory hard right now want Johnson to move to a 'no deal' position.

Nicola Sturgeon set out her Programme for Government. There will be bills on Defamation, Good Food, the European football championships, etc. Nothing radical, all pretty uninspiring. There is a paltry £10 million additional cash to deal with the drugs deaths crisis.

Culminating three years of chaos, the big Brexit vote took place today. In the debate, Rees-Mogg was terrible, Clarke and Grieve were excellent. The atmosphere in the Commons was like a Celtic v Rangers match minus the pleasantries. The government was defeated by 328 to 301. In response Johnson ranted and raved and said he would bring forward an election.

4 September At Westminster the shenanigans go on with the Commons backing a bill to prevent a 'no deal' Brexit. At Prime Minister's Questions Johnson was embarrassingly bad. The MP Tanmanjeet Singh Dhesi attacked Johnson's racist writings when he was a 'journalist'. It was a thing of beauty and left Johnson absolutely floored.

An image of the epitome of elitist entitlement went viral: Jacob Rees-Mogg lounging across the green benches of the Commons like a Roman Emperor waiting to have the silver spoon removed from his mouth and a grape dropped in.

5 September I had a discussion with US mesh surgeon Dr Veronikis this morning. The Scottish Government is putting completely unnecessary barriers in his way to prevent him from coming here. The good news is Claire Daisley is on her way home after her operation and she did not need to lose her bladder or bowel.

I asked a question of Joe FitzPatrick on the drugs crisis finding out that the drugs deaths task force hasn't met in six months.

Having good fun goading the Tories about their Scottish leadership campaign, it is rumoured Michelle Ballantyne MSP is going to stand. That will be 'interesting'.

Johnson spoke in front of a group of police officers today. They must have wondered what on earth he was talking about.

6 September Went to Billy Kane's funeral at Livingston Crematorium. What a shame for the family losing their mum and dad in such a short space of time. Billy was Communist, community activist, trade unionist, stalwart of the Loganlea Miners' Club and a great character. There were many great stories and much banter in the club afterwards.

7 September Amber Rudd resigned from the Tory Party saying she could not stay in following the sacking of 21 of her colleagues by Johnson.

8 September *The Sunday Post* carried five pages of stories about mesh. They covered Claire Daisley's story, the Veronikis saga and the failure of the Scottish Government to bring him here. Outstanding campaigning journalism from Marion Scott.

9 September Did an interview with STV on the mesh issue. The Scottish Government failed to put up a minister, which is telling. They issued a statement claiming they are doing 'due diligence'.

The bill blocking a 'no deal' Brexit passed through its final stage today. The House of Commons will now have five weeks off. The 'mother of all parliaments', indeed.

9 September John Bercow, the Commons Speaker, announced he will stand down at the election or on 31 October, whichever comes first. The Tories hate him because he stands up to them.

Visited West Lothian Drug and Alcohol Project to discuss drugs and the organisations' funding crisis.

10 September I visited the Penumbra mental health drop-in centre in Leith. This is a first-class centre where people can walk in off the street and if necessary stay for a night or two to get away from a crisis. They are then supported into services. Astonishingly, this is the only such facility in Scotland.

My 'double jobbing' bill was lodged today and the good news is all of the Greens, four SNP and six Labour MSPs have signed up already.

Trump sacked his third National Security Adviser via Twitter.

11 September The Court of Session found against Johnson proroguing parliament. The case will now go to the Supreme Court.

Went to the Glasgow Film Theatre to speak at the launch of the new documentary about the Durham Miners' Gala.

12 September At FMQs the Sick Kids Hospital debacle was the main topic. No one in the SNP ever takes the blame, apparently it's all down to 'the matrix', whatever the hell that is.

I spoke in the debate on the drug deaths. Joe FitzPatrick took a hammering from opposition speakers, there was not a single word of criticism or even concern from his own side. FitzPatrick's response to the debate was his worst since… his last response. He is completely out of his depth, can barely string a coherent sentence together and is unable to think on his feet. He is on the ropes and the government's failure is exposed. We need to bring about a change of minister.

13 September Jeremy Corbyn was awarded a lifetime achievement award from Strathclyde University in recognition of decades of work with refugees and asylum seekers. It received almost zero media coverage.

15 September Over to Auchengeich Miners Welfare for the 60th anniversary of the mining disaster. Councillor Willie Doolan was overseeing events. There were about 500 in attendance with children and families taking part.

16 September Boris Johnson was in Luxembourg trying to woo EU leaders to support his Brexit plan. It was a complete disaster with the Belgian President humiliating him at the post event press conference.

17 September After previously claiming she couldn't instruct a public inquiry into the Sick Kids Hospital debacle, Jeane Freeman announced… a public inquiry into the Sick Kids Hospital debacle. She was given a torrid time in the chamber.

During a staged visit to a hospital, Boris Johnson, the father of a sick child lambasted him for holding a PR event instead of addressing the crisis in the NHS. Johnson claimed there was no media there, only for the man to ask what about the entourage of cameramen, reporters and photographers.

19 September After months of controversy and opposition the SNP are scrapping the 'Named Person Legislation'. Of course, this is not their fault, it's the opposition's fault: they never take responsibility for anything.

Met with the Law Society to discuss the SNP's Referendum Bill and to investigate whether I could move an amendment for a third option and a confirmatory ballot. The Bill excludes the involvement of the Electoral Commission, who are very unhappy about this, leaving it to the Cabinet Secretary to dictate terms through regulations.

20 September Got a response to a parliamentary question today advising 67 per cent of drug deaths involve street benzodiazepines. There is no strategy for addressing the street benzo death toll.

It's been five years since the Independence Referendum. The issue still dominates every single political utterance, divides our country and paralyses rational debate.

I was supposed to meet Jeane Freeman about mesh but she cancelled.

There was a global climate strike today. I went to the local event in Livingston where around 50 children and parents turned up to protest. There were big demos in Edinburgh and Glasgow.

21 September To the Labour Party conference in Brighton. On the way there, I read astonishing news that at the NEC there was a move by a Corbyn ally, Jon Lansman, to scrap the post of Deputy Leader. It's all about getting rid of Tom Watson. This cack-handed attempt is a gift to the right wing. The only thing we should be discussing this week is how to get rid of the Tories. I texted Jeremy and John McDonnell to this effect.

22 September Andrew Fisher, Corbyn's Head of Policy, is to stand down citing infighting, a lack of professionalism in the team, too many egos and an unbearable working atmosphere. This is a real shame as Andrew is a very capable, decent guy.

23 September Into the hall for Richard Leonard's speech, which was decent, then for John McDonnell who delivered a list of policy commitments including a state-run pharmaceutical company, sectoral bargaining, a living wage for all, a million new homes, free prescriptions and a revolution in workers' rights. Great stuff, delivered in his unflappable style.

I spoke at a lunchtime fringe before going into the hall for the big Brexit debate. There were a number of decent speeches. Keir Starmer's style is odd and stilted and dull but he knows his stuff. At the end there was chaos when the Chair, Wendy Nichols, failed to call a card vote (this is done when a show of hands is close). She then called the result wrong. Jenny Formby, the General Secretary, was sitting next to her and advised her of the mistake, so Nichols reversed her decision. I think she made a genuine mistake but all hell broke loose. The pro-EU zealots were furious. She could have resolved it easily by accepting the call for a card vote but dug her heels in and created unnecessary animosity.

24 September At 10.30am the Supreme Court delivered an 11-0 ruling stating the Prime Minister had broken the law by proroguing parliament. The Commons is being recalled tomorrow. Johnson's humiliation is complete. Corbyn's speech was brought forward a day.

The hall which was buzzing after this morning's events. Corbyn gave a speech full of policy announcements – Crossrail for the north, nationalised rail, Post Office, water and pharma, net zero emissions by 2030, £10 per hour living wage, end of zero hours contracts, a new Trade Union Act, expansion of electric cars, municipal bus services and free personal care. It set the scene for the election that is coming.

Home on the 'sleeper' to Edinburgh – one thing about the sleeper is you don't get much sleep.

25 September The House of Commons returned to extraordinary scenes. MPS were screaming and bawling at each other, some in tears talking about the threats they have received from extremists online. Paula Sherriff MP called out Johnson for referring to the murdered MP Jo Cox in one of his answers. It was dreadful.

26 September At the meeting of the Standards Committee today. The new Standards Commissioner was there to give her annual report. She hinted that all was not well before she took over, so I asked her to elaborate on this and she went into a big long list of issues she uncovered – 70 per cent staff vacancies, a huge backlog of cases, major problems with administration and much more. We asked her to return so we could investigate things further.

27 September An announcement was made today advising that the proposed re-opening of the St John's children's ward on a 24/7 basis in October will not now happen. This has rumbled on for seven years.

28 September The newspapers full of the St John's children's ward story.

29 September The *Sunday Times* put the boot into Johnson over an affair he had with a woman who won contracts when he was Mayor of London. He then claimed his government is building 40 hospitals when in reality it is six.

I got a letter today from Dr Veronikis saying because of the games being played by the Scottish Government he is no longer prepared to come to Scotland. He gave a damning critique of the Chief Medical Officer and senior surgeons. This is devastating news for the women who need his skills.

30 September I phoned Dr Veronikis. He is despondent at the way he has been treated but even more despondent at the fact that so many women who are living in pain will not be able to access mesh removal treatment. He is convinced that the senior Scottish surgeons do not want him here as it would expose bad practice.

Spoke to a constituent at my surgery who is in temporary accommodation. The owner has 40 rooms let out to homeless people, there are no cooking facilities in the rooms, only a kettle. He pays £98 per week – god knows what the council pays. The owner is coining it and people are cooped up for long periods waiting on being placed on a housing waiting list of over 10,000.

2 October Labour led a debate on the disastrous Scotrail franchise. When the vote came, SNP and Tories voted together to ensure Abellio keep the contract. So much for the 'progressive' SNP.

3 October Green MSP John Finnie's Bill to ban smacking was passed today.

4 October Went to the local mental health advocacy project to speak to them about the crisis in mental health. It was even more shocking than I had expected.

My Members' Bill to restrict MSPs from 'double jobbing' has received 35 signatures from Labour, Greens and the SNP – no Tories or Liberals signed.

5 October Huge Independence march in Edinburgh today.

6 October In the *Sunday Post*, Marion Scott covered the Dr Veronikis's withdrawing his offer. I have called for a public inquiry into the whole mesh debacle and for Freeman to resign for her role in it. She has known since last Monday that he is not coming and has chosen to say nothing. I did lots of media clips.

7 October I spoke at length this with mesh survivors about the Veronikis withdrawal. They are furious about the government's handling of this.

Met West Lothian council officers to discuss the case of a child with special needs who, due to the retendering of a taxi contract, has lost his driver and trusted escort of eight years. This is an example of the often unseen impact of austerity. It might seem trivial to some but for this young boy it is huge.

8 October It has been reported that the Provost of Glasgow, Eva Bolander, spent £8,000 on eight blazers, 23 pairs of shoes, five coats, eight pairs of trousers, underwear, 20 nail treatments and designer hats – all paid for by the taxpayer at a time when her council were cutting homeless services and social care budgets in a city with the greatest level of disadvantage in the UK. I took the opportunity of the business motion being moved to raise the mesh issue and call for a debate on the fiasco.

Scottish Tory leader Jackson Carlaw told me that there will be a challenge to him soon.

9 October Sat for eight hours through the Transport Bill, discussing powers for councils to run bus services, low emissions zones, a car-parking levy on workers, etc. after voting for all of these positions, SNP ministers jumped into a line-up of large chauffeur driven ministerial cars to take them home.

The Provost of Glasgow says she will repay the £8,000 she spent on clothes.

8 October At FMQs, Richard Leonard and Jackson Carlaw raised the mesh scandal and Dr Veronikis. Sturgeon expressed her desire to ensure he comes here and that women get the best treatment possible. The reality is that she has not once taken up the many requests for a meeting.

Coming out of the chamber, I read on Twitter that Kezia Dugdale has left the Labour Party, claiming it was Brexit that did it. She was the one who demanded a second referendum and now that it is Labour policy, she leaves. She also said she didn't vote Labour in the Euro elections, despite the people she claimed as her close friends, David Martin and Catherine Stihler, being top candidates.

11 October Met with West Lothian IJB mental health service heads today, to discuss the lack of drugs and addiction support, the absence of emergency mental health provision, waiting times, lack of psychological appointments and the police being forced to pick up the pieces.

13 October Dani Garavelli wrote a brilliant piece in *Scotland on Sunday* on the Portuguese experience of decriminalising drugs. This is what we should be doing here.

14 October It was Queen's Speech day at Westminster. With 22 bills listed, none of them will be enacted. It's all about an election.

At the SNP conference Jeane Freeman was not given a speaking slot – the Cabinet Secretary of the biggest spending government department with no speech. Well, no wonder. Waiting times and delayed discharge are at record levels, the Sick Kids fiasco rumbles on, we have the worst drug deaths in the developed world and a mental health crisis.

15 October Spoke to Dr Veronikis today. He has a phone call with Sturgeon on Thursday. I am hopeful his offer to come here can be saved. I ran through some of what she might say and how he should approach the conversation.

Sturgeon gave her conference speech, claiming she will call for a Section 30 order next year to hold another referendum. This is a pre-election move to try and rally SNP voters.

16–23 October In Crete for a week with Fiona.

When I was away Johnson tried to get another Brexit deal. There was a Saturday sitting of the House of Commons for the first time since 1982. It all fell flat when an amendment to delay Brexit passed. Johnson is now supposed to write to the EU and ask for an extension but says he won't. The timing of the vote coincided with a huge 'People's Vote' rally.

Johnson brought forward his new Brexit Bill, all 110 pages of it, with just two days of scrutiny. The second reading was passed by 30 votes but the programme for the Bill was rejected, delaying it.

Spain is in turmoil following the jailing of Catalan nationalists and there is crisis after crisis breaking out across the globe, including Lebanon, Chile, Turkey, Syria, Yemen, Bolivia. We live in increasingly worrying times.

The Northern Ireland Assembly passed legislation on same sex marriage. This is huge progress.

Richard Leonard is in New York with his wife. He tweeted a photo taken with Bernie Sanders and was immediately attacked by Scottish Labour right-wingers.

Despite all the Brexit chaos, Johnson is getting a bounce in the polls.

Thirty-nine people were found dead in a lorry trying to get into the UK, what a horrific situation.

24 October Back to work to deal with the case of the young refugee women living in completely inappropriate temporary accommodation with her young son. I assured her I will do everything I can to get them into better accommodation.

Audit Scotland published a damning report into the state of the NHS. Six years ago I called for a comprehensive review of the NHS in Scotland and had we done that we would have been in a much better position. As it stands, there is a £200 million black hole, waiting times and delayed discharge are increasing, performance falling and staff are under pressure like never before.

Ruth Davidson has taken a second job earning £50,000 a year for 24 days' work with a lobbying and PR company. This is perfect timing for my Members' Bill on 'double jobbing'. The media and social media went wild at this news. I put out a statement calling for her to resign from the Scottish Parliament Corporate Body and from parliament. She is now under immense pressure. She has set up a company for tax purposes the same as Alex Salmond did.

25 October Great news today as my mum has been offered a place in the local sheltered housing complex. I really hope she will accept it although it will be devastating for all of us to leave behind the family home.

26 October The Ruth Davidson story is not going away. She claims she got approval from the Scottish Parliament to take up the role. If this is true then the system is not fit for purpose.

27 October My mum is going to accept the offer of sheltered housing. We are all delighted.

The Sunday papers are full of calls from the SNP and Liberal Democrats for a

General Election, yet only two days ago SNP Westminster Leader Ian Blackford said a General Election would be a terrible idea.

I got an email from someone who said they were an SNP supporter: '*Why don't you just fuck of ya Tori bastard kidden on your Labour total wanker an answer would be nice but that aint gonna happen is it no money in it for you ya fucking areshole hope you get hit by a bus ya bastard*'. Charming.

28 October I spoke to a woman today who has extreme nerve pain shooting through her skull and into her tongue. She has been waiting on a neurological appointment which is supposed to be based in the new Edinburgh hospital, which lies empty with no sign of it opening. Her employer provides private medical insurance that would pay for the procedure but since it would have to take place in the same NHS facility that is currently closed this route is also unavailable. She has suffered like this for a year.

29 October The General Election will take place in December. I have real fears for what may happen to the Labour Party. Jeremy Corbyn is talking up Labour's chances but of course Jess Phillips MP and the rest are putting the boot in. Owen Smith is standing down; others will follow.

Ruth Davidson will not now take the £50,000 a year PR job, presenting herself as a victim.

Went to the Labour Group for the first time in weeks, it was as dreadful as ever.

30 October I spoke to some of Tory members, apparently none of them supported Ruth Davidson taking the PR job.

I asked Jeane Freeman about women being told that they have had full mesh removals when they haven't. This is the new emerging scandal: women have it on their medical records that they have had a complete removal, only to be informed later that they still have mesh inside them. It looks like there will be some sort of review into this following my question and letter.

At PMQs the Tories mocked Jeremy Corbyn for wearing a green tie, which was a tribute to the survivors of the Grenfell Tower tragedy.

The Lord Provost of Glasgow resigned after the clothing expenses scandal.

31 October To FMQs for predictable pre-election knockabout. I managed to raise the case of my constituent who cannot get treatment for her extreme neurological pain Hopefully this intervention will ensure that she is seen soon.

Trump has attacked Jeremy Corbyn and given his support to Boris Johnson and Nigel Farage. Corbyn gave a good speech saying Labour would take on vested interests such as bad employers, rogue landlords, tax avoiders and polluters.

I had an extended Twitter exchange with Andrew Wilson of Charlotte Street

Partners today, who claims that they are not a lobbying organisation and that his involvement in the SNP's Growth Commission was public service. Hmmm.

1 November Over the last few weeks we have been working with a young woman who is a refugee. Today, we managed to get her two-year-old son into nursery and an appointment with the Refugee Council legal team.

We had an excellent fundraising event at the Bay Leaf restaurant in Pumpherston. We raised a decent amount of money towards the election campaign for our candidate Caitlin Kane.

3 November Fiona's nephew Leo's christening today. We are his godparents.

4 November Tory MP Ross Thomson has resigned as their candidate in Aberdeen following allegations made by Paul Sweeney MP.

Lindsay Hoyle was elected as the new House of Commons Speaker.

5 November Lib Dem Leader Jo Swinson claimed that she will be Prime Minister. In reality, she will be lucky to retain her seat. Farage was in Bolsover, an area where 70 per cent of the people voted leave. I am very worried that Dennis Skinner may lose his seat after 50 years of outstanding service.

Jacob Rees-Mogg said that the Grenfell Tower residents shouldn't have listened to the fire service and instead should have left the building. Then another Tory MP said that Rees-Mogg was cleverer than the people of Grenfell.

6 November Attended the Scottish campaign launch in Glasgow which went well.

The Tory campaign launch was overshadowed by Rees-Mogg's comments. The Welsh secretary resigned and James Cleverly was empty chaired on Sky TV after turning up at the studio, then refusing to go on live. Not a good start for them.

7 November Tom Watson resigned as an MP and Deputy Leader of the Labour Party; then Ian Austin, a Labour MP for many years, urged people to vote Tory. What a charlatan.

8 November The SNP launched their campaign, talking up a progressive alliance to keep out the Tories. What they really want is another Tory government with Scotland voting SNP.

9 November Helped launch Pat Egan's campaign in Fife then to Dundee for Jim Malone's launch. At each event my job was to rally the troops and get them fired up for the election.

10 November Attended two Remembrance Sunday events.

11 November This morning the BBC showed a clip of Boris Johnson from three years ago laying a wreath at the Cenotaph. They showed this instead of his appearance yesterday, as he was a shambles. Can you imagine the outcry if this had been Corbyn?

12 November There was a cyber-attack on the Labour Party website today. The big policy announcement was on student support with students to receive the equivalent of £10 per hour.

13 November Jeremy Corbyn was in Scotland and was heckled by a church minister who asked him why he was wearing 'a jihadi head scarf'. The media were all over this until they realised the guy was a homophobic bigot whose social media is full of bile. It turned out Jeremy was in fact wearing a scarf provided by the 'Who Cares Scotland' charity.

14 November At FMQs, Anas Sarwar raised the case of a young child who has died of an infection she got from the ventilation unit at the brand-new Queen Elizabeth Hospital in Glasgow. Apparently, the Health Secretary knew about the source of the infection but never told the parents.

To Edinburgh University for the Labour election rally with Jeremy Corbyn, Richard Leonard, Leslie Laird and others. About 1,000 people turned up, the atmosphere was excellent.

15 November Results came through today of two by-elections in Fife. The SNP won both with Labour fourth in oney. This does not bode well.

I got a Freedom of Information response showing that the NHS is paying private agencies up to £150 per hour for nurses, this at a time when the NHS has a huge black hole in its budget.

I heard today that Ruth Davidson is getting a huge fee from ITV for appearing on the election night show.

Labour announced a policy of free broadband for all.

16 November Went to Midlothian for Danielle Rowley's campaign launch where I spoke alongside Grace Blakely.

The polls are looking grim for Labour and I fear a bloodbath.

The BBC showed an interview with Prince Andrew discussing allegations about his relationship with Jeffrey Epstein and the abuse of young women. It was brutal, he is rightly in huge trouble.

17 November The fallout from the Prince Andrew interview is astonishing: references to suicide, orgies, sex trafficking, doctored photographs, 17-year-old girls – the list goes on and on.

The *Sunday Mail* ran a story we gave them about private nursing agencies receiving up to £1,715 for each shift.

18 November In my home village canvassing. On the doorstep, we are getting too much of the 'Corbyn is a terrorist' line coming through. It just shows how certain messages cut through and others don't. It is utter nonsense, all his life Jeremy has campaigned for peace. The media hostility to him is incredible.

19 November At Stage Two of the Scottish National Investment Bank Bill I moved amendments to try to ensure companies involved in tax avoidance, that use zero hours contracts and umbrella companies and don't recognise trade unions do not receive public funding from the bank. The SNP and Tories voted down every measure, plus a proposal for pay and pensions to be covered by public sector pay policy.

Jenny Marra raised with the Labour Group concerns that we (i.e. me) attacked Ruth Davidson over her money grabbing enterprises. She said it was 'bullying'. It is nothing of the sort, it was a political attack on a politician who is using her position and contacts for self-enrichment.

In the TV election debate between Johnson and Corbyn, Johnson repeated 'Get Brexit done', time and again. Clearly this is polling well for them. He had no answers about his personal integrity, the NHS, austerity, housing and poverty, and showed zero understanding of ordinary people's lives. He lied his way through the whole thing.

20 November The media is full of post-debate comment. Corbyn came out on top with the pollsters. Johnson's tedious lines about Brexit and talking over people went down badly. Corbyn was weak on Brexit, strong on the NHS, morality and climate. Johnson was very poor on the NHS and telling the truth. The Tories have changed their Twitter account to something called 'Fact Check UK' which is spewing out anti-Labour content.

Jeane Freeman is under pressure from all sides over the Queen Elizabeth hospital scandal, the delay to the Sick Kids Hospital, waiting times, delayed discharge and workforce shortages.

21 November Mesh campaigners in Australia have won a huge victory over Ethicon: 1,350 women have received substantial payouts. This is excellent news.

This morning Alex Salmond was in court charged with 14 sexual offences following complaints made by ten women.

The Labour manifesto was launched with Jeremy Corbyn setting out Labour's position as being on the side of working people and against the establishment who back the tax avoiders, polluters, exploiters and those who seek to divide us. The manifesto is full of commitments and there was a decent feel to the launch – fairness, hope, equality and real change are the themes.

Went to the Scottish Politician of the Year awards at Prestonfield House. Just after dinner I got a phone call from Fiona to say my mum has had a stroke and was in hospital. She came through for me immediately and we went to St John's, where mum was in A&E. She was given clot-busting drugs and transferred to the medical admissions unit. She is weak and paralysed down the left side. When it happened, she had the presence of mind to press the emergency button on her pendant and speak to NHS 24. Fiona and Chloe were up at her house within five minutes and called an ambulance. My sister Anna and I stayed with her until 5am and left her sleeping.

22 November Back to the hospital to see mum. She will be moved to the stroke unit later. Lots of people contacting us to ask how she is and all the family are around.

23 November Mum was not good today, much weaker and very difficult to hear, she cannot swallow food so has an intravenous line in. I am really worried about her.

24 November It doesn't look like the drugs have had much effect on my mum. We will speak to the doctor tomorrow. Fiona did her hair for her and freshened her up a bit.

25 November Went into Glasgow for the long-awaited meeting with Nicola Sturgeon and the mesh women. For eight years they have been ignored. It is, of course, a 'complete coincidence' that she agreed to a meeting during a General Election. At the start of the meeting, government press officers tried to stop Marion Scott from the *Sunday Post* entering the room but she refused to leave. The campaigners were excellent and raised many issues, including surgeons misleading patients, patient pathways, the need for safe mesh removal and for financial and emotional support. There were painful testimonies and fierce criticism of Sturgeon and her government's approach over the years. She nodded and empathised and said the right things but we need action.

Did my surgery at Whitburn before visiting mum in hospital. Her voice was a bit stronger.

Andrew Neil dismantled Sturgeon in a TV interview today. She was not a happy bunny.

Internal polling is not good for Labour.

The Chief Rabbi made an appalling statement saying Labour and Corbyn are antisemitic.

26 November I drafted a long letter to Sturgeon about yesterday's mesh meeting, raising a long list of concerns.

The fallout from the Chief Rabbi's comments are dominating the news. Corbyn has been an anti-racist campaigner all his life. In the '70s and '80s he was vilified for supporting the black community, the anti-apartheid campaign and the gay community. Now that this is mainstream, he is attacked as an antisemitic racist. Later, he went on the *Andrew Neil Show* and took a battering, I couldn't watch. It makes me so angry to see a decent, honourable man attacked on the very thing he prides himself on: his commitment to equality, justice and diversity.

I welcomed the 'Be Herd' group from Whitburn Academy to parliament. They have totally changed the culture of the school to one where mental health issues are spoken about openly and where people share their anxieties with each other. They were very fantastic.

27 November Mum had a peaceful night, we will find out more from the doctor later.

Sturgeon launched the SNP manifesto with commitments on Independence, Trident and a 50p tax rate at a UK level where they can't implement it but no 50p rate in Scotland where they can.

To Addiewell for canvassing, good response in Caitlin's home village.

A big YouGov poll came out showing a Tory majority of 68, Labour down to 211 seats with just two in Scotland. I fear this is pretty accurate. I felt sick reading it.

28 November I was not called at FMQs today but made a point of order afterwards about the new Chair of the Scottish National Investment Bank, who moved his business from Edinburgh to Bermuda. He was fined a record amount by financial regulators for a conflict of interest and now has been appointed to this role.

Channel 4 hosted an election Leaders Debate. Johnson didn't turn up so they replaced him with a block of ice. Gove went along with a camera crew to take his place but was refused entry.

Later it emerged that the BBC told all the political leaders they would all be interviewed but now Johnson is refusing. Every trick in the book is being played.

The SNP candidate for Kirkcaldy and Labour candidate in Falkirk were sacked for antisemitic comments.

29 November Campaigning all morning in Livingston, the latest polls have Labour 7 per cent behind.

A terrorist incident at London Bridge saw a man with a knife attack passers-by. He was tackled by a member of the public despite appearing to have a suicide vest on and was later shot by a police marksman. It was all caught on video. It turned out he had been released from prison on terror offences and was at a rehabilitation event. Campaigning was suspended.

30 November My mum's 80th birthday. We went into the hospital where they gave us a room so she could see her family and friends and have a wee tea party. She is very weak and her voice is difficult to hear but she enjoyed seeing people. We all sang Happy Birthday, it was very emotional. She was shattered by the end of it. All of the family came back to our house for dinner.

1 December Campaigning in Livingston, Brexit is hardly mentioned but the demonising of Corbyn is having a real impact. I spoke to Tommy who is Jeremy's Scotland adviser. He said Jeremy was hurting badly over the claims of antisemitism. I urged him to feed back to the leadership that they need a plan for after the election as there will inevitably be an all-out attack on the left.

4 December 3 hours of leafletting before visiting my mum who was in a deep sleep and unresponsive when I held her hand. I stayed for a while then left her to rest.

5 December Susan Deacon resigned as the Chair of the Scottish Police Authority citing a lack of scrutiny and accountability. Every day I regret voting for the creation of Police Scotland.

The unity in SNP is beginning to fray with the obnoxious Wings over Scotland blog attacking Sturgeon over the candidate sacking in Kirkcaldy. The Salmond trial will bring many of these tensions to a head.

Visited mum tonight, I can see her making a little progress.

6 December After the BBC debate Johnson was ahead by 52 per cent to 48 per cent.

7 December Canvass session in Livingston village, the latest poll has Labour 6 per cent behind.

9 December Footage emerged today of ITV reporter Joe Pike interviewing Boris Johnson about the plight of a young boy who is very ill and was forced to lie on a hospital floor. Johnson refused to look at the pictures and then grabbed the reporter's phone from him. Laura Kuenssberg described the incident as an 'awkward moment'. If this had been Corbyn it would have run for days. Then Health Secretary Matt Hancock went to hospital and claimed he had been punched by a protestor, which turned out to be completely false.

It has emerged that in 2004 Boris Johnson wrote a novel that depicted Jews controlling the media and repeated racist tropes and stereotypes, but this barely made a ripple in the news.

I heard tonight there is zero progress on bringing Dr Veronikis to Scotland.

10 December The *Daily Record* claims Sturgeon was interested in discussing a third option in any future Independence referendum. I will hold her to that. Labour should now own that third option.

Jonathan Ashworth, the Shadow Health Secretary, was recorded slating Corbyn and saying Labour had no chance of winning the election. He then had to go on TV for excruciating interviews where he tried to claim it was a wind-up by a friend.

In the Scottish TV debate Richard Leonard savaged the Tories on austerity. This was his best performance by a long way.

11 **December** My reflections the day before polling day are that the media campaign against Corbyn has been massive and effective. People are feeding back the attacks on the doorstep and I really fear the result. Johnson has lied repeatedly but the media ignore this with, 'It's just Boris'. He has avoided interviews and scrutiny. Research has shown over 80 per cent of the Tory social media output has been misleading.

The SNP campaign has focused on Independence, which is of course deliberate, intended to polarise the debate. The Liberals have been woeful and I hope Swinson is booted out. Let's see what tomorrow brings. I am doing the STV election night show.

12–13 **December** Up at 6am for an early leaflet run then door-knocking before visiting my mum for half an hour. Lots of people helped get the vote out, we worked at it all day until I had to go to get ready to head to party headquarters for the exit poll and results.

I spoke to Karie Murphy, who seemed upbeat and optimistic, but she is in London and will be getting a very skewed view of the world. Then came the exit poll predicting a 70-seat Tory majority. How the hell do I face this up on national telly? Well, I can only tell the truth and answer straight questions with straight answers.

I made my way over to Pacific Quay, it was grim. I went on with MSPs Shirley Anne Somerville of the SNP and Tory Dean Lockhart. The discussion was hosted by Bernard Ponsonby. As the night unfolded the full horror of the result became apparent. Working-class Labour seats in the north of England and the Midlands fell like dominoes – Durham, Blyth, Bolsover all gone to the Tories; West Bromwich and Dudley too. Ian Murray was Labour's only victory. In Livingston and Linlithgow we were third, despite a huge effort by Wendy Milne and Caitlin Kane.

The repercussions were immediate, with all those who have attacked Corbyn for the last four years saying I told you so and attacking him again. There was zero self-reflection on their role and how this contributed to the result.

Later, Corbyn said he would resign after seeing through transition to the new leadership. I went home knackered and thoroughly depressed. Slept all day then went for a curry with Fiona.

14 **December** The result was a disaster with Labour losing 60 seats and the

Tories winning a majority of 80. In Scotland Labour lost six seats, the SNP took 48, Swinson lost her seat and resigned as Lib Dem leader and the Tories lost seats to the SNP.

The fallout from the election disaster went on, with all the Blairite right wingers who advocated the Better Together disaster coming out of the woodwork. I wrote an article for the *Sunday Mail* saying Labour must face up to the reality of a demand by the Scottish people for a referendum on Scotland's future, that we must take part positively in discussion around it, end our sour attitude and argue for a devo max third option, which, I think, would win. I don't want Independence but if the people choose it so be it, that's democracy, and we should campaign for a radical Labour government in that independent Scotland.

Shock and awe was launched against Corbyn and McDonnell, and the backroom team, especially Seamus Milne and Karie Murphy. Potential leadership candidates are jockeying for position with David Lammy, Rebecca Long-Bailey, Richard Burgon, Jess Phillips (God help us), Yvette Cooper and Keir Starmer (who is clear favourite), all being touted.

Went to Pitlochry for our annual Christmas weekend away with pals, to rub buckets of salt into open wounds the band at the hotel was called 'Independence!' It did make me laugh.

My *Sunday Mail* article has caused a stir. Monica Lennon and Ged Killen who lost his Rutherglen seat supportive of my position. Colin Smyth, Daniel Johnson and Ian Murray attacked me.

John McDonnell did an interview and took the blame for the election on the chin and didn't dodge a single question. A very dignified and honest approach.

Visited my mum tonight, she is getting a little stronger each day.

16 December An asylum seeker we have been representing came to see us. Her temporary leave to remain in the UK has been lifted, she can now stay and get access to social security and public services. She was very emotional and thankful for the help of my office staff, Mhari, Caitlin and Mary Theresa and the Scottish Refugee Council. Just the tonic needed after the grim weekend.

Anas Sarwar joined the attacks on me and others and called for a reality check on the constitution. The unionist ultras have been out in force. Sarwar will soon challenge Richard Leonard.

Lesley Laird, who lost her Kirkcaldy seat, stood down today as Deputy Labour leader in Scotland.

I spoke to Angela Feeney, our candidate in Motherwell and Wishaw where she was trying to overcome a very small SNP majority of 318 but lost by 6,000. She said they never saw it coming as canvas returns were good. She is being attacked by right-wingers in her constituency.

I saw an interview on TV with two guys from Burnley who live in a run-down bedsit and work on zero hours contracts. They voted Tory because of Brexit and they believe the Tories will help them get on. I almost wept.

17 December Met with parliamentary officials about my 'double jobbing' bill. I know they don't like it but I am pressing on with it.

Labour MSPs were clearly miffed by my article at the weekend, but Alex Rowley came for a chat and was supportive. There is a Labour Group meeting tonight, which will be grim, but I gave up going to them as life is too short.

Nicola Sturgeon made a statement on the election. I got in with a question saying I respected the sovereign right of the Scottish people to determine their own future but that if there is to be a referendum it should only take place after we find out what is happening with Brexit. I also appealed to her to work cross-party on this. She said she would speak with MSPs of different parties. I won't hold my breath as she has barely broken breath to me in nine years.

18 December I spoke to a senior SNP MSP today who advised me that one senior Special Adviser made 50 complaints about Alex Salmond. The person told me 'Salmond would bring the house down with his evidence'.

I heard that tonight's Labour Group meeting was just one long attack after attack on Richard Leonard, Lesley Laird, Jeremy Corbyn, John McDonnell, our staff and anyone associated with them. It went on for over three hours. It is clear that Sarwar will launch a leadership bid; the only question is when.

At the same time as all of this the cost of the ferries contract with Ferguson's in Inverclyde has doubled, 2,000 families are waiting on post-mortems being carried out on dead relatives, the railway franchise is a shambles and the SNP get away with it. Good governance is out of the window, replaced by flag waving.

19 December Sturgeon made a statement and called for powers to be transferred to Holyrood so that another Independence referendum can be held in 2020.

It was the Queen's Speech at Westminster today.

To the chamber for Stage Three of the Referendum Bill. I would have voted for it but Mike Russell tried to fix the question and prevent the Electoral Commission having a say on the wording. This was just wrong. I spoke in the debate and raised the points I have repeatedly made about Labour's failure to provide a credible alternative to Independence and the status quo and for there to be other options rather than a binary referendum. When the vote came Monica Lennon and I abstained.

Clive Lewis declared his candidacy for the Labour leadership today.

Went to see Mum. Her voice was much stronger, which is great.

20 December I had a horrible night but had to get up early to do the Radio 4 *Today* programme on Brexit and Independence. Afterwards, I almost fainted in the shower. I went to bed and stayed there all day.

Johnson's Brexit Bill passed today with a huge majority, the Tories are cock a hoop.

Today the SNP released a 'guide for journalists' on how to interview Tories. Absolutely incredible, a political party telling journalists how to do their job.

The media carried coverage of my speech and abstention on the referendum bill. Criticism from the usual quarters but I couldn't give a toss.

Ian Murray has said he might stand for Deputy Leader of the Labour Party. I would rather stick very long, sharp pins in my eyeballs than vote for him to be Deputy Leader of the local scout troop, never mind of my political party.

23 December Visited Mum in hospital. She told me that the doctor had told her to get all things in order and that she should consider signing a 'Do Not Resuscitate Order', which rocked me a bit as no one discussed this with any of the family who all have power of attorney.

24 December Visited Mum before going to the Christmas vigil mass and carol service.

25 December Visited the hospital with all the family to see Mum for Christmas. We took her to the hospital chapel for a while, she was in good form and enjoyed seeing everyone. Fiona gave her communion. Then Christmas dinner at Fiona's sisters

28 December Ian Duncan Smith, the former Tory leader, has been awarded a knighthood in the New Year's Honours list. A failed Tory leader who introduced Universal Credit, cut disability benefits and thinks the bedroom tax and rape clause are good ideas rewarded with a knighthood. It is sickening.

2020

I HOPE AND pray there will never be another year like 2020.

Following a stroke at the end of 2019 that left her very debilitated my mum had to move into a care home. As we helped move her belongings into her new room, we could not have imagined what was to come. Just a few weeks later the world was hit by the Coronavirus pandemic.

Covid-19 changed everything. Every citizen was impacted in some way by this unprecedented global health crisis. Schools were closed, the NHS was overwhelmed, civil liberties were suspended, huge state intervention in the economy took place, people were told to stay at home and the streets were deserted. Over 6.5 million people worldwide died, many unnecessarily. The UK and Scotland had some of the worst death rates anywhere across the globe.

As an elected politician during this period, the sheer volume of casework that came my way was phenomenal. People needed information about their jobs, their kids' education, how to access food, how to keep within the law, how to help their friends and neighbours who were vulnerable, how to keep safe and avoid contracting the disease. The list of queries was endless.

In such times, governments understandably seek to create an atmosphere on national unity; however, this can also be used to avoid scrutiny and shut down dissent.

I was more determined than ever to speak out when bad decisions were made, or contradictory advice given. I saw it as my job to hold those in power to account, no matter how hard they tried to close down debate. I became a point of contact for many people who had information about the way those in power were trying to evade scrutiny over their decision-making. With a personal interest in the care home sector, this was to become a major focus of my work.

Away from Covid, the miners' justice campaign took a huge step forward and we saw progress in the campaign for fair treatment for mesh injured women.

Keir Starmer was elected leader of the Labour Party, Alex Salmond was acquitted of all charges against him and the Boris Johnson's Brexit bill finally pass.

1 January Fiona was nightshift at the hospital last night so she nipped along to my mum's ward at the bells to see her, but she was sound asleep. At least she wasn't alone as the New Year came in.

3 January Starmer looks like the favourite to succeed Jeremy Corbyn.

4 January Had a long chat with Angela Rayner today. She has done a deal with her pal Rebecca Long-Bailey, who will stand for Leader and Rayner for Deputy. We discussed Scotland and what needs to be done. I appealed to her to get Rebecca to drop her 'progressive patriotism' guff.

5 January Watched Jess Phillips on *Andrew Marr*. Marr describes her as 'one of Britain's most charismatic politicians'. I really must be missing something. Starmer was also on the show. He has released a video expressing support for striking miners and print workers, poll tax protesters and Lawrence family. It was clearly pitched at the left and trade unions.

6 January There is a horrific story in the news today of a man in Manchester who has raped over 200 men plying them with the GHB drug then assaulting them. Police found 1,500 videos of assaults on his phone.

7 January Rebecca Long-Bailey launched her campaign, saying she supports the Corbyn agenda. I like her but she doesn't inspire confidence.

Jackie Baillie will stand for Scottish Deputy Leader. Anas Sarwar is pulling the strings.

Spoke to a senior journalist today who said the coming Salmond trial will be sensational and really damage Sturgeon. I'm not so sure it will.

8 January Went in to parliament for the debate on the Legislative Consent Motion on the EU Withdrawal Bill. Mike Russell and Adam Tomkins were beating their chests and braying at each other in faux outrage.

Got a text from Keir Starmer who said he wants to speak to me, but he never followed it up with a call and I'm certainly not chasing him. He's no chance of getting my vote anyway.

9 January At FMQs I had a question about my constituent who is suffering with extreme neurological pain and cannot get an NHS appointment. She has private health insurance through her employer but any private treatment would be conducted at the new NHS neurological centre, which has been delayed again.

This was the exchange:

Neil Findlay (Lothian) (Lab)
In October, I raised with the First Minister the case of my constituent who has been waiting for an operation. She has severe neurological pain,

has been off work for a very long time and has to take 48 tablets a day to try to alleviate the agony that shoots through her head and face every few seconds. Following my question, the Cabinet Secretary for Health and Sport wrote to me, saying: 'There is no suggestion of any kind that the delay to the new department of clinical neurosciences has anything to do with the case of your constituent' and that my constituent's case 'would be resolved by NHS Lothian'.

Well, my constituent's case still has not been resolved by NHS Lothian. She remains in agony, has had her operation cancelled again and has again been told by NHS Lothian officials that that is due to a lack of staff and a lack of theatre space because of the debacle around the Sick Kids Hospital and the neurology centre. Will the First Minister take this opportunity to speak directly to my constituent – who is watching this session – and give her some hope that her living hell will end soon?

The First Minister (Nicola Sturgeon)

When any individual does not get the standard of care that they have the right to expect from the national health service, I always apologise to them readily, and I will do that to Neil Findlay's constituent.
As Neil Findlay has said, he raised the issue before, and the health secretary wrote to him. Neil Findlay and his constituent clearly and understandably do not consider that the issue has been resolved. I will therefore ask the Health Secretary today to look again at this issue and liaise with NHS Lothian and respond as quickly as possible to Neil Findlay once she has had an opportunity to do so.

The newspapers are reporting that Richard Leonard will host a one-day conference to agree Labour's constitutional position. I think this is a decent move, but the unionist ultras are attacking the idea.

10 January The Labour right are attacking the plan for a one-day conference to determine Labour's position on the constitution.

Went to see mum today. She is going to have to go into a care home. It is devastating that she won't be able to move into her beautiful wee sheltered house, which is sitting ready for her.

Sinn Féin and the DUP have struck a deal to return to power-sharing in Northern Ireland.

11 January I got a call from *The Herald* to advise that Labour's Executive rejected Richard Leonard's plans for a one-day conference. He did zero preparatory work to brief allies on the Executive and failed to explain the rationale for it. I think, privately, Richard should stand down and get on with his life. He is a good man and a friend, who has been undermined and attacked by his own side since the start and he doesn't deserve that. The pressure on him has been intense. For me, I really wish the election was this year as I would only have three months of this torture to go.

12 January After reading Kenny MacAskill's interesting *Scotsman* column on the constitution, I made contact with him to set up a meeting.

Richard is taking a hammering in the media today over yesterday's vote.

One paper ran an interview with Ian Murray who says 'he is no Blairite'. I agree, he is far more right-wing than that.

13 January Met with the Refugee Council to discuss the Elections Bill and asylum seekers right to vote.

There is talk of Jackie Baillie and Pauline McNeil sharing the deputy leadership to avoid a contest. I was asked my view and said I really couldn't give a toss as the way we are going they will be deputy leader of a party that barely exists.

14 January Boris Johnson issued a letter saying there will be no Indyref2. Sturgeon responded saying she will set out the way forward soon, meanwhile public services are crumbling.

I had a look at the election results again today. In Leave seats in England, we lost massive numbers of voters. There has been no comment on this from those who said Labour should have taken a 'Remain' position.

The *Daily Record* reported that Lesley Laird's report into the Scottish Labour Party's organisation and campaigning capacity was leaked to the media. Everything is leaked, indeed, the more private a meeting or report, the quicker it is leaked.

15 January Jenny Marra's brother Michael, a councillor in Dundee is going to run for Deputy Leader, if this happens it scuppers the Baillie/McNeil joint bid. Later, Matt Kerr, a Glasgow councillor on the left, called to say he is going to stand. He will get my support.

Went into the Education debate to hear SNP MSPs saying that anyone who criticises the government on education is talking down Scotland's children! It is the job of the opposition to hold the Scottish Government to account.

16 January The Standards, Procedures and Public Appointments Committee sat for Stage Two of the Elections Bill where I moved amendments to give asylum seekers voting and candidacy rights; all voted down by the SNP and Tories. Gil Paterson of the SNP claimed the Parliament didn't have the powers to do it. Utter nonsense.

I also moved an amendment to end the ban on councillors who previously stood down and took a severance payment from standing in future elections. This was passed unanimously. Good result.

In response to my idea of establishing a fund for mesh-injured women's, Jeane Freeman has said she is considering it. This is positive news.

At decision time Alasdair Allan raised a point of order on the removal of the EU flag after Brexit. Mike Russell and the cybernats are going mad about this. I wish there was the same level of outrage over homelessness, drugs deaths and mental health services.

Home to celebrate Chloe's 24th birthday.

17 January I was emailed by Michael Marra seeking support for his deputy leadership bid. I replied asking him who he nominated and voted for in the 2015 leadership election when I stood, of course the answer was Jim Murphy. I never heard from him again.

18 January Saw clips of the first UK leadership hustings on TV where candidates, including Jess Phillips were urging unity. This is the same Jess Phillips who said she would 'stab Corbyn in the front'.

19 January Pauline McNeill has withdrawn from the deputy leadership contest. Jackie Baillie has played her like a fiddle. The people who nominated Pauline can't now nominate anyone else, so Matt Kerr will be seen to have only one MSP nomination: me. It will now be Kerr versus Baillie, as Marra couldn't secure the required nominations.

21 January Jess Phillips has withdrawn from the Labour leadership contest. Starmer is running the best campaign. Rebecca Long-Bailey's campaign is poor but I will vote for her as the most likely to carry on Corbyn's policy agenda.

Went in for Stage Three of the Scottish National Investment Bank Bill. I moved amendments to ensure this publicly funded bank will pay the living wage, does not fund tax avoiders or organisations that employ people on zero hours contracts or use umbrella companies. Every amendment was voted down by an alliance of SNP and Tory MSPs. Derek Mackay, the Cabinet Secretary, launched a series of personal attacks on me. He had nothing else in his locker.

Trump impeachment proceedings started today.

22 January Salmond's pre-trial hearing took place.

I went to see my mum and spoke through what we have been told about her needing constant care. She was disappointed at not getting into her new house but accepted the doctor's advice. A tough conversation.

23 January The list of charges against Alex Salmond have been published. There are allegations of groping, forcing himself on women, attempted rape and sexual assault.

I spoke to Rebecca Long-Bailey's team today and raised concerns about the campaign but said I would come out in support of her when Starmer is in Scotland.

I heard from the NUM today that they are meeting the Justice Secretary to discuss the campaign for miners' pardons. I really hope we see progress.

I received a briefing pack with all the information about my involvement in the forthcoming 'Justice for Colombia' peace monitor visit. It looks like a very interesting trip to check on the progress of peace process and the political violence scarring the country.

24 January A new disease called Coronavirus is causing panic across the world. There are now suspected cases in Glasgow. I tweeted: 'Coronavirus is of course a huge potential threat to the population and the authorities must act quickly to prevent spread and threat to life – it will be interesting to see the response to this compared to the approach to 1,200 drug deaths.' The cybernats attacked me but sensible people who understood my point, including Darren McGarvey, gave support.

25 January I spoke to a Chinese constituent who works as an NHS Nurse. She is very worried about Coronavirus and her family in China.

27 January Went to see mum tonight. She had asked me to bring in some chips from the chippy. She said they were delicious.

28 January In this week's parliamentary business the government proposed a one-and-a-half-hour debate on the drugs death crisis. I urged our Business Manager, Elaine Smith, to oppose this and call for an extended debate when the bureau met. The government only agreed to extend the debate for half an hour on the proviso they got a debate on flying the EU flag. This made me so angry. We have four people dying every day and their priority is flying a flag.

Went to the Labour Group for the first time in ages as Starmer was there to give his leadership pitch. He played to his audience and hinted at dropping a lot of the economic policy developed under Corbyn and McDonnell. I really do not trust him.

29 January I went into the chamber for the most nauseating waste of time I have experienced since going into Parliament, the 'debate' on flying the EU flag. Fiona Hyslop led for the government and refused to take any interventions.

We then had a debate on a motion about another Independence referendum. I was denied a speaking slot by the Labour whips, so I intervened on Sturgeon to get it on the record that the Scottish people are sovereign but that a referendum should not take place until after the outcome of Brexit is known. This was all about Sturgeon trying to give something to her base to take attention away from repeated policy failures.

30 January Audit Scotland published a scathing report on PFI/NPD. Richard Leonard led with this at FMQs, leaving Sturgeon an open goal to hammer him on Labour's record on PFI.

Michelle Ballantyne is going to stand for Scottish Tory Leader. She is very, very right wing.

I took part in the first debate in government time since 2012 on drug deaths. Joe FitzPatrick's performance was nervous and bumbling. He refused to take a single intervention, so much for it being a debate.

When I spoke, I suggested if we can have an annual debate on fish quotas we should have an annual debate on drug deaths. I offered 19 policy ideas for change, including decriminalisation, all based on my discussion with drug users, families, clinicians, support workers and academics.

This was the last day for British MEPs in the European Parliament, there was a lot of coverage of Farage and his band of zoomers waving union flags and SNP MSPs being led out by a piper.

31 January Today is Brexit day with lots of flag waving outside Holyrood and Westminster.

On a day to bury bad news, Brian Houston, the Chair of NHS Lothian, was sacked by Jeane Freeman. He is being blamed for everything. None of the mess will be the government's fault.

1 February UNISON's Scottish Executive came out in support of a second referendum.

Three people died in a terror attack in London and in China over 200 are dead from Coronavirus.

2 February Visited Mum with my brother John to discuss the move to the care home, she seemed OK about it.

3 February I went to API Foilmakers Plant at Livingston to try and get into the mass meeting they called to discuss closure plans but the management wouldn't let me in. The factory has been in the town for decades and was a good employer. I hope a way forward can be found. I have secured a meeting with Jamie Hepburn, Minister for Business, Fair Work and Skills, to see what support can be given.

4 February I visited the Maggie's Centre in Edinburgh; what a beautiful, calming and welcoming place providing support for cancer patients.

At topical questions, Jeane Freeman simply refused to answer questions about Brian Houston's resignation. Zero accountability.

I bumped into Murray Foote, the former editor of the *Daily Record*, who was behind 'The Vow' in 2014 and was Editor of the paper when I convinced them to support Corbyn in 2015. I like Murray and tried to get him as our Director of Communications. He told me he has just become Sturgeon's chief spin doctor. How interesting.

Later, I spoke to a senior journalist who told me about the coming Salmond trial and said that a number of senior people in the SNP are up to their necks in some very questionable things. I have to say Salmond's ego and thirst for publicity is such that it would not surprise me one bit if he was to win his case and seek to return to politics.

5 February Met Jamie Hepburn and representatives from UNITE to make an appeal for intervention to save API Foilmakers. All the fair work protocols the government claims are in place have been by-passed. There wasn't much commitment from him to act.

6 February Scottish budget day. The *Sun* ran an explosive story about Finance Secretary Derek Mackay sending texts to a 16-year-old boy asking him to meet him and go to events. The texts were creepy and highly inappropriate. Sturgeon initially supported him but the pressure grew and by lunchtime he had resigned. This is big news, as Mackay saw himself as successor to Sturgeon. At FMQs Jackson Carlaw raised the issue of Mackay 'grooming' a young boy and Richard Leonard called it 'predatory behaviour'. I hope the young victim is being supported and protected.

At FMQ's I asked about NHS Lothian.

Neil Findlay (Lothian) (Lab)

This week's appalling report on mental health services at NHS Tayside is evidence of the need for openness and transparency in our greatest public service, the National Health Service. In that vein, does the First Minister agree that patients and staff of NHS Lothian have the right to know why the chair of the board has resigned and, more important, why the Health Board that spends their taxes and treats their children has been put into special measures? On Tuesday, the Cabinet Secretary for Health and Sport refused to answer questions from members across the chamber on that extremely important issue. Will the First Minister now instruct the Health Secretary to release all information on Mr Houston's resignation and, more important, on the decision to invoke special measures for NHS Lothian?

The First Minister (Nicola Sturgeon)

As I understand it, the Chair of NHS Lothian resigned because he disagreed with the assessment of his performance as chair that had been made by the chief executive of NHS Scotland. Regarding the decisions around the escalation to Level 4 of aspects of NHS Lothian's performance, the Health Secretary has spoken about that on many occasions in the chamber, and she continues to be prepared to answer members' questions. I give an assurance that, if there is particular information that the chamber wants, that information will be made available.

In the budget debate, Kate Forbes stood in for MacKay and did a decent job under the circumstances. Tucked away in the detail was a £1million commitment to fund my proposal for a 'mesh-injured women's fund'. I am over the moon about this.

There was lot of media coverage of the Mackay scandal and over-the-top plaudits for Kate Forbes. I tweeted a light-hearted comment – 'And on day two Kate Forbes will part the Red Sea, run the 100 metres in four seconds and whip Kim Jong Un at golf.' The cybernats went crazy with SNP MSP Jenny Gilruth saying I was a 'disgrace' and that Kate Forbes has achieved more in one day than I had in eight years. It seems that standing up and reading out a speech written by the civil service is a modern-day miracle.

7–14 February On holiday with Fiona in Egypt.

15–22 February I spent a week in Colombia as part of an international delegation to monitor the peace process. The visit was organised by the London based NGO 'Justice for Colombia' and their brilliant team led by Hasan Dowdell and Nick MacWilliam. I was joined by Labour MPs Clive Efford and Lloyd Russell Moyle, a Spanish Senator, Italian, Danish, English and Irish trade unionists and two Scots, Douglas Chalmers, President of the University and Colleges Union, and Susan Quinn of the EIS. Our role was to visit numerous places and speak to politicians, civic leaders, activists, trade unionists, indigenous people and government representatives, then report on our findings in relation to the peace progress.

Having experienced decade upon decade of civil war, the right-wing Colombian government signed a carefully negotiated peace accord in Havana in 2016 with the former left-wing guerrilla organisation, FARC. There was great hope that the agreement would be fully implemented, ending years of violence replacing it with sustainable and lasting peace.

Given the history of corruption, violence, political assassinations and gangsterism involving hugely powerful and well-armed drug and business cartels, often in cahoots with multinational corporations and right-wing political leaders sponsored by the US, it was inevitable that unravelling all of that, facing up to past atrocities and delivering a reformed, democratic state based around human rights for all would be complex, controversial, difficult and uncertain.

As we know, having seen the progress made in Ireland, building peace out of war can be accompanied by crises, outbursts of violence, disagreements and stand offs but with support, encouragement and occasional threats from the international community real and lasting progress can be made.

We heard from representatives of youth and students groups who told us that Colombia had the worst human rights record in the western hemisphere and relayed stories of violence and murder perpetrated against human rights defenders.

We heard from lawyers representing families of the hundreds killed every year in political violence. We spoke to indigenous leaders, some of whom had walked for a week from their home village to meet us, about land distribution and the exploitation and control by multinationals who hire violent paramilitaries to drive peasants from their land or force them to grow coca.

We visited the UN mission, where we met ambassadors of the Norwegian and Cuban governments who sponsor the peace accord.

We met with political leaders of FARC who emphasised their total commitment to peace and the end of the armed struggle. They appealed for us to put pressure on the Colombian government to deliver on the peace accord.

Trade union leaders told us of the daily violence, assassinations and intimidation of their members and that Colombia is the most dangerous place in the world to be a trade unionist. While we were with them, news came through that two young members of the oil workers union had been murdered.

We visited the Truth Commission, who oversee a truth and reconciliation process which provides an opportunity for former combatants, paramilitaries, police and army officers to confess to offences carried out during the civil war and try to establish the whereabouts of the bodies of thousands of 'disappeared people'.

We met with the Progressive Coalition for Peace, a group of left and centre parties committed to the implementation of the peace process and we flew to Medellin, then by bus into the countryside, to see a truly inspirational UN-sponsored project where displaced former FARC combatants have built from scratch, a new village with housing, a school, shop and a successful fish farming cooperative providing jobs and income to families.

All of the social activists we met mentioned the extent of political violence against them; some raised the issues of land distribution, the absence of progressive economic reform and the endemic corruption and collusion between the government, police, drugs cartels and multinationals.

In contrast, political advisers to the government denied state involvement in corruption and violence and claimed the peace process was progressing well.

The desire in peace was powerfully and movingly expressed to us by the young people of the country, indigenous groups, teachers, health workers and former FARC soldiers who have laid down their arms in favour of peaceful coexistence with their former enemies.

23 February The *Sunday Mail* ran a front-page story using information we provided on the Scottish National Investment Bank Chair having been appointed without proper scrutiny or any reference to the Commission for Ethical Standards.

Lots of fallout in councils following the budget. More swingeing cuts are being voted through. Left-wing Labour councillors Matt Kerr in Glasgow, Angela Feeney in North Lanarkshire and Gordon Munro in Edinburgh refused to support more cuts. Good on them. They will likely be suspended by their respective groups.

There is a story in the papers about SNP MP Mhairi Black accompanying a drag queen called 'Flo job' to do readings in a school for P1 children during LGBT awareness month.

25 February Monica Lennon's 'Period Poverty Bill' had its Stage One debate today. The Tories, who were previously critical of the bill and the SNP who were outright opposed said they would now support it. Last week they were claiming there would be cross-border tampon raids with marauding, menstruating English coming north to pillage free Scottish sanitary towels. The U-turn is welcome, though.

I was told that a few weeks ago Tory leader Jackson Carlaw was doing a live Facebook event and Joe Cullinane, the excellent Labour Leader of North Ayrshire Council, sent in a question urging him to support the Period Poverty Bill. He had nowhere to go and gave support – a very smart move by Joe. This left the SNP isolated. They simply had to change their position.

Monica Lennon's performance inside and outside of the chamber was really first-class. To take a Members' Bill through against government opposition then bring on board all parties requires skill and dogged determination. A very impressive achievement.

26 February I voted in the Labour leadership ballots, supporting Rebecca Long-Bailey for Leader, Angela Rayner for Deputy and Matt Kerr for Deputy in Scotland. My greatest hope is that Matt wins.

I met Mark McHugh from BFAWU (Bakers Food and Allied Workers Union). He was with some of his members who work as interpreters. They are employed by agencies to deliver interpreting services in the NHS, the courts, etc. They are being exploited with no guaranteed hours, traveling time or expenses. I agreed to raise their case.

I bumped into Justice Secretary Humza Yousaf in the canteen and asked about the miners' review. He said the report would be published soon and that I 'wouldn't be disappointed'. This sounds very promising.

27 February At the Standards Committee the Commissioner for Ethical Standards in public life was present. I asked what her role was in appointing the Chair of the Scottish National Investment Bank. She said that as the appointment was made prior to the legislation going through, it was deemed as an 'unregulated appointment' and would remain so until a piece of subordinate legislation was passed, which has never been done. Apparently, Derek Mackay asked three times for the Commissioner to get involved in the appointment. Each time, correctly, she refused. She also refused to comment on whether she would have rubber-stamped the appointment of Wille Watt as CEO of the Scottish National Investment Bank.

I met Jim McColl, the owner of the company involved in the ferries contract fiasco. He was angry at comments I made about him being a Monaco-based tax exile (which he is). We had a frank exchange of views on this and agreed to disagree. He then told me all about the ferries shambles. He is furious with Sturgeon and Mackay who he believes have shafted him.

At Stage Two of the budget, shock, horror, the Greens have done a deal. There will be a less big cut for councils but it is still large, a study into free bus travel for under 19s and a few minor environmental measures. They really have no idea how to use the power they have as 'kingmakers'.

Gail Ross, one of the SNP MSPs elected in 2016 has announced she is standing down for family reasons. She lives in Caithness and finds being away from family all week intolerable.

28 February I got a call from *The Herald* who asked me to comment on Ruth Davidson receiving £7,500 for appearing on the ITV election show. I got two Tunnocks Teacakes for two hours on STV.

29 February Spent a sad morning helping pack up mum's house. My dad bought it for £4,000 in 1974 and knocked bits down and built extensions. It will be hard seeing someone else live in it.

1 March Met Kenny MacAskill. He is very frustrated and keen to build an anti-Tory, anti-austerity alliance. We agreed to try and to build support across party boundaries. He thinks Salmond will get off with the charges against him and Sturgeon will be gone soon.

2 March Mike Russell announced he will be standing down at the next election. I have always enjoyed my battles with him. In his book *Grasping the Thistle* he promoted a neoliberal free-market manifesto Scotland with flat taxes, privatisation of the NHS and civil service, education vouchers and a 'new union' – not Independence. I enjoyed reminding him of this in debates and watching him squirm.

Jackie Bailie had an article published in the *Scotsman* attacking me for pandering to the SNP. This is because of my belief that the Scottish people are sovereign and that Labour should promote a third option in any future referendum. She ignores the fact that 'the claim of right' signed back in the '90s by almost every Scottish Labour MP stated the people were sovereign.

3 March Three Scottish Coronavirus patients have now been identified.

5 March The Covid death toll in Scotland has reached nine.

After FMQs I had a members' debate on mental health provision for young people. Whitburn Academy pupils were in to hear it. They have done fantastic work in their school.

The budget passed with the Greens supporting more cuts for local government.

Tensions are breaking out in the SNP. This is all a preamble to the Salmond case.

Over the last few days we have had contact from the Council Social Work Department to discuss the discharge of my mum from hospital. A senior manager tried to convince us that the only care home place available was in Avonbridge, about 12 miles away from the family and not accessible by public transport. My brother, who is in a wheelchair, would have no way of seeing her. I made it clear that we will not accept Mum being admitted to Avonbridge. The guy tried to pressure us into accepting. We then discussed the funding for her place. When it emerged she would be self-funding her care from the sale of her home, a few hours later we were called back to be told a place had 'been found' at the care home 400 yards from her house. This is the two-tier care system at work. Had she been state funded, no place would have been available but because the owners can charge her more they have offered her a place. She will now be ripped off to the tune of around £1,000 a week.

6 March Today is my 51st birthday.

I heard today that letters offering a financial settlement have been sent out by the mesh manufacturers. This is good news but nothing will bring back quality of life for those affected.

Mum moved into the care home today. She was transferred by ambulance on a stretcher, which must have been very frightening for her but the staff were great and got her settled. It was very emotional being there and knowing that she would not be going home.

7 March Went over to see Mum, took her a gin and tonic, which she loves.

8 March The Sunday papers are full of the Salmond trial, which starts tomorrow. The SNP is increasingly fractious but my prediction is that whatever the outcome of the trial it will make zero impact on their poll ratings. In *The Herald*, Neil Mackay's article about the trial was accompanied by photos of Ian Brady and

Myra Hindley and made references to Rose and Fred West.

9 March I went with hernia mesh patient Roseanna Clarkin to meet Terry O'Kelly from the Scottish Government about hernia mesh. Roseanna is not my constituent but said she asked her local SNP MSP for help but he refused. The issues with hernia mesh are similar to transvaginal mesh. O'Kelly said he would look into issues raised but I don't expect much from him.

The Salmond trial started today with him strutting into court in that cocky, gallus manner of his. Initial exchanges centred around an alleged attempted rape.

10 March Italy is in complete lockdown because of Coronavirus. The scenes on the news are awful. God knows where this is going.

I hosted the PCS union low pay drop-in to coincide with the budget. Not a single SNP, Green, Lib Dem or Tory MSP turned up to listen to low-paid workers.

At topical questions, Jeane Freeman was quizzed about the resignation of Brian Houston as Chairman of NHS Lothian. At the weekend he gave a newspaper interview saying Freeman was lying. Freeman's response was to attack Houston, denying any responsibility for NHS failings. I asked for all documents relating to his sacking to be published. She repeatedly claims his performance was not acceptable, which is a bit rich from someone who has overseen record A&E waiting times, two-thirds of NHS boards in special measures, record drug deaths and the Sick Kids Hospital fiasco.

There were more lurid revelations in the High Court today about Alex Salmond's alleged predatory behaviour.

11 March Coronavirus is getting huge coverage; 15,000 people in Italy have it.

In Parliament the government was defeated on their proposals for nursery education.

UK Health Minister Nadine Dorries has coronavirus. Now this in itself may be shocking but frankly I'm more concerned that Nadine Dorries is a minister.

There are TV reports of people fighting in supermarkets over toilet rolls.

12 March Nicola Sturgeon made a statement saying that events with over 500 people will be discouraged from Monday but the Celtic v Rangers match, which will have over 50,000 in attendance, can go ahead on Sunday. Where's the logic in that?

Trump has halted all flights from Europe to the US, the stock market is down 11 per cent, the second greatest fall on record. We have reports of the first covid cases in my village. St John's Hospital has set aside two wards and social occasions like birthday parties are being cancelled.

13 March Coronavirus is now a major global crisis. Care homes are stopping visitors from entering, employers are trying to arrange home working, shops are selling out of basic items like pasta and rice.

After a meeting in Edinburgh, I walked through the town. There was a very eerie feeling, people looked nervous and glanced suspiciously at each other.

Told all my staff to go home early.

I went to see Mum in the care home. The manager told us they are now restricting access to essential visits only. This will be very difficult for residents and their families, especially those who are near the end of their lives.

The first Covid death was recorded in Scotland.

16 March At Boris Johnson's daily press conference, he advised that the UK death toll was 55. Everyone has to avoid gatherings and crowded places like pubs, theatres and clubs. All who can, should work from home. Ccare home visits are only to be made when necessary and if anyone in a household has symptoms, everyone has to isolate for two weeks.

Macron has put France in lockdown, Germany has closed its borders and the UN is saying test, test and test again. These are unprecedented times.

At the Salmond trial, one of the charges against him was dropped. A woman gave evidence saying Salmond had asked her to re-enact a Jack Vettriano christmas card with him.

17 March In Parliament all events have been cancelled, no one can enter the public gallery and it will only be government business for the next few weeks. Nicola Sturgeon and her entire cabinet were available for questions after a statement and there was a lot of unity in the face of this crisis. However, there were a lot of mixed messages over schools remaining open, while at the same time we are being told to avoid social contact. If something is not done fast there will be an unemployment crisis. I am receiving call after call and hundreds of emails from individuals and businesses who are really scared. I asked Nicola Sturgeon why the government was not following the World Health Organisation advice to test, test and test again. The answer seems to be we don't have the resources. The WHO has extensive knowledge of pandemic management, surely we must follow their advice.

I got a message from Mum's care home to tell me that only one visitor at a time can see her.

In summing up at the Salmond case, his lawyer claimed that everything said by the witnesses was false and politically motivated and his client is misunderstood and innocent.

18 March The world has turned very surreal. There are hardly any passengers on the trains, the roads are empty and people are panic-buying in the shops. Everyone is feeling tense and frightened.

I went to an MSP briefing with Jason Leitch, the NHS National Clinical Director and David McGill, Chief Executive of the Scottish Parliament. Leitch is loving the limelight and is starting to get carried away. He kept mentioning 'this new-found media career of mine' and wallowing in the adulation from SNP members. He took lots of questions; I got the last one and asked why we were not following WHO advice to test, test and test again. He said, 'We are testing frontline staff but we won't be testing everyone.' It seems like they have been completely unprepared despite warnings.

At lunchtime, Nicola Sturgeon announced all Scottish schools would shut on Friday and remain closed until after the summer holidays.

19 March FMQs was dominated by coronavirus issues and the news that for the first time in history school exams are being cancelled. With no school, there are questions about how vulnerable children will be fed and kept safe. I asked about why patients suspected of having coronavirus are not being tested. The answer was unconvincing.

I spoke to MSPs Donald Cameron and Alex Cole-Hamilton, who are both members of the committee that's looking into the government's handling of complaints against Salmond. I advised them that at the outset they should move that all witnesses be put under oath before they give their evidence. They didn't know you could do this, but as a former committee chair, I was aware of it. I hope they follow through on this.

20 March I closed my office and advised all my staff to work at home until further notice.

The mixed messages coming from the Scottish and UK governments are confusing but at least Sturgeon speaks with confidence, unlike Johnson who is incoherent and incompetent.

After major lobbying by the trade unions and concerned MPs, the Chancellor made a huge announcement that the state would guarantee 80 per cent of the wages of those who could not go to work and are unable to work from home. This is the biggest-ever state intervention to shore up pay. The self-employed and freelancers will surely have to be helped too.

As the number of deaths increase, doctors, nurses and social care staff cannot get the proper PPE and we are still not testing everyone suspected of having the virus. I find this incredible.

The news carried coverage of a hotel at Coylumbridge firing workers and putting them out of tied accommodation. Meanwhile an English doctor has made £2 million in a week selling Covid tests by mail order.

21 March The weather is fine, people are going to parks and heading to the countryside in caravans and campervans, ignoring advice, thinking it doesn't affect them.

I got an email from a constituent who lives near me saying that payday lenders are now putting out leaflets offering loans at 500 per cent APR. They know people are terrified of going without money so are exploiting vulnerability. I gave the story to the *Sunday Mail*, hopefully this will put a stop to their predatory practices.

In Glasgow the G1 Group started paying people off but quick work by UNITE forced them to put an end to this.

John Mason MSP spoke publicly opposing the closure of churches, claiming 'Jesus will sort things out'. Now, we all have our beliefs, but this is very dangerous.

22 March The scenes from Italy are horrendous with bodies piling up. On the Andrew Marr show, the WHO director repeated the message that we should be testing extensively and chasing down every case of the virus. Why on earth are we not doing this? Doctors are complaining that they are like lambs to the slaughter with inadequate PPE.

Later, I saw footage of Cuban doctors arriving in Italy to provide humanitarian medical support. It really is remarkable that wherever there is an international crisis the Cubans immediately respond.

23 March It's been an extraordinary day. I fielded hundreds of emails from people seeking advice on so many different issues. The problem is there is little I can tell them and can only refer them to agencies such as the Citizens' Advice Bureau, councils and the NHS.

I spoke to Doctor Devi Sridhar, a public health expert from Edinburgh University, about the lack of testing and failure to follow WHO advice. She is very much on the same page as me regarding this. Why are we not learning from China, South Korea and Taiwan, where mass testing is taking place? South Korea is doing 10,000 tests a day, Scotland is doing 450, hopelessly inadequate.

After lunch came the news that Alex Salmond has been acquitted on all charges. He says he will provide evidence in due course to support his belief there was a conspiracy against him. Alex Neil MSP and MPs Joanna Cherry and Kenny MacAskill called for resignations, a police inquiry, and an SNP investigation. This is going to run and run.

In the evening, Boris Johnson and Nicola Sturgeon came on TV to announce that the country is going into lockdown. People can only leave home for essential shopping, medical care or if they are key workers. We are allowed out to exercise once a day and the police will help enforce these restrictions. These are extraordinary measures and it is likely they will have to go on for weeks and weeks.

24 March The motorway was very quiet but clearly some companies were ignoring advice: construction workers were still going to work.

Salmond is claiming there was a conspiracy against him involving senior people in the civil service and the SNP.

Spent all day taking calls from workers who have been told they must go to work but feel they shouldn't be. Companies are trying everything to get round lockdown. While I can understand they are trying to keep their businesses going, they are also endangering the lives of workers. The government will have to step in and clarify who should and should not be working.

I went into the chamber for the First Minister's statement, which covered health, justice, the economy and education. I asked about the failure to follow WHO advice on testing and again got no clear answer.

A temporary hospital which can hold 2,000 patients is being built in London.

I spent the evening answering hundreds more inquiries.

25 March Fielded calls all morning from factory and warehouse workers who are scared for their wellbeing and jobs.

Prince Charles has tested positive for Covid. It seems like the aristocracy can get access to Covid tests but key workers can't.

I watched Jeremy Corbyn's last Prime Minister's Questions today. I am very sad to see him go. He is an honourable man who deserves peace and happiness in his life following five years of the most outrageous attacks on his character, his family, his friends and his comrades. The media assisted by the right wing of the Labour Party have played a shameful role. In hindsight, I think he should have stood down after the 2017 Election, leaving John McDonnell in pole position to take over. That would have ensured his legacy. But without doubt his term as leader gave so many of us hope and a belief that the Labour Party could radically change our country for the better. Those were exciting times, and I am proud to have played my party. Jeremy will always be a good friend and comrade to me.

The bloodletting following the Salmond case continues with attacks on civil servants and senior figures within the SNP.

There are 719 Covid cases and six more deaths in Scotland.

Social Care and NHS staff continue to complain about the lack of PPE. Jeane Freeman is denying there is a shortage. This bears no relation to reality.

26 March In Scotland, 894 people have Covid and 25 people have died. At the

Scottish Government press conference, it was said that 40,000–50,000 people are infected but don't know they have it. 1.5 million medical masks that were deemed out of date are now OK to use. Why would they do this if there is no PPE shortage? Not a word about testing.

I spoke to Mum over Skype.

We are now entering a major phase of the infection and we will see a high number of deaths. Italy is a few weeks ahead of us and they have a crisis on their hands dealing with the volume of dead bodies.

The whisky industry is claiming it is an essential business and their staff are key workers.

27 March I can't help being worried. Every day I see my wife and daughter go out to work in NHS wards where there will be Covid patients. They say that hospitals are being emptied of patients to make way for an expected Covid influx.

Lots of media coverage today about the lack of PPE for health and social care staff.

I spoke to a major employer today about the concerns raised by their staff and urged them to ensure that they had procedures in place to protect their workers.

Sturgeon said testing will increase next week. Next week? We need it massively increased now. Where is the media in holding the Scottish Government to account over this crucial issue?

Prime Minister Boris Johnson, Health Secretary Matt Hancock and the Chief Medical Officer in England have all tested positive.

29 March The *Sunday Times* has an exclusive story about Alex Salmond's QC Gordon Jackson being caught on film referring to Salmond as a bully. The women involved in the case have made a joint statement about their treatment and how they have been portrayed.

30 March I was contacted by constituents who have received texts and letters from their GP practice with links to end of life care and 'do not resuscitate' notice guidance. This is not something that should be done via text message. I will be raising this with the GP practice and the government.

Scotland is still only testing 700 people a day.

I heard today that Devi Sridhar is being recruited to the Scottish Government Advisery Group. Her public interventions are gaining traction and they will want to keep her inside the tent.

The Scottish Exhibition Centre is going to be used as a temporary field hospital. Meanwhile, the Sick Kids Hospital in Edinburgh lies empty.

The trade unions are doing some fantastic work on behalf of their members, making sure they are being treated properly and getting paid.

Hospitals are now almost empty with some wards down to just one or two patients.

31 March The Coronavirus Bill was published. It is without doubt the most oppressive and restrictive legislation outside of wartime but much of it entirely necessary. We will have to give it close scrutiny as there are so many impacts on people's liberty and rights. Proposals to suspend trial by jury and the restrictions on freedom of information are steps too far for me.

1 April I spoke to Carol Ewart from the Freedom of Information campaign about the emergency legislation and will work with her on amendments.

I asked a question in the chamber about whether the Scottish election can possibly take place with such a restrictive piece of legislation in place. I can't see how it can.

We then had Stage One of the Covid Bill with just two hours to put forward Stage Two amendments. I worked with Carol on the Freedom of Information ones and went to see Mike Russell about them. He rejected my call to shelve the plans for a non-legislative solution.

By the start of the Stage Two debate, the proposal to abandon trial by jury had been dropped because of the strength of opposition. I moved around 15 amendments on the proposals to restrict FOI and called for a pragmatic solution similar to New Zealand; I pointed out that not even Boris Johnson has tried this. On the key amendment, 29 the Greens bailed the government out. Some of the other amendments were tied 41-41 with the Presiding Officer casting his vote for the government position.

2 April I received lots of emails supporting yesterday's amendments on FOI.

At a press conference, Nicola Sturgeon said testing would increase to 900 a day by the end of April. It is woeful but at last the press are taking an interest.

Football teams are getting pelters today as they are using the furlough scheme to pay 80 per cent of their workers' wages, while multi-millionaire footballers receive full pay.

3 April I spoke to Mum again on Skype. She is in good spirits despite not being able to see anyone, but she can't wait until this is over.

At last testing is all over the news.

I spoke to Marion Scott at the *Sunday Post* today. She has a story of a Scottish company funded by Scottish Enterprise who are exporting millions of coronavirus test kits abroad but producing none for Scotland. This is very telling and confirms that the government has been completely caught out.

Jackie Baillie was named Scottish Labour's new Deputy Leader. She secured 58 per cent of the vote to Mark Kerr's 42 per cent. Matt did brilliantly well against a high-profile MSP of 20 years' standing. But this is a disastrous result.

4 April Dreadful news today that 13 residents in a Glasgow care home have died in the last two weeks because of Coronavirus.

This morning Keir Starmer was announced leader of the UK Labour Party winning 56 per cent of the vote with Rebecca Long-Bailey second on 27 per cent with the others trailing behind.

Angela Rayner was elected deputy with Ian Murray trailing behind in fourth which is a shame as I really hoped he would be fifth.

Starmer made commitments during his campaign to continue with policies he supported during Jeremy Corbyn's time, but we will see if this was campaigning rhetoric or genuine conviction.

5 April A Sunday newspaper had a massive scoop. The Chief Medical Officer, Catherine Calderwood, has been caught visiting her second home in Fife, defying her own guidance to stay at home. Her credibility and the government's messaging has been hugely damaged. If this was an ordinary member of the public they would be facing criminal charges. I cannot see how she can survive.

Mike Russell went on *Politics Scotland* and tried to play down the story, as did Jason Leitch on the radio but this is not going away.

Keir Starmer was on the *Andrew Marr Show* and I have to say the alarm bells are already ringing. He sounds desperate to ditch the manifesto he has just been elected on. He also announced the appointment of Ian Murray as Shadow Secretary of State for Scotland.

Later at a press conference with the First Minister, Catherine Calderwood apologised and tried to sound contrite. However, it emerged that she had gone to her second home not once but two weeks in a row. At 11pm her resignation was announced.

Boris Johnson was admitted to intensive care suffering from Covid.

6 April 6,000 people in the UK have died from Coronavirus. Parliament is to be reconvened to discuss the crisis.

The UK Chief Medical Officer is now saying we can learn from Germany on testing. A bit late.

8 April At the weekend I wrote to Presiding Officer Ken MacIntosh calling for the Scottish Parliament to be recalled from Easter recess to discuss the mounting crisis. I released this to the media and it got picked up. Later, I received a response rejecting my request. Instead there will be a virtual Leaders' question time on Thursday. In the middle of this crisis, journalists can ask questions of the First Minister and get answers, yet elected members of Parliament can't.

9 April At the first virtual FMQs, Richard Leonard asked about the inadequacy of the testing regime and Patrick Harvie raised the 'do not resuscitate' issue.

A worker from one of the companies I have been pressing to improve their health and safety provision has died of Covid.

Nurses are advising me their wards are empty, with no patients.

Starmer has appointed the rest of his frontbench team, which is full of Blairite ultras, like Wes Streeting, Pat McFadden and Stephen Kinnock.

10 April My brother-in-law Jim's brother, Larry has been admitted to intensive care in London with Covid.

11 April A very quiet Easter Sunday.

Sky News are running a story about an internal Labour Party report showing how party staff set about undermining Jeremy Corbyn, anyone associated with his team, candidates they didn't like and election campaigns.

13 April Over the weekend the UK death toll reached 10,000, one of the worst rates in the world. Scotland has followed the UK in almost every way. The governments have been warned for months that Covid was coming and completely failed to prepare.

Johnson is out of intensive care and being hailed as some kind of hero.

I wrote to Michael Sharpe, the Scottish Labour Party General Secretary, demanding an inquiry into the conduct of Scottish Labour officials to establish whether over the last five years any senior party staff were involved in attempts to undermine the 2017 and 2019 election campaigns. I am not accusing Michael of this as he is a big supporter of the Corbyn project but I do want to know why for example, John McDonnell as Shadow Chancellor was prevented from speaking at the Labour conference; why campaign finance was diverted into some seats and away from others; and why those on the left were ignored in favour of New Labour and right-wing candidates. In Leith, where Gordon Munro was crying out for help, resources were diverted to Ian Murray's seat which had plenty of volunteers and money.

The report from London shows that party staff deliberately sat on complaints of antisemitism to make the party look bad. I read the full report today, it is sickening. Anyone to the left of Gordon Brown is dismissed as a Trot.

14 April There is a big scandal brewing over care home deaths. I am terrified for my mum.

Jim's brother is still on a ventilator in a London hospital, he is very ill.

Went on the Labour Group meeting call and raised the need for a Scottish inquiry into the conduct of staff during elections. Jackie Baillie claimed there is nothing to see here, move on.

15 April Testing is back on the agenda – 25 per cent of current deaths are in care homes where staff and residents have not been tested. We are all holding our breath in the hope that the virus does not get into my mum's home.

Scottish Labour Party right wingers are attacking me for calling for a party inquiry. They protesteth too much.

Fiona and I helped the local community development trust deliver food to pensioners. All were very pleased to get it and have a chat.

I went out for a walk with Fiona and Chloe. Both work in hospitals and are just getting on with things but I worry about them every day.

16 April Covid deaths in Scotland reached 1,000.

People were urged to go out onto their doorsteps and clap for the NHS this evening. Lots of people in my street did it, the scenes on TV were amazing.

17 April I was contacted today by a constituent who has very little food in the house. I offered to provide some to get the family through the next few days and then spoke to the food bank who are going to help with an urgent delivery.

Heard from the owner of two care homes that they are having problems with PPE, testing, funding and staffing. I wrote to the government raising my serious concerns.

There was an online question time with ministers. I was able to ask Jeane Freeman why the government was still ignoring WHO advice on testing. She claimed WHO are happy with the Scottish Government approach.

I spoke to an ex-miner from Dalkeith whose GP has asked him to consent to a 'do not resuscitate' order in the event he ends up unwell.

18 April I had a chat with a senior government adviser who told me that officials have been completely caught out by Covid and were committed to a 'herd immunity' strategy. They have made no preparation for testing and will have to stick to their anti-testing approach or admit their failings. They don't want to go into lockdown or close schools, but were forced to do so because of public opinion.

19 April I am going to keep pushing on testing as the government is in complete denial.

21 April Went into Parliament. After FMQs, the government sought to bring forward the Agriculture Bill and Stage Three of the Coronavirus Protection

Bill. We have had zero time to debate the Covid strategy and our questions to ministers get no answers. All of the written questions that we have sent and letters to ministers have gone into a black hole.

We are now being asked to rush through this legislation unquestioningly in a context where thousands of our citizens have died, there is a PPE crisis, testing is a shambles and the economy is in meltdown. I raised this with the Presiding Officer and called for a two-day debate to allow as many members as possible to raise issues on behalf of their constituents. Rejected. I voted against the motion. However, all other parties supported the government approach.

The oil price dropped to minus $32. They are paying people to take it away.

20 April Richard Leonard appointed Jackie Baillie as Finance Spokesperson. She is now in poll position to kill off his leadership and usher in Anas Sarwar.

21 April The *Financial Times* is reporting that the real death toll in the UK is 41,000 and not the 17,000 being reported.

I spoke to my mum today; she is looking well and seems content enough. I really feel for the staff in the care homes, theyare under so much pressure.

23 April The Scottish Government published its Covid exit strategy. Good in parts, but it says: 'We are clear that an assumption that there is a proportion or section of the population that is safe and it is acceptable to allow it to be infected forms no part of the Scottish Government's policy or approach.' This is a 100 per cent U-turn on the 'herd immunity' approach that senior officials previously espoused. In recent weeks, Jason Leitch advised that it was okay for the Old Firm football match to go ahead and for his wife to go to a Stereophonics concert; he opposed the closure of schools, said the over-70s did not need to stay at home, claimed there was no PPE shortage and that community testing was unnecessary. On every one of these issues, he has had to reverse his position. The fact that he maintains a calm and assertive manner does not mean that what he says is correct.

26 April *The Times* is saying that Scotland is 19th out of 25 countries in Europe for testing provision.

27 April Boris Johnson was back at work today trying to sound upbeat but there is not a great deal to be optimistic about. We are going to have one of the worst death tolls in the world.

28 April After weeks of saying that face masks don't help the Scottish Government has changed its advice. Is it any surprise that people are confused?

It also announced that the outcome of its review into Curriculum for Excellence was to be delayed until after the Scottish election. Education is supposed to be the First Minister's priority.

I joined the online International Workers Memorial Day event. More relevant than ever.

29 April Had a tough day today. For the first time I feel things are getting to me mentally. My brother John, who has multiple sclerosis, hasn't been out of the house for seven weeks. My mum is in a care home and can't get any visitors and my wife and daughter are working in hospitals with Covid patients.

British Airways announced they are paying off 12,000 workers.

30 April There has been a 23 per cent increase in excess deaths in Scotland.

The Herald has reported the Scottish Government testing target is being missed by 90 per cent.

Ryanair is making 3,000 staff redundant.

Attended an online briefing with Sir Hugh Pennington. The microbiologist was scathing about much of what has gone on, particularly the lack of urgency from the government and the advice they are getting from their officials.

1 May I submitted a motion calling for an extra bank holiday as a mark of respect for key workers.

2 May A poll has the SNP on 52 per cent and Labour on 12 per cent. It is remarkable how the Labour Party does not understand that having no credible position on the constitution for the last ten years has brought us to this position. Everywhere you look public services are in crisis and inequality is growing, yet the SNP are miles ahead.

3 May The crisis in care homes is getting worse with 16 Covid deaths at a Kirkcaldy home and 56 cases at a home on Skye.

There is a lot of speculation in the papers about a potential split in the SNP and a new Independence Party being formed. Jim Sillars has said the SNP is rotten at the top.

5 May Jennie Formby stood down as the General Secretary of the Labour Party.

6 May It has emerged that 59 per cent of deaths from Covid in Scotland are in care homes, a clear failure of strategy and policy on testing. The wellbeing of our elderly loved ones has been sacrificed and I am so angry at this.

In Parliament, I questioned Nicola Sturgeon saying:

> Can I ask why on earth we are continuing to discharge patients from hospital to care homes without establishing whether or not they are positive for Covid-19? I am not one that ever pleads with the First Minister, but I will now. Please, stop this practice now to save the lives of residents and the great people who look after them.

Sturgeon appeared to become emotional as she responded:

> Every single one of us is deeply, deeply concerned and moved by what's happening in our care homes. And that is particularly the case for people like him who have relatives in care homes. But I don't think there is a single one of us who does not think this a deeply and profoundly upsetting situation. So please do not ask these questions in a way that suggests we are not all trying to do everything we possibly can to do the right thing.

So, the First Minister, who should be accountable for the decisions she and her government have made, tells an elected opposition Member of Parliament not to ask questions in a way she doesn't like. Well, my concern is not for the sensitivities of Ms Sturgeon, they are for the hundreds of older people who are dying as a result of her government's NHS discharge policy. It is my duty to ask these questions on behalf of the people I represent and no matter how much abuse I get online from her sycophantic supporters I will go on asking hard questions and holding those in power to account for their decisions.

7 May On Facebook and Twitter I have been called 'slug', 'fanny', 'scumbag' and 'prick' for putting a very pertinent question to the First Minister yesterday. I have also received a lot of support from families of care home residents and those who work in them, many telling me horror stories of their experience. Had a good long chat to John McDonnell today about the future. John is someone I always enjoy talking to.

8 May Spoke to my mum on the phone today. She is very upset about the situation in the care home sector and has heard lot of what has been on the news and radio. Hearing this and seeing staff wearing masks all the time is making residents very anxious.

Did another session at the food project today with Fiona. We sent out ready meals to be delivered by local taxi drivers. They have been brilliant.

9 May Johnson announced that people who can go back to work should do so on Wednesday. Scotland, Wales and Northern Ireland are taking a different approach. Quite right too.

10 May The press is full of stories about the rest of the UK diverging from Johnson. There are more mixed messages.

This evening *Disclosure Scotland* exposed how the virus came into Scotland in February but the public were not told. It covered mistakes over testing, care homes and hospital discharge. Nicola Sturgeon was asked to appear on the programme but refused. Professor Allyson Pollock said that she had written to the Scottish Government about the lack of contact tracing but never received a reply. Ireland set up test and trace rapidly, while we are still pissing about. One family spoke movingly about the loss of three grandparents to the virus. Ninety per cent of people who have died are over 65 years of age. Older people have been let down by those in power.

12 May I submitted an urgent question asking why the Covid cases affecting people who attended a conference of Nike workers in Edinburgh in February were not made public. Jeane Freeman cited client confidentiality.

Stewart Stevenson gave the first ever online speech in Parliament. It was every bit as bad as his in-person ones.

13 May London and the rest of England are opening up. The Tube was rammed with people.

After FMQs we had a statement from the Lord Advocate about the recording of Covid deaths. MSPs had all of ten minutes to raise questions. Parliament is not covering itself in glory.

We then had another Covid Bill introduced, covering things like weddings, student accommodation, justice and support for carers. Earlier, Adam Tomkins had advised me that he would be introducing an amendment on FOI to repeal the previous legislation. I intervened on Andy Wightman's speech to see if the Greens would support this and he said they would. Good news.

We are months down the line, and we are still not routinely testing all care home staff.

14 May Worked all morning on a series of amendments to the Covid Bill on trade union access to companies receiving Scottish Government grants, the creation of a health and safety fund, the living wage for workers employed on Covid-related work and the repeal of FOI restrictions.

I was told today that the Covid testing centre at Gartnavel Hospital is closing because of a lack of people attending for tests. What is going on?

15 May Spent another few hours volunteering at the food project. It's a lifeline for many people.

I took a lot of calls from journalists. They keep phoning me because of the questions I am asking about Covid policy.

I spoke to a constituent today whose partner worked at a kilt shop in Edinburgh where a number of the Nike conference delegates visited. She measured 17 of them for Highland outfits over 90 minutes and has still not been tested.

16 May Took a very distressing phone call from a constituent about a care home in my region where ten residents have died, two staff are infected and there is a lack of PPE. She reported poor practice, a lack of social distancing in lunchrooms, staff being pressured to return before their isolation period is over and patients being accepted from hospital untested. I immediately wrote to the care inspectorate and the care home owners, HC1.

18 May Apparently, the Nike store in Livingston was deep-cleaned around the time of the Edinburgh conference but workers were not advised why.

The length of time the government is taking to respond to parliamentary questions is dreadful. I have some going back to 31 March, on behalf of people who desperately need answers.

19 May Got up very early to be in for 7:20am for Stage two of the Covid emergency legislation. It was pretty depressing. The SNP and Tories had done a deal to oppose almost every progressive amendment put forward. They opposed a rent freeze, introduction of collective bargaining in the care sector, trade union rights for companies engaged in public contracts, a health and safety fund, free bus travel for the low paid and unemployed and so on. Mike Russell led for the SNP and Adam Tomkins for the Tories. The SNP Covid-19 Committee members Stewart Stevenson, Annabelle Ewing and Willie Coffey never uttered a word during the entire proceedings. We did, however, have one small victory with the previous FOI restrictions being overturned.

In the afternoon, I received confirmation from Livingston Shopping Centre that the Nike Store had indeed been deep cleaned after the conference in Edinburgh. All of this is having to be dragged out of the authorities.

20 May The government announced that the mesh-injured women's fund that I have campaigned for will pay £1,000 to each victim. This is not a compensation payment, but it is to help with additional expenses that women experience because of their injuries or disabilities. It is a small but helpful amount. I am delighted that they agreed to my proposal.

At FMQ's, the Nike conference and testing dominated.

We had Stage Three of the Covid Bill in the afternoon with Michael Russell at his arrogant worst. I resubmitted all my Stage Two amendments and was attacked for doing so. He claimed it was impossible to set up collective bargaining in the care sector so quickly, despite the fact that the unions support my amendments. So we can do all sorts of things in this emergency situation, but setting up a form of collective agreement for the care sector is one of the things that is beyond the wit of man.

21 May Nicola Sturgeon announced the beginning of the phased end of lockdown. From next week, people will be able to meet other people outside and travel more.

Health Secretary Jeane Freeman has been caught out giving the wrong numbers of people discharged from hospital untested. The correct number is over 1,000. An urgent question was put down about this and I was able to ask how the government managed to eradicate a 20-year-old problem of delayed discharge overnight in March and April? Freeman claimed it was all down to 'digital improvements' and 'changes in practice'. I don't believe a single word of it. For years, families have been told that their mums and dads who were ready to leave hospital couldn't because there were no care home places or care at home available. Now we are expected to believe that 'changes in practice' and 'digital improvements' eradicated this problem almost overnight.

Lots of new bedrooms in care homes or new home carers did not appear overnight providing increased capacity. The reality is what they did was provide money. And that money freed up places that were already there.

Year-on-year cuts to council budgets have reduced the amount of money available for social care, leaving older people stranded in hospital at a cost of up to £4,000 a week to the NHS, compared to £1,000 a week in a care home and £350 being looked after at home. This really is a scandal and I'm going to pursue this vigorously.

22 May I spoke to seven journalists this morning about the discharge scandal.

Dominic Cummings, Boris Johnson's most trusted adviser, has been caught traveling 250 miles to Barnard Castle in Durham for a holiday whilst suspected of having Covid. One rule for us plebs, another for the arrogant elite. It is Catherine Calderwood all over again.

23 May Cummings apparently drove to Durham when his wife caught Covid. He had his kids in the car and went sightseeing when he was there. He was seen at different locations by a number of people. This is a major crisis for the Tories.

At 5pm Johnson defended Cummings at a press conference and refused to sack him. Public opinion is raging against them.

Scottish Television has released a video of children saying 'thank you' to Nicola Sturgeon for her leadership during Covid; 2,700 people have died, over 1,000 elderly residents were discharged into care homes untested, resulting in the virus running like wildfire through the system, and now we have a major broadcaster getting kids to say thank you to those who have directed and overseen this disaster.

May 25 Dominic Cummings gave a press conference in the Downing Street Rose Garden. It was something else. He read a long statement about his wife and him being ill, how they drove to Durham with their children where they stayed until they recovered. He said he went for a half hour drive to Barnard Castle to 'test his eyesight before driving back to London'. He made no apology and was put through the wringer by the press with charges of hypocrisy, double standards, illegality and so on. Afterwards, Johnson did another press conference where the focus transferred to his judgment.

The *Daily Mail*, of all newspapers, called for Cummings to be sacked.

26 May There is wall-to wall-coverage of the Cummings story. The consensus is that his press conference was a disaster and has opened up more questions than it answered. The Scottish Tories are trying to ride it out by saying nothing. Jackson Carlaw is under huge pressure. Out of the blue, Moray MP Douglas Ross, a junior Scotland Office minister, resigned from his ministerial role. This was followed by Tory MSPs calling for Cummings to resign. They have apparently been inundated with emails from furious constituents. Michelle Ballantyne MSP then popped up to support Cummings.

May 27 The Wings Over Scotland appeal regarding the defamation case against Kezia Dugdale was unsuccessful. Good news.

Johnson appeared before a House of Commons committee to discuss the Cummings case and was torn to pieces.

At FMQs, Richard Leonard pushed hard on the care homes discharge policy. Sturgeon, clearly on the back foot keeps repeating the line: 'If we knew then what we know now then we might have done things differently.'

Later I asked this question:

Neil Findlay (Lothian) (Lab)

For years, patients have been stuck in hospital and told that their discharge has been delayed because a care home place or a care package is not available. However, in March, 1,000 such cases were resolved almost overnight, not because new care home rooms were suddenly built, or because new staff were recruited overnight, but because money became available to purchase places.

Does the First Minister accept that all those delayed discharge patients and their families, who for years were told that they were delayed because no care home place or care package was available, were in fact misled, and that the real reason that they were stuck in hospital was because integration joint boards and councils did not have the money to purchase the care packages that they needed?

First Minister (Nicola Sturgeon)

We always have to work within the resources that we have, and we do so to the best of our ability. Within that, the government that I now lead has prioritised health and social care all along. We have lived through many years of austerity along the way, which has made it very difficult.

We received additional funding through the consequentials route at the start of the crisis to help us to deal with the health and social care impacts, and we took decisions to try to mitigate the impacts as much as possible.

We continue to take the best decisions that we can, based on the best evidence, and will continue to do so. I will not shy away from doing that, even though I know that, often, whatever decision I take, somebody in the chamber will say that it is the wrong decision and that I should have taken another one. Particularly at times of crisis, the job of somebody like me is to take those decisions, based on the best evidence that we have and with the resources that we have at our disposal, and to be accountable for them. I will continue to do that every step of the way.

28 May Sturgeon announced the lifting of some Covid restrictions. People will be allowed to meet members of another household outside; some sports are resuming and bits of the economy opening up.

In the US cities are like a tinderbox following the death of George Floyd, a black man who died after his neck was knelt on for an extended period by white police officers. It has all been caught on camera. Trump is blaming everyone expect the police.

29 May At the NHS Lothian MSP briefing, I asked how they eradicated delayed discharge in April. The officials were very defensive but accepted that money had freed up places, confirming what I have said all along. I also asked about the low usage of intensive care beds but high death rate of care home residents and why residents had not been admitted to empty ICU beds. They did not like this question at all.

A huge forest fire occurred near my house. Firefighters have been working in sweltering conditions all day trying to put it out.

30 May The forest fire is still going on. Lots of local people are providing drinks, food and ice lollies to the fire fighters. The heat from the fire and sun must be brutal.

Met some family members for the first time in ages, great to see them.

1 June There has been ongoing rioting and unrest in the US as the George Floyd video goes viral.

2 June The Scottish Government refused to provide me with details of meetings between the Scottish Chief Medical Officer (CMO) and UK counterparts. Tommy from my office had also submitted an FOI asking for briefings from the CMO and Jason Leitch to Sturgeon and Freeman. The response was astonishing with the government claiming that no written briefings exist and that they were all done verbally! At the government briefing, James Mathews of Sky asked about this and Sturgeon said she did get written briefings after all. Later, a government spokesperson claimed: 'It was the wording of the FOI that resulted in it being denied.' This is garbage, as the wording was advised on and agreed by the Scottish Government FOI unit. This is now quite a big media story.

In the afternoon debate on health, I raised the social care crisis and the delayed discharge scandal, but Jeane Freeman made no attempt to address my points in her summing up.

I had a parliamentary answer today confirming that the cost of keeping someone in a hospital bed is around £4,000 a week, compared to £1,000 a week in a care home. This shows the scandalous waste of resources over many years as people languish in hospital when they could be home.

3 June Protests go on in the US. Trump held a bible in front of church in one of the most crass photoshoots I have ever seen.

Mike Russell gave evidence to the Covid Committee and was asked about some of the regulations put through in his name – he didn't have a clue and was completely shown up, it was a joy to behold. He also advised everyone to 'stare at people in shops who were not wearing a mask'. I would like to see him staring down people in my local Lidl.

Scotland reached a tragic milestone with care home Covid-related deaths outstripping hospital deaths, a consequence of the appalling decision to discharge so many elderly people untested from hospitals to care homes in April.

It was decided that over the summer parliament will meet once a week and that the recess will be curtailed.

4 June I got a reply to a parliamentary question on the Nike conference. They could not tell me the number of workers who came into contact with delegates as this would breach confidentiality. More cover-up.

5 June The *Daily Record* ran a story about Richard Leonard saying Labour are totally opposed to an Independence referendum. This is such a stupid and self-defeating position. It leaves the SNP to hoover up Yes voters and the Tories No. We should be saying we will respect the democratic will of the people, take part positively in the debate and put forward a credible, third option of devo max. The party seems to be on a kamikaze mission.

At the daily press conference, Freeman and Sturgeon said they would name and shame NHS boards that failed to deliver on testing. They seem to forget seven out of 11 boards are in special measures, effectively run by the government.

6 June Black Lives Matter protests continue. In Bristol the statue of slave trader Edward Coulson was toppled into the water.

7 June The *Sunday Times* is reporting on the gross under-occupancy of ICU beds while hundreds of older people are left to die in care homes and denied hospital treatment.

8 June The *Daily Record* ran an excellent piece on my visit to Colombia and the situation there.

9 June Got a parliamentary answer back about the Rangers v Leverkusen match. Not one of the almost 50,000 fans were contact traced after the game.

10 June Got such amazing news today: Larry Doolan, the brother of my brother-in-law Jim woke up and spoke to his sister after nine weeks in a comma caused by Covid. He was lucid and coherent.

11 June Still only 11,000 out of 50,000 care home staff have been tested.

I got another answer to a PQ back today. It showed 108 people were contact traced around 1–2 March after the Nike conference in Edinburgh and yet the government allowed the Scotland v France rugby match and Rangers v Leverkusen game to go ahead over the following two weeks with no contact tracing of any fans.

12 June A number of new Labour commentators have come out in the media pushing for Anas Sarwar to take over from Richard Leonard. This has been coming for a long time. I heard that, on Saturday at the party's Scottish Executive meeting, Richard cut a deal with Ian Murray on opposition to another referendum. He is now a very isolated figure.

Did a conference call with government Ministers Maree Todd and Ash Denham on the Children's Bill and pushed them on sibling contact for children in care and building standards in contact centres. They gave a commitment to act on these issues.

15 June Did a conference call with Alex Neil and Jackson Carlaw and the General Medical Council. We raised the cases of women told they had 'full mesh removals', only to find later they still had very significant amounts of mesh still in them. They agreed to investigate every case put before them.

Afterwards, I spoke to Dr Veronikis, who withdrew his offer to come to Scotland to do mesh removals after being repeatedly mucked about.

16 June Spoke to Mary McLaughlin who advised that a report has recommended the Canadian government fund mesh removals in the US from Dr Veronikis. This will now become our ask.

At topical questions, John Swinney failed to clarify the situation with next year's schooling. Some councils are saying children will have a few days at home and few at school but the situation is really unclear.

Man Utd player Marcus Rashford has used his experience as the son of a poor single mum whose family were reliant on free school meals to call for Johnson's government to provide them over the summer holidays. He is articulate, honest and principled and got huge traction with this call. After initially refusing and a day of appalling headlines, Boris Johnson was forced to capitulate. Brilliant.

18 June Iain Gray MSP for East Lothian announced he is standing down at the election.

More lifting of restrictions today but still no care home visiting.

19 June Got my van back from the joiner. He has done a brilliant job converting it into a camper. I hope we get to use it over the holidays.

20 June Met my brother, sister and their partners for a chat, the first time in ages. It was great.

21 June The *Sunday Post* ran the story about Dr Veronikis not coming to Scotland. I have submitted a motion and FMQ on this.

22 June I spent the morning working on speaking notes for my Stage Two amendments on the Children's Bill. They relate to the experience of my constituent Emma McDonald, who brought forward a petition on family contact centres following an appalling experience where there were major issues around the health and safety of children left there. She has been excellent and has really helped push this issue to the fore.

23 June I moved around eight amendments to the Children's Bill; all were voted down by a coalition of SNP and Tory MSPs. They rejected regulatory control of family contact centres, opposed a publicly owned system leaving centres in private hands and rejected professional training and accreditation for staff.

Swinney has done a major U-turn on schooling next year. A few days ago it was to be part-time and blended learning, now pupils are going back full time.

24 June At FMQs I got a question about mesh and the failure to bring Dr Veronikis and got the usual flannel.

Neil Findlay (Lothian) (Lab)

In November, after eight years without meeting mesh-injured women, the First Minister asked for a meeting in the middle of the general election campaign. She said all sorts of sympathetic things and gave those women her personal commitment to do all that she could to ensure that Dr Veronikis, the United States mesh surgeon, came to Scotland to help them. He made his offer in good faith more than a year ago, and all that there has been since is delay, deliberate blocking and inaction by vested interests that never wanted him here in the first place. He has walked away in disgust at that behaviour.

For those women, who have been horribly injured and disabled, the prospect of Dr Veronikis coming to Scotland is their last hope of ridding their body of this poison. The First Minister should listen to what one woman said this week in an email to me and her:

> For years, I thought I had some kind of mental problem as I didn't know other people were similarly affected. I had to retire from the job I absolutely loved in a school. I had to give up the gym. I used to do Race For Life every year and the MoonWalk. I danced my socks off at family gatherings. That person doesn't exist anymore and I'm left a pain-ridden shell of the person I was. I hate me and suffer from depression.

For a decade, the government has failed those women and I am sorry to say that the First Minister has too. Does her government intend to do anything to help hundreds of women live a life that is free of the brutality of mesh pain?

The First Minister (Nicola Sturgeon)

I know how strongly Neil Findlay rightly feels about the issue, and I pay tribute to the way in which he has consistently brought it to the Parliament. I take very seriously the commitments that I made to the women when I met them and I will continue to do so. We have already taken steps, including the creation of the fund to help women who have been affected by mesh.

On Dr Veronikis, I genuinely say to Neil Findlay and to others who are interested in the issue that they should try to work with us on it. First, we have not received any correspondence from Dr Veronikis to say that he has withdrawn his offer to come to Scotland – that is a statement of fact. The former chief medical officer wrote to him on 24 and 27 February, and the international recruitment team at NHS Greater Glasgow and Clyde wrote to him on 3 March. We did not get responses to those letters. The interim CMO wrote to Dr Veronikis on 24 April to reiterate that the invitation still stood and that we looked forward to welcoming him when restrictions around Covid were lifted. On 5 June, there was a response that expressed frustration at a lack of progress. There seems to be an issue here. We thought that we had made progress, when Catherine Calderwood spoke to him, around the need to ensure that a surgeon cannot simply operate on a woman with whom he has had no prior contact and that pre-operative and post-operative care need be in place. Those seem to be the arrangements on which we have struggled to make progress with Dr Veronikis.

The offer is still there and we have been trying to get those arrangements finalised. I repeat today my personal willingness – although I am not a clinician – to speak to him directly, as I did before, to try to get the arrangements in place that would allow that visit to happen. It is not the case that that has not happened because of blockages or an unwillingness on the part of the Scottish Government to have him here, and it is an unfair and inaccurate characterisation to say that. My personal opinion is that the contrary is absolutely the case. I hope that others who have a genuine concern about the issue will help with that rather than try to characterise the situation in an inaccurate way.

25 June Lots of mesh women and their families have been in touch. They are rightly furious about the way Dr Veronikis has been treated by the Scottish Government.

Rebecca Long-Bailey was sacked by Starmer today for taking part in a newspaper interview with the socialist actress Maxine Peake. In a wide-ranging piece, Maxine compared the action of the police in the George Floyd's case with the actions of the Israeli Defence Force – and for that, Rebecca was sacked. On this basis, if someone you know says something about the Israeli government, you too are held to account.

26 June I took part in the NHS Lothian MSP briefing where staffing problems at the St John's children's ward were raised. The Royal College is saying that if the staffing issues are not resolved, NHS Lothian should not expend any more energy on it to the detriment of the pan Lothian service. I think the plan all along has been to downgrade the service to an assessment centre.

28 June The papers are full of stories about Labour battles and Starmer's sacking of Rebecca Long-Bailey. Lots of left-wing members are leaving which, is exactly what the right want.

29 June Did an online meeting with key members of the Scottish left. We agreed to put out a statement urging people to stay in the party and fight back against attacks from the leadership and their supporters.

1 July 12,000 jobs were lost today in hospitality, aviation, and engineering.

I had another very interesting call with Alex Neil and Kenny MacAskill to discuss the possibility of building an anti-Tory campaign against cuts and austerity. It was a positive meeting and we agreed to meet up again soon.

It was confirmed that all witnesses that come before the Salmond inquiry will give evidence under oath. This follows a tip-off I gave to opposition committee members, which was followed.

The SNP and Tories have worked together to kill Pauline McNeil's Members'

Bill on restricting private rent rises.

I had to show potential buyers around my mum's house today. It was sad.

3 July Worked at the food project and took in a donation of 100 bags of food from Whitburn Church, a brilliant boost to stocks.

For the first time in four months someone was able to visit Mum. My sister said Mum was overwhelmed and crying but calmed down and they had a good chat. Families across the country will be experiencing the same thing.

4 July TV and radio are reporting huge crowds on the streets, on public transport and in trains in London. This is pretty scary and will stoke fears of a second wave of Covid.

5 July I got a call from a constituent about a young relative who is terminally ill and if there is anything that can be done to allow more people to attend funeral services. I immediately got on to the government about this. What an awful situation.

6 July The young constituent who was ill has passed away. What devastating news. I put a call into the First Minister's office seeking immediate and up to date guidance for the family on funeral numbers.

7 July Got a reply back from the First Minister's office about funerals. Sadly, little has changed but I passed it on to the family who appreciated the effort made.

Reach PLC, owner of the *Daily Record*, announced 550 redundancies. This was met by hundreds of social media posts from nationalists gloating and abusing journalists.

8 July A big day today for the mesh campaigners. Baroness Cumberlege published her report into medical devices with a big focus on mesh. It was an excellent piece of work and stands in stark contrast to the completely discredited whitewash review that the Scottish Government published. The report vindicated the women and their complaints, exposed the MHRA as a failed and compromised regulatory body, highlighted the conflict of interest of mesh surgeons and how patients were treated with contempt by many in the medical establishment. She has published a long list of positive recommendations for improvements in care, practice and the appointment of a patient safety commissioner. The report was all over the news which shows how far we have travelled from when we could barely get a journalist, other than the brilliant Marion Scott interested.

9 July More easing of restrictions were announced today.

At questions I raised the mesh report and called for its recommendations to be implemented the Scottish Government to fund women to have mesh removals in the US.

10 July Worked at the food project this morning, the numbers needing emergency food is shocking.

11 July Went to the funeral of my young constituent who died of cancer. A moving service with hundreds of people outside the church, where the service was being relayed. It was uplifting to see so many young people there showing their respect and solidarity, it must have given the family a lot of comfort. Afterwards, a number of us met outside at the golf club and despite the sad circumstances there was a great sense of mutual support and people were so pleased to see each other for the first time in months.

12 July The *Sunday Post* ran a front-page and four inside pages of excellent coverage of Baroness Cumberlege's report on mesh.

14 July Good news. Luath has accepted two book proposals I have submitted, one for my granda's memoirs or life in a shale mining village and the other my interviews with people on the frontline of major social justice campaigns.

15 July Alex Neil, Jackson Carlaw and I did a call with Jeane Freeman about the outcome of the Cumberlege Report. Freeman is of the belief that an offer is still on the table for Dr Veronikis to consider. I made it clear that he has withdrawn and there would need to be very significant change if there is to be any progress. We expressed our anger and frustration at the treatment of him by the government and officials.

17–30 July On holiday, touring in Scotland in the campervan.

While we were away on holiday the Labour right and their friends launched further attacks on Richard Leonard with George Foulkes and of all people Archie McPherson calling for him to stand down.

The SNP blocked Joanna Cherry MP from standing for the Scottish Parliament, leaving the path clear for the return of Angus Robertson.

30 July There have been 2,400 excess deaths in Scotland's care homes.

After just five months, Jackson Carlaw announced he is resigning as Scottish Tory Leader. In no time, Douglas Ross MP declared for Leader. It is clear this has been in the making for some time and was cooked up by Ross and Ruth Davidson. It looks like Ross might go unchallenged. Once, when asked what was the first thing he would do if he was Prime Minister, said: 'Clamp down on gypsy travellers.' What a lovely guy.

I watched a recording of the *Disclosure Scotland* programme on the care homes scandal. It was a very tough watch. The criticism of the government and their policies around care of the elderly was spot-on. How can ministers remain in post?

2 August Nicola Sturgeon has said that she privately met Alex Salmond and his adviser Geoff Aberdein to discuss allegations against Salmond. This information was not given to parliament. Henry McLeish as First Minister was forced out of office over a mix up about an office lease, yet Sturgeon, who helped force him, out gets away with this.

4 August School exam results day. A major scandal has emerged. The lack of exams this year meant teachers had to submit grade predictions for each child. However, an algorithm used by the SQA meant downgrading a quarter of pupils, overwhelmingly from deprived communities – results amended by postcode. MSPs are receiving hundreds of emails from angry pupils and their parents. Swinney and Sturgeon are insisting the system is fair when it clearly is not. The stories I am hearing from constituents are awful. Some consistently A grade students are being awarded an F grade. One pupil who has had As all through school and needed an A to get into Cambridge was downgraded to a B. Her dreams are now in tatters.

5 August The school exams system is rigged against poorer pupils. Why should someone's address or their schools' exam history determine their individual performance this year?

I put an appeal out on social media for constituents to get in touch if they feel disadvantaged and was inundated with emails from distraught pupils.

6 August Swinney and Sturgeon are still adamant the exams system was fair and are advising pupils to appeal. I got another hundred emails today telling of apprenticeships lost, job offers withdrawn and college and university places in doubt. In the media, Ruth Wishart and Iain MacWhirter are defending the SNP's handling of this fiasco. Not a single SNP MSP or MP has raised a cheep about it. There is a demonstration in Glasgow tomorrow. Sturgeon said if she was a young person she would be attending it. She has no shame.

Douglas Ross was named new Scottish Tory Leader.

Another day clearing mum's house. Soon this will no longer be our family home. We have so many good memories and funny stories from over 40 years.

7 August I went to Glasgow to show support for the school exams protest. It was very good and got a lot of coverage. It emerged today that 46 per cent of pupils in North Lanarkshire had their results downgraded. Sturgeon is refusing to budge. Iain Gray has called for Swinney to resign. There will be a confidence debate next week.

Robin McAlpine of Commonweal has launched a scathing attack on the SNP, saying its central office is 'rotten to the core'. He says it is undemocratic and Sturgeon acts like a president. He also said that despite having differences with me, that I was one of the most effective MSPs asking the right and difficult questions.

8 August I heard from a constituent today whose daughter went to Forrester High School, the same school John Swinney attended. She is a straight A student who was projected to get an A but because of the school's postcode she was awarded a C. The result is a very competitive scholarship she secured has been withdrawn. Meanwhile, pupils from schools in more affluent areas had their grades marked up – this is sheer class prejudice.

9 August For a week Swinney and Sturgeon have dug in defending the indefensible, then over the weekend, as talk of a no confidence vote in Swinney grew, the backtracking began. He now says he 'hears the anger of young people' – it seems his hearing improved as his job became more precarious.

10 August Still getting lots of emails about the exams.

I spoke to a constituent today whose 91-year-old father was transferred from the Edinburgh Royal Infirmary to St John's hospital in Livingston untested, only to find out he had Covid. Later he died and following a discussion the family established a 'do not resuscitate' notice was on his record without any discussion with them as next of kin.

A U-turn over the exams fiasco. While this is very good news, it is not about the integrity of the exams system, it is about one thing, saving the skin of an Education Secretary who deserves the sack.

11 August Got the train back to Parliament, it was empty with almost no passengers. Edinburgh's streets, normally full of tourists during the Festival, were eerily quiet.

At 11.30am, Lesley Brennan came to see me to advise that Jackie Baillie, James Kelly and Mark Griffin had gone to see Richard Leonard to advise him that ten members of the Labour Group want him to resign, 8 support him and the rest haven't expressed a view. I'm not sure how they can say this, as no one has ever asked me. Baillie and her little helpers have been plotting since the day Richard was elected. Later it was floated that they were willing to support Monica Lennon as successor but this is nonsense, they can't stand Monica and are simply trying to use her.

Over to the chamber for John Swinney's statement, which was a defence of his position of last week. He claimed the methodology was right and that the SQA was an independent body, however he was overriding them so that pupils received grades based on teacher estimates. Pupils who have already received good grades based on their postcode will keep them. The Greens are now claiming their demands have been met and will now support Swinney in Thursday's vote of confidence. What a surprise.

12 August A train derailed at Stonehaven. Three people have died, one of them the driver.

I haven't heard any more about the coup against Richard, but it won't go away. The motivation for many of those attacking him is their place on the regional list.

A poll out today has support for Independence on 57 per cent, another has the SNP in line for a 25-seat majority. Amazing, given how badly they are governing.

13 August The *Daily Record* has been leaked internal polling that was only sent to Labour MSPs. The paper ran three stories attacking Richard. I put out social media attacking those behind the leaks and their destructive briefings.

In the chamber, we had the confidence debate on Swinney. Richard Leonard and Ruth Davidson set out Swinney's litany of failures in the role. Angela Constance and Annabelle Ewing were rolled out to laud 'honest John', 'a man of integrity and decency' blah, blah... nothing about the shambles of working-class pupils' life chances being ruined by his incompetence. Ross Greer performed verbal gymnastics to justify the Greens becoming de facto SNP backbenchers supporting a dreadful Education Secretary. The best speech by far came from Johann Lamont. It was full of substance and passion based on her own teaching experience. We then had Mike Russell summing up with a bizarre speech. He listed four tests that he said Swinney had to pass to stay in office and it was clear to anyone listening that he failed three out of the four. When the vote came the Green Party rode to the rescue and Swinnney survived.

14 August Last week Sturgeon announced that care homes could have more visitors, so my brother and sister tried to visit my mum today. It turns out that Public Health Scotland has not given permission for the home to have more visitors so they were turned away. Families are getting desperate; the system is failing them.

To Innerleithen in the campervan for a beautiful peaceful night in the sunshine.

15 August Day in Peebles with Fiona.

Michael Sharpe, the Labour Party General Secretary, emailed all Labour members in Scotland advising them of the ongoing issues with the Parliamentary Labour Group and the leaking of information. A much-needed move.

17 August I had another very interesting meeting with Kenny MacAskill, Alex Neil and a few others to discuss how we can build links across parties in opposition to the Tories. We had a very good discussion about respecting each other's position on the constitution and the legitimate call for a third option to be on the ballot. There was little disagreement. We agreed to meet again.

18 August I watched the start of the Salmond Inquiry. Permanent Secretary Leslie Evans was the first witness. She refused to answer some questions and Linda Fabiani in the chair helped her by ruling them out of order. Not a good start.

At topical questions, I asked Jeane Freeman who was accountable for the decision to release Covid positive patients into care homes untested. She used 'the clinical decisions of doctors' defence and came over all offended when I said they were 'clearing the decks' when they discharged all those older people.

19 August It emerged today that only 0.8 per cent of the 3 per cent promised to social care staff as a pay rise is being funded by the Scottish Government; the other 2.2 per cent has to come from IJB budgets, which means cuts in other areas.

Richard Leonard gave an interview to Borders TV and said he would not resign and that Labour would go into the election opposed to another Independence referendum. Well, that's 50 per cent of voters lost right away. This is a strategy that has failed us since 2014 and is doomed to fail again.

20 August At FMQs, under pressure from the opposition, Sturgeon claimed that she had no input into the decision to discharge untested patients into care homes and that all patients were clinically assessed beforehand.

21 August Caitlin in my office has unearthed a letter that shows Jeane Freeman wrote to IJBs in April to congratulate them on meeting the 'challenging target' of 900 patients being discharged from hospital to care homes, including those who tested Covid positive. This letter proves the point that these were government-driven targets, the Health Secretary signed them off. This completely contradicts claims of a clinically driven policy. I will have to think about how to get this very important information into the public domain.

23 August The *Sunday Post* is running the story about Freeman's letter and the care home targets on its front page. The government is under real pressure now over the scandal.

SNP MSPs Roseanna Cunningham and Alex Neil announced they were standing down at the election. Alex is a good friend, a very clever operator who is not afraid to speak his mind, he will be a big loss to Parliament. I never really had many dealings with Roseanna Cunningham; however, as keen fisherman I was delighted to play a part in stopping her introducing rod licensing for freshwater fishing in Scotland.

24 August Received the first draft of my book of Granda's memoirs today, very exciting.

Jeane Freeman announced she is to stand down from Parliament at the election. I've had many battles with her, especially over the care homes crisis and mesh. I will continue to pursue these issues, but I do respect her ability and I think she respects me.

25 August At topical questions, Jeane Freeman was under pressure over the revelations in the *Sunday Post*. I asked, if the discharge of patients was all down to 'clinical decisions', then why was the 'clinical decision' made to discharge untested patients into care homes last April? She bumped her gums a lot and said nothing much but the reality is it was all about money.

In the afternoon I moved seven amendments at Stage Three of the Children's Bill and managed to get one through on consultation. The bill is so much better for the pressure a number opposition MSPs put on.

26 August The Parliament tried out hybrid voting with some people online and others in the chamber, but the system appears to have a lot of problems. The Presiding Officer is telling people that it is robust, stable and working well. I have yet to be convinced.

28th August Went to a briefing with NHS Lothian. I asked about delayed discharge. Contrary to their previous briefing, they are now admitting they were able to reduce numbers because money was made available. This is what I have argued all along but it's the first time anyone had admitted it.

30 August Liberal Democrat MSP Mike Rumbles has apparently been living in Tuscany for two months 'working remotely'.

The *Sunday Times* has all the details about James Kelly, Mark Griffin and Jackie Baillie meeting with Richard Leonard giving him an ultimatum to resign. Another leaked story.

31 August Andy Whitaker was appointed as Richard Leonard's Head of Comms, a very good appointment that will really piss off his critics in the Labour Group – good.

I heard today that Jenny Marra, who hasn't been seen in Parliament or online, and who hasn't asked a question or taken part in a Labour Group meeting since March has found time to speak to the newspapers calling for Richard Leonard to stand down. What a trooper.

1 September Sturgeon set out her Programme for Government with a number of policies that have previously been announced, including a youth jobs guarantee, support for businesses and renewables funding. There is another Referendum Bill and a review of social care. The response from her backbenchers was flat. I asked her to implement collective bargaining across the social care sector immediately. She didn't rule it out but I don't expect progress.

Jeane Freeman made a statement about social care. I asked her why the Minister for Older People has said and done nothing throughout the pandemic, despite the biggest crisis facing older people in decades? Freeman attacked me, actually saying I don't care about social care!

2 September Well, well, well the 'chicken coup mark II' (the chicken coup was the name the left gave to failed coup against Jeremy Corbyn) is under way with right wing MSPs in the Labour Group trying to force Richard's resignation.

James Kelly was the first to resign from the frontbench. The reality is he has done the sums and can see his future as an MSP is likely to be over when the election comes, and this is his last throw of the dice. He hopes that by replacing Richard someone will come to his rescue. This was followed by Daniel Johnston and Mark Griffin. I took a number of calls from the media asking for comment on Kelly's resignation, so I gave them an on-the-record quote, saying it was 'treachery with a snarl' and that this was all about reselections.

3 September We now have those great champions of democracy – Baroness Ramsay, Lord Foulkes, former NATO General Secretary Lord Robertson and Dame Helen Liddell – calling for Richard to go. Not exactly surprising, as democracy is an alien concept to these unelected members of the House of Lords.

Richard, obviously under the advice of Andy Whittaker, came out swinging, saying this was a concerted attack on him, he was the elected leader and that his critics might not be fit to be Labour candidates. He should have been dealing with them like this all along. Interestingly, Ian Murray, Anas Sarwar and Jackie Baillie said nothing.

At my CLP meeting tonight not, a single member called for Richard Leonard to resign.

4 September Hilarious story in *The Herald* today, no wonder Ian Murray has been keeping his powder dry in Parliament. The paper has published a picture of him practising his speech before the launch of 'Change UK', the breakaway party made up of bitter ex Labour and Tory MPs. Murray had been ready to jump ship but bottled it at the last moment. He must have thought he had got away with it but the footage has been passed to a newspaper (how ironic). Absolutely priceless. He is being ridiculed any credibility he had has just evaporated. Apparently, he had approached the Liberal Democrats before Change UK. A 'man of real principle'. indeed.

I got to visit my mum this afternoon for the first time in six months. It was great to see her. She looked and sounded healthy, we had a great chat. My brother John and I took her outside into the sunshine. It was lovely. I hope we are getting back to regular visits.

6 September Someone sent me an article from former *Scotsman* editor John McClellan, saying that I am the person in Labour who should be by taking on Sturgeon. Not likely, as I won't be there much longer.

Rumours abound that there will be a confidence vote in Richard at the Scottish Executive on Saturday.

7 September My staff team came back into the office for the first time since March. It was good to see them all again.

There was an online rally tonight called by the Campaign for Socialism. John McDonnell MP and Craig Anderson of the CWU spoke along with a good number of young activists. There was a real fighting spirit and disgust at what was happening.

8 September At lunchtime, James Kelly, Daniel Johnston, Neil Bibby, Jenny Marra and Mark Griffin called for a leadership contest.

I was asked to lead and close today's debate on Baroness Cumberlege's review as Monica Lennon was not available. The government motion only mentioned two of her recommendations but I and others asked Jeane Freeman to commit to all the recommendations. My amendment called for the temporary suspension of the new Scottish mesh service until serious questions are answered about those who will staff it, their training, competence and credibility. There were excellent speeches from Jackson Carlaw, Alex Neil, Clare Adamson and Alex Cole-Hamilton. Bob Doris asked many of the right questions. When the vote came, opposition parties supported my motion but there was a complete shambles with the hybrid voting system which was not working properly, some people got their vote and others didn't. My amendment was defeated by one vote. I immediately challenged this and was supported by, of all people, Mike Russell, who said we had to have confidence in the system. I moved that we rerun the vote but the Presiding Officer refused, saying he would do a debrief and announce the result tomorrow.

9 September At 2pm the Presiding Officer announced that the mesh vote from yesterday would stand as only one person who had tried to vote was unable to do so and even if they had it would have been a tie and he would have voted for the government, as is convention. There was a flurry of points of order including from me. I said that I would be laying a motion of no confidence in the new hybrid system. He really did not like that as he sees the system as his baby.

It was reported today that the SNP at Westminster abstained on changes to fire regulations following the Grenfell fire.

For the first time in ages I attended a Labour Group meeting. The lynch mob were out in force attacking Richard. Neil Bibby as group chair led the way and was supported by James Kelly, the Ronald Villiers of Scottish Labour. Anas Sarwar rewrote history to make himself appear squeaky clean. Rhoda Grant and Elaine Smith were excellent in their contributions. I asked Bibby to name the replacement candidate if they got their way. There was no answer. When the time came, he bottled calling a confidence vote.

10 September As expected, *The Herald* carried a full report of yesterday's Labour Group meeting and attacked Michael Sharpe, the General Secretary, for supporting Richard Leonard for leader three years ago. The barrel is being well and truly scraped. Former MEP David Martin had a good article on social media supporting Richard. It looks like this will all come to a head at Saturday's SEC meeting.

Sturgeon announced new restrictions with only six people allowed to meet up, face coverings to be worn in certain places and Phase Four of opening up postponed.

11 September As expected, a vote of no confidence in Richard has been tabled for Saturday's Scottish Executive meeting.

The new 'Protect app' to alert people of Covid contacts does not work on older mobile phones. This is a problem as many do not have the latest smartphones.

There have been all sorts of things going on today ahead of the vote of no confidence tomorrow. The left are pulling out all the stops to help and the right wing pulling every trick in the book.

12 September The Scottish Labour SEC meeting is being leaked line by line to the waiting media, what a surprise. The confidence motion was withdrawn, this must have been because the plotters were going to be defeated. They will be furious. It made my day.

Richard must now put his foot down, show real leadership, bring in a host of new and supportive candidates and be ruthless in clearing out his dead-wood opponents.

14 September Reports from yesterday's meeting of the SEC confirmed that Jackie Baillie and Ian Murray spoke in favour of removing Richard.

There is a huge row going on at Westminster over Boris Johnson's decision to break international treaty obligations in relation to Brexit. He was brutally savaged by none other than Ed Miliband in the debate. Five former Prime Ministers – Major, Blair, Brown, Cameron and May – all spoke out against this absurd move.

15 September At topical questions, I asked Jeane Freeman about increasing access to care homes for families wanting to visit residents. She advised she is working on it.

Police Scotland are refusing to release the latest drug death statistics, an outrageous abuse of position.

16 September I went to the Burton's biscuit factory in Edinburgh to support GMB members who are on strike following the award of a measly 14p an hour pay increase.

17 September I met Jeane Freeman for breakfast as agreed. We regularly clash in the chamber over policy but get on personally. I raised social care and the desperate need for families to be able to visit loved ones. I also called for her to fund women to travel to the US for mesh removal treatment from Doctor

Veronikas as there is no treatment available here. I advised her that that women will not use the new Glasgow service for removals as they have no confidence in the people who will staff it, since they are the very ones who advised them to have mesh implants in the first place. I hope to see progress on these very important issues.

At FMQs I mentioned the strike at Burton's – hopefully by raising the profile of the dispute it will force the company to increase its pay offer.

Keir Starmer was in Scotland today. I think I know where he stands in relation to Richard Leonard's future.

18 September I spoke to Paul Hutcheon, who has been leaked a copy of John Scott QC's review into the conviction of miners during the 1984–85 coal strike. The report makes one recommendation: that there should be a pardon. This is fantastic news and exactly what I proposed to the review. I put my heart and soul into this and expect the government to accept the recommendation. We can then work on the issue of compensation.

It looks like we are heading for another lockdown, how depressing.

Kenny MacAskill MP has leaked private WhatsApp messages that were sent to him showing Nicola Sturgeon's husband Peter Murrell calling on people to pressure Police Scotland over the Alex Salmond case.

19 September The *Daily Record* led with 'Pardon the Miners' and inside there was a spread and editorial, it was fantastic. Reaction has been brilliant, lots of media coverage.

21 September There is more speculation about the country going back into lockdown.

Met with a constituent, Aidan Martin. He has written a book about his journey through trauma, addiction and mental illness. I want to help him as much as possible and will try to promote his book and his work. He is a really smart and likable guy who I believe will make a real impact.

22 September Keir Starmer made his first conference speech as Labour leader. It was flat and uninspiring.

Nicola Sturgeon announced the reintroduction of restrictions on meeting other households, sharing cars, public transport, etc.

Presiding Officer Ken Macintosh is standing down at the election. He has always been a pleasant man. I have had a few run-ins with him, nothing serious and I wish him well for the future.

Boris Johnson, Nicola Sturgeon and Mark Drakeford all made TV statements tonight explaining why they are introducing further lockdown.

23 September Humza Yousaf confirmed the government's U-turn on the Hate Crime Bill after a lot of public opposition. Serious concerns had been raised about the impact of the bill on freedom of speech. Opponents said the full implications of the bill had not been thought through and that it was too vague and open to interpretation. The bill's proposals also became embroiled in the polarised debate over trans rights.

Keir Starmer gave an interview where he said it was for Scots to decide on the future of the country, just as John McDonnell had done previously. However, this time there was no all-out attack from the Labour right, what a surprise!

I took part in a call with the Orgreave Truth and Justice campaign to update them on the situation in Scotland with the miners' inquiry.

24 September At FMQs, I asked Nicola Sturgeon if she would guarantee that the miners' pardons bill would be introduced before the Scottish elections in May, she failed to give a commitment on this.

I received an email from the STUC to advise that they want to interview me for the post of Assistant General Secretary. This is one of the first jobs I have applied for, so I am pleased to get an interview.

26 September There is speculation in the newspapers that the Scottish elections may be delayed by six months. I raised this last year, and the possibility was dismissed out of hand – I really hope it's not true.

29 September I appeared on *Scotland Tonight* along with former Tory MP Peter Duncan and Fatima Joji, an SNP candidate, to discuss diversity and the need for more BAME, working class and independent minded MSPs. It was a decent enough discussion.

30 September Lots of media coverage of the Salmond Inquiry being frustrated by the Scottish Government refusing to hand over key documents. In the chamber, Oliver Mundell, the Tory MSP for Dumfries, was thrown out for calling Nicola Sturgeon a liar, as she had previously said she would make all information available to the inquiry.

I spoke in the debate on social care and recapped what had happened over the last seven months and the situation in care homes now. I feel absolutely compelled to keep raising this issue because the treatment of older people has been a serious human rights abuse.

Watched the Trump v Biden debate on TV. Dire.

1 October It was reported that former SNP Finance Secretary Derek Mackay, who has not appeared in Parliament for months, has been claiming expenses for renting a flat in Edinburgh over the summer.

Nicola Sturgeon had her worst FMQ in a very long time. She was attacked by the Tories for failing to release papers to the Salmond Inquiry and by Richard Leonard for the confused Covid guidance given to students and I asked her about the failure to routinely test all NHS staff. A bad day for Sturgeon soon got worse when it was reported that SNP MP Margaret Ferrier had tested positive and instead of isolating, travelled by train from London to her home in Lanarkshire, potentially infecting many people. This, from a woman who had previously called on Dominic Cummings to resign for doing the same.

Kenny MacAskill and others in the Salmond camp are gunning for Sturgeon, attacking her for failing to release the key documents; it is now open warfare.

2 October Donald Trump has been diagnosed with Covid.

The Margaret Ferrier story is huge. Apparently, Ferrier travelled 500 miles on public transport before visiting shops, a gym and a beauty salon, while knowingly positive.

3 October Trump has been admitted to hospital.

There are calls for Margaret Ferrier to resign. The SNP tried to protect her and prevent the story from coming out.

4 October The *Sunday Mail* had a piece on the abject failure of Ministers Shirley-Anne Sommerville and Christina McKelvie, who are supposed to have responsibility for older people, but who have done absolutely nothing during the entire Covid period. It leads me to wonder what Age Scotland have been doing during this period?

5 October National Clinical Director Jason Leitch said today that pubs may be able to open late if the Scotland v Israel football match goes to penalties. He tells us that these decisions are based on 'the science'.

Heard today from staff and families linked to Redmill Care Home in Whitburn about a major Covid outbreak.

6 October Three people have died and 53 staff and patients have Covid at the Redmill Care Home.

Did my interview for the STUC job. I was pleasantly surprised at how well it went. Later I got a phone call to say I was a very close second for the job. This is the first interview I have done in about 12 years.

7 October New restrictions brought in – all pubs and hospitality venues closed across the central belt for three weeks. Last week Jason Leitch was saying pubs might be able to stay open late for a football match, today they are being closed down.

I received a remarkable letter from HCI, the owners of Redmill Care Home, advising that there have been four deaths and 54 Covid cases, and six staff are waiting on results. The management advised NHS Lothian of the outbreak on 28 September but there was no comprehensive home testing until a week later. They said tests couldn't be done right away because they had no labels, then 20 tests were returned negative with no information about who they belonged to, one staff member got someone else's test, another got three different results. I immediately raised this with the Cabinet Secretary Jeane Freeman who said she would look into it.

8 October I spoke to more staff and patients at Redmill. They are really struggling and scared.

Nicola Sturgeon has claimed that she forgot about the meeting with Alex Salmond's adviser Geoff Aberdein when he told her about the complaints made about Salmond. She also tried to claim she didn't mention this meeting, which took place in her house, to her husband who just happens to be the Chief Executive of the SNP!

9 October STV came to my house to do a piece on the situation at Redmill. I then got an email from the Scottish Government who have brought together HC1, NHS Lothian and the IJB so they can control the release of information.

10 October The death toll at Redmill is now seven. The government is denying the testing problems HC1 reported.

11 October Sturgeon was on the Sophie Ridge show reading out private WhatsApp messages between Alex Salmond and her, all a bit bizarre.

Margaret Ferrier gave an interview in *The Sun* saying she won't resign. Well, of course she won't, she will take her wages until she stands down in a few years' time, just like MacKay.

13 October Professor James Mitchell and I met with Gordon Brown to discuss a third option in any future referendum and the need for Labour to have a credible, coherent position. We urged him to use his influence to move things on.

Got the final version of my granda's memoirs through from the publisher today. It is looking great.

14 October A poll out today has support for Independence at 58 per cent. The need for a credible third option is vital.

Steve Rotheram and Andy Burnham have reacted with fury over Johnson extending lockdown on Merseyside and Greater Manchester without any consultation. Wales is also locking down and Northern Ireland schools are closing.

For me, the last seven months have been utterly surreal and so busy, but the last few weeks have seen case work go through the roof.

15 October Over the last two days, I have read Aidan Martin's book *Euphoric Recall: A True Story of Grit and Hope*. It's powerful, raw, scary and desperate but ultimately uplifting. It deserves to be read widely.

Nicola Sturgeon introduced new regulations. For the first time she admitted 'the science only takes us so far, then we have to make political decisions'. At last some honesty. I asked if she would now make the 'political decision' to ensure every care worker and NHS staff member are tested every week. I have been calling for this from day one. She said they are 'considering it'. Seven months on and just considering it!

Thirty-three Labour MPs rebelled and ten resigned over Starmer's insistence they abstain on the Covert Human Intelligence Bill. This is an outrageous decision by the Labour Leader, a former lawyer who previously worked on behalf of clients who were victims of the Spycops scandal. I am sickened.

21 October A law to make it compulsory to have mains-linked smoke alarms in every Scottish home has been shelved for another year. The contract for building the latest offshore wind farm has gone abroad while Scottish manufacturing capacity lies redundant.

22 October The government in Wales is taking the railways back into public ownership. The Scottish Government claim they don't have the powers to do this, which has now been exposed as a lie.

Jason Leitch said today that people will have to have 'a digital Christmas'. There will be a major revolt on their hands if they impose this.

At the Petitions Committee, we had a session with Dr Veronikis, the US mesh surgeon. He was uncompromising in his criticism of the former CMO, Catherine Calderwood, Dr Karen Gueurro and Jeane Freeman, and made it clear that they deliberately prevented him from coming to Scotland. I urged the committee to ask the Scottish Government to pay for Scottish mesh victims to be treated in the US.

I was told that Police Scotland have been interviewing staff over care home deaths in Scotland. I have written to them to ask if government ministers, civil servants, NHS chiefs and special advisers will also be interviewed?

23 October Nicola Sturgeon announced a new, complex, tiered lockdown system.

Keir Starmer and Angela Rayner met with the Scottish Parliamentary Labour Group today. Warm words but little substance.

Chaired an online event on drugs with academics Iain McPhee and Barry Sheridan to discuss how we can expose the failings in drugs policy. Around 200 people were on the call.

Fourteen people have now died at Redmill Care Home.

24 October Peter Krykant, a former drug user who set up a safe injecting van with his own money, was cautioned by Police Scotland. I cannot express how angry I am at this. Here is a man trying to stop people dying and he gets picked up by the cops. Meanwhile, 1,200 are left to die in manky alleyways and useless Scottish ministers claim there is nothing they can do. They are the ones who should be arrested.

25 October The *Sunday Times* published an extensive piece looking into the way older people have been dealt with throughout Covid. It makes my blood boil. If an individual GP failed to test for diseases despite suspecting a person was infected, or refused to treat a patient who was clearly ill, or denied them hospitalisation despite beds being available, or put a 'do not resuscitate' notice on a patient without their or their family's knowledge, they would be investigated and struck off. Yet this is exactly what has happened to our loved ones under guidance issued by the government.

The *Sunday Post* ran a brilliant article on *Life in the Raws*, my granda's memoirs.

27 October The stream of constituent emails and phone calls is relentless. We had people contact us about help for gyms, boxing clubs, football teams, care homes, home carers, schools, jobs, hospitality, colleges and universities.

I was contacted by a source who apparently had been copied into an email by mistake, advising that there will be a rollout of a Covid vaccine in December. If correct this is massive. I worked with the *Sunday Mail* to try to get to the bottom of it. They plan to run the story on Sunday if it holds until then.

At topical questions, I asked Jeane Freeman about the situation at Redmill, where 15 people have now died with Covid. I raised testing, communications, transparency and care of residents.

Tomorrow is the miners' review statement. I have fingers, toes and everything else crossed for a positive result.

28 October The government response to the Miners' Review was published. They have accepted my proposal for a pardon based on the scheme I set out to John Scott and Dennis Canavan. I met with around 20 former miners outside the Parliament to do media interviews. When I went into the chamber, Humza Yousaf came up to me and said, 'You should be very proud today, well done,' which I appreciated. His statement when it came was excellent. He paid tribute to the miners and their communities and was measured and clear. When I spoke, I said:

> I have campaigned on this issue for most of the ten years that I have been in this Parliament, but that is absolutely nothing compared with the 36 years of campaigning by former miners and their trade union.

The release of the Cabinet papers under the 30-year rule and the information that came out of the Hillsborough inquiry were the game changers in this campaign, confirming the long-held view that the miners' strike and the arrests during it were politically motivated miscarriages of justice. Scotland was the scene of one of the biggest mass arrests anywhere in the UK, with 300 arrested in one day at Stepps in Lanarkshire.

The Cabinet Secretary was right in saying that Scottish miners were just 7 per cent of the workforce but they made up 30 per cent of those who were dismissed after arrest. Most of those were on trumped-up charges of minor breaches of the peace, but the effect on miners was that they were made redundant and lost their jobs and livelihoods, many were blacklisted and many never recovered.

I am delighted, proud and, I have to say, moved that the pardons scheme that I put to the review has been accepted in full. I give my unequivocal thanks to the panel led by John Scott and to the previous Justice Secretary, Michael Matheson, who met us, listened to us and took the bold move of initiating the inquiry. I also pay absolute tribute to the Cabinet Secretary for accepting the recommendations of the report in full. From the bottom of my heart, I say thank you.

The demand for justice does not diminish through time. Today shows us that determined, dogged campaigning works, and I hope that this decision today will put pressure on the UK government for a full inquiry into the events at Orgreave and the policing of the strike in England and Wales, because burning injustices will not go away.

Enacting the pardons will require legislation. Will the Cabinet Secretary agree to meet party representatives to discuss how we could expedite that before the end of this parliamentary session, because the numbers get fewer every year, and time is of the essence?

Finally, if the pubs were open, I would be going for a pint tonight, but I will have a few beers at home instead.

I was quite emotional, this meant so much to me. The strike inspired me to get involved in politics and when elected to Parliament I made a pledge to myself to do what I could to help the miners and their union. I am delighted to have fulfilled that pledge.

Sturgeon claimed there was no link between discharging people untested into care homes and the disease spreading, this is nonsense.

29 October Lots of brilliant media coverage about the miners' pardon.

Starmer made a statement about the Human Rights Commission report into antisemitism in the party. It said Labour had failed to adequately roll out training and investigate complaints, and that there had been intervention from the centre into cases. Jermey Corbyn then made a comment agreeing that antisemitism was a serious issue and that there was no place for it in society or the Labour Party, but that in relation to the Labour Party some reports had been exaggerated for political reasons. Starmer then took the astonishing step of suspending Jeremy from the parliamentary party. One of the country's foremost anti-racist campaigners of the last 30 years has been suspended from Labour and meanwhile, Tony Blair, with the blood of tens of thousands of dead Iraqis on his hands, is offering the Labour Leader advice.

30 October Starmer is doubling down on the Corbyn suspension.

31 October Sean Connery died today aged 90.

Got a reply to an FOI today advising me that it would be too expensive for the government to tell me when Nicola Sturgeon and Jeane Freeman first knew of Covid positive patients being discharged into care homes. All I want is a date. They are withholding essential information.

1 November The *Sunday Mail* ran the vaccine story but strangely it is not getting the pickup in the media I expected. A vaccine against Covid is a massive issue given what we have been through. So why is it not the biggest news in town?

2 November I went into the office to prepare for this week's members' debate on the Amnesty report on care homes in England. It details major human rights abuses of older people. All of this happened in Scotland and at times things were worse, yet there is no Amnesty report on Scotland.

England will go into full lockdown on Thursday and Scotland will follow. The tiered system takes effect today, with the Central Belt in Tier Three, meaning no visits to other households, working from home where possible and pubs and hospitality venues closed.

Tomorrow is the US election. I really hope Biden wins but fear it will be Trump.

3 November I got a letter today from the Scottish Government in response to a Freedom of Information request that I submitted, asking what they knew about the Margaret Ferrier debacle. The response claims it would not be in the public interest to release this information. I'm sure the people who sat on the train next to her believe it is in the public interest! But this is the usual secrecy.

I led the members' debate on the Amnesty report on care homes in England. It was a damning critique of the conduct of the UK government and its treatment of older people during the pandemic. Shocking that there is no report on human rights violations in Scotland. NGOs who work with older people are shamefully silent. Only one of them has sent in a briefing for the debate. Christina McKelvie, who is supposed to be the Minister for Older People, summed up for the government. In my ten years in Parliament, I have never witnessed a government minister summing up a members' debate refusing to take a single intervention, yet this is what she did. She wouldn't answer legitimate questions about key government decisions. They can run but they can't hide.

5 November The US election is neck and neck, but Biden is ahead. Trump is claiming fraud.

Went into the chamber for the debate on the government's failure to release papers in relation to the Salmond Inquiry. Swinney was sent out to defend the indefensible.

Afterwards, there was a debate on care homes and a call for an immediate public inquiry into the government's conduct during the pandemic. The government was defeated on both issues, which is very significant.

This was my speech in the debate on care homes:

> I declare an interest as my mum is a resident in a care home and my wife and daughter work in the NHS.
>
> I have never worked in a care home and have never been a resident in one. With that in mind, I have to relay what carers and those for whom they care have told me and try to put myself in their position.
>
> Imagine that it is March of this year and that you are an 81-year-old patient in hospital. You have been there for six months and have been ready to go home for 12 weeks but have been told repeatedly that the reason why you cannot leave the hospital is that there is no care home place or package to support you. Imagine then being told at short notice that a place has become available and that you are moving today, although not to your own community, among the people you know, but many miles away, and that you have to move there, as it is the only place that is available.
>
> Imagine watching TV on that same day and hearing that a virus that results in the deaths of hundreds of thousands of older people just like you is sweeping the world. You see the news bulletins that show multiple deaths at care homes across Europe, and the haunting image of undertakers removing bodies. Imagine then being discharged alone, with limited family contact and without an assessment of your needs and without being tested.
>
> Imagine working in a care home on minimum wage, in a place that is regularly short staffed and has been for years. Imagine that you have to take in more residents and that the company that you work for cannot provide you with appropriate and safe PPE to protect you, keep your residents safe and allow you to do your job. Imagine that that company

is registered in a tax haven, pays negligible corporation tax and posts regular, healthy profits. Imagine going home at night – every night – to see the news headlines of more and more people dying in care homes just like the one you work in.

Imagine reading newspaper reports of multiple care home deaths – such as happened on Skye – and wondering, 'Are we next?' Imagine listening to politicians who claim that we have the best testing capacity in the world at a time when neither you nor the residents you care for have ever been tested. Imagine caring for Covid-positive people who have become seriously ill and then being told that they must not be admitted to hospital for treatment.

Imagine being Covid-clear as a patient in hospital but finding yourself ill from Covid a few days after you are moved to a care home. Imagine realising that, as you worked and tried to keep people safe, you were inadvertently spreading Covid because you had never been tested.

Imagine being vulnerable, living among new people you do not know and seeing the Covid crisis growing. Feeling scared and alone, you are unable to hold the hand of your son and daughter or even to speak to them. Imagine being asked to agree to a do not resuscitate order without a discussion with your general practitioner or your closest family. Imagine seeing your friends and neighbours – other residents – die without their family around them and being laid to rest with a handful of mourners.

Too many of our mums, dads and grandparents, our friends and our family have no need to imagine those things – they happened to them in Scotland in 2020, and that is to our eternal shame.

5 November Looks like Biden has won the election.

England goes back into full lockdown today.

6 November Trump went on TV making false claims about ballot rigging and corruption. It was so outrageous that the main TV channels cut him off.

7 November More than four days after the US elections, there is still no result. Trump is going to court to try and get the results overturned but now even the Republicans are turning on him.

8 November As the Democrats celebrate victory, the US far right and armed militias are patrolling the streets. Scary stuff.

9 November Pfizer has produced a new Covid vaccine.

10 November Liz Lloyd, one of Nicola Sturgeon's advisers, apparently met one of the complainants in a sexual harassment case against Alex Salmond, in

Sturgeon's office a day before the government's sexual harassment policy was extended to politicians. Previously, Sturgeon claimed she only knew this when Salmond told her.

STV did a nice piece about the publication of my grandad's memoirs.

11 November The government's Test and Trace app is operating five times worse than claimed. There is nothing they will not attempt to spin.

In the afternoon, there was a Labour-led debate calling for routine regular testing of all health and social care staff, the government has resisted this since the outset but facing defeat and capitulated. All their backbenchers, who for the last year and a half have been attacking me and others who were calling for exactly this, are now reading the same supportive lines from a script they have been given.

12 November The Care Inspectorate report from Redmill care home is out today and it is damning. It shows that three weeks after an incident management team went in, the inspector found major areas of weakness with infection control, health and wellbeing and staffing levels.

Scotland qualified for the Euro football championships tonight following a playoff victory against Serbia, the first major tournament we have qualified for in a very long time.

Boris Johnson sacked Dominic Cummings.

15 November *Scotland on Sunday* published an article I submitted on devo max, provoking the usual abuse from nationalists and unionists, both of whom gain from a polarised debate. My proposal is for a third option to be on the ballot paper in a two-question poll.

16 November Still getting abuse on social media for yesterday's column.

I spoke to a woman whose sister died in Redmill Care Home. She told me that at the end of her sister's life she was offered a Zoom call to see her as she lay dying.

Richard Leonard appointed Anas Sarwar to his shadow cabinet, with responsibility for the constitution. I nearly fell off my chair when I heard this. What is he playing at?

Boris Johnson is isolating, having contracted Covid again.

17 November I spoke to BBC journalist Alison Walker who has been very vocal about the treatment of her parents, who are care home residents. Her situation is like that of so many families.

I also spoke to the families of more residents at Redmill. What they have been telling me is appalling.

Jeremy Corbyn was readmitted to the Labour Party today by the NEC.

18 November Keir Starmer has refused to admit Corbyn back into the parliamentary party following the lifting of his suspension. This is vindictive, immature nonsense.

After just a few days in post, Anas Sarwar has stated that there should be no Independence referendum until after 2026 at the earliest.

I was contacted by a constituent whose mum is in a care home. She was hospitalised then told she was to be discharged back to the home, Covid positive. After all the cases, all we have learned, they are still doing it. I cannot believe this and will try to raise it tomorrow at question time.

Enjoyed a very good session with the Red Paper Collective and Professor James Mitchell discussing multi-option referendums. There have been a hundred held across the world and there is much we can learn from them.

19 November At FMQs I raised the case of my constituent's mum being discharged into a care home Covid positive. Sturgeon said this was not policy and should not be happening and that I should send her details of the case, which I will.

I spoke in the debate on the new Covid restrictions which are really restrictive:

> For almost nine months, people across Scotland have cooperated. They have been careful, taken advice and been tolerant. They have implemented unprecedented measures and have sacrificed their rights, freedoms, relationships, jobs, businesses and much more. Their physical and mental wellbeing has suffered. It has been brutal, painful, dispiriting and, all too often, devastating, with 5,000 friends, relatives, parents and grandparents dead and laid to rest at services with only a handful of mourners. Despite all that sacrifice, and with no idea about the long term consequences, we now have to accept more restrictions, more anguish and more social and emotional trauma. I can only imagine how difficult it is for governments across the world. I do not question their good faith, and I have never questioned their effort. However, our job, which is essential at a time like this, is to hold the government to account for its decisions and to raise questions on behalf of our constituents. Mine are asking why, when the science does not support it, West Lothian is going from Level Three to Level Four, or why Edinburgh is still in level Three. A few weeks ago, the First Minister said that the 'science takes us so far, after that, decisions are political'. My plea is for the government to make it clear that non-science-based decisions are, indeed, political decisions. That would be honest, open and transparent.

I also want to object, in the strongest possible terms, to the way in which the emphasis of government strategy sees the cause of virus spread as individual behaviour and not as a failure of planning, governance and year-on-year cuts to the public services that protect and civilise us. The greatest failure has been the failure to take on board the WHO's advice to test, trace and isolate, which is something that I have banged on about from day 1. From the outset, every case should have been tested, traced and isolated – not doing that has been a major failure. It is not the doctors and nurses who took the policy decision to discharge Covid-positive older people to care homes or the students who, by themselves, rushed back to university; they were told to do so, following pressure and lobbying by Universities Scotland for financial purposes. It is not the citizens who are responsible for the inadequacy of the test and trace system, and it is not the health and care staff who are responsible for the failure to test them routinely and weekly.

We were told that Scotland could eradicate Covid by the end of the summer, but the actions that we have seen and the actions in the strategy are self-evidently not working and we are back to the situation that we are in. I cannot support a plan to put the emphasis of blame on individuals and to absolve those in positions of power of the mistakes and bad decisions that they have made. I will tell members what will happen with the legislation that we are about to agree – are we about to agree it? I do not know. The greatest impact will be on the low paid, the young, teenagers, the old, the poor, the isolated, the lonely, the weak and vulnerable, those in care homes, those with addictions and the people at the coalface of the pandemic. For those reasons, I cannot support what is being proposed to Parliament.

20 November My constituent confirmed that yesterday her mum was transferred from hospital back to the care home and she was indeed Covid positive. It is unforgivable.

22 November The *Sunday Mail* has a big piece today on Covid positive patients still being discharged to care homes. It looks like my constituent's case was not a one-off after all. The government is claiming that this happens only when patients are at the end of their lives, but this is not necessarily true. Jeane Freeman went on TV to say this was all down to 'clinical decisions', more buck passing. They will do anything but take responsibility.

23 November I did an interview on BBC Radio Scotland discussing the care homes discharge scandal. I was then emailed by a care home manager and families who told me this is happening in their areas too. NHS Lothian put out a statement which never once mentioned end of life care. They are making it up as they go along.

24 November At topical questions I raised the care home discharge policy with Jeane Freeman. She claimed the policy had not changed. In my supplementary, I pointed out if someone is discharged into a home while Covid positive, homes will prevent any visitors visiting for 28 days, penalising residents who are clear of Covid and desperate to see relatives.

I sat in for Stage Three session of Monica Lennon's Period Poverty Bill, which was passed unanimously. An outstanding achievement.

Spoke to my mum tonight on the phone. She is desperate to see us all.

Tory MSP Michelle Ballantyne resigned from her party over disagreements on many issues.

25 November Diego Maradona, one of the greatest footballers ever, died today.

26 November At FMQs, Ruth Davidson who was standing in, attacked the Scottish Government for refusing to release the legal advice on the Salmond case, despite Parliament voting for it.

The SNP conference is this weekend. Sturgeon rolled out her standard line that she may call a referendum next year. Surely delegates will not fall for this one again?

27 November The Labour Group awayday. We heard from Professor Linda Bauld, the public health specialist. It was very useful. Then we had a session on electoral strategy, which was depressing. Not a bit of it was about the need to come up with a credible position on the constitution. The strategy appears to be if we ignore the constitution and talk about jobs and health, then people will forget the national question. This is the same nonsense I have listened to since 2011. It has failed every single time. Alex Rowley, Monica Lennon and I completely disagree with this approach.

28 November I took part in a very good discussion on social care at the Marxism 2020 event along with Professor Allyson Pollock.

Jenny Marra announced she is not standing for re-election.

29 November Nicola Sturgeon appeared on the *Andrew Marr Show*. She was under a great deal of pressure over Scotland having the third-highest level of Covid deaths in Europe, the educational attainment gap and the Salmond case. She looked very unhappy.

30 November 30 At the SNP conference, Nicola Sturgeon announced a £500 payment for Health and Social Care staff and challenged Boris Johnson not to tax it – which was quite extraordinary given that income tax is levied in Scotland.

I met with a group of care home families along with Patrick Maguire and Bruce

Shields from Thompsons Solicitors to discuss care home visiting.

Lewis McDonald announced he is standing down at the next election, having been an MSP since 1999.

Today is my mum's birthday. It is really sad that we can't see her but everyone spoke to her on the phone and we did our best to cheer her up. It is really frustrating as her home is only about a hundred yards from my house, yet we can get in and see her.

1 December I listened to Nicola Sturgeon's conference speech. There was not a single mention of care homes, the biggest scandal that has emerged over the course of the pandemic.

2 December The government was defeated by one vote on their handling of BiFab in Fife.

3 December Spent the day drawing up an open letter on the care homes scandal and getting signatories.

Jeane Freeman gave some details of the rollout of the new vaccine, which will be a huge logistical exercise.

Sad news today that Maria Fyfe, the former Labour MP for Maryhill, has died. She was a marvellous woman and a principled advocate of equal opportunities and women's rights. She was a great friend who encouraged me greatly.

3 December I took a call from Michael Settle, *The Herald* Westminster correspondent, who said there was talk of Keir Starmer wanting Richard Leonard to stand down.

4 December I have spent a good bit of time securing signatures for the open letter on care home visiting and the treatment of older people. All the opposition parties have signed up, we also have lawyers, sports stars, families of residents and celebrities.

5 December There is more speculation in the papers about Richard Leonard's future. Having brought back Sarwar and Baillie against the advice of his allies, he will now struggle to get the left to support him if the right move against him.

The *Sunday Mail* ran a very good front page and two further inside pages on the care homes letter. I will send it to Sturgeon, it has been a good exercise to try and increase pressure for a change of approach.

Lots of speculation in the media about serious splits in the SNP and unhappiness about a number of issues, including Salmond, trans rights and the ostracising of MP Joanna Cherry.

7 December NHS vaccine booking opened today. The phone lines are jammed, the system is down with people left holding for ages on a pay for phone line.

8 December Took a call from a constituent who told me about a shocking case of neglect of her father by a care home company. I will be raising this with the company and the care inspectorate.

Fantastic scenes on TV today as a 91-year-old woman became the first person in the UK to receive a Covid vaccine.

I went into the chamber to ask my Topical Question on care home visiting. I asked it in a calm and considered way but was heckled by SNP MSPs Keith Brown and George Adam. I lost my temper and called Brown a clown. As we were leaving the chamber, I asked Adam why he didn't like me doing my job by asking important questions about the care of older people. He started ranting and raving and pointing and shouting but was restrained by Linda Fabiani. Later I got an emailed rebuke from the Presiding Officer for shouting at Brown. It seems he is more sensitive about the language used in the chamber than the disgraceful policies inflicted on older people.

Peter Murrell, Nicola Sturgeon's husband, gave evidence to the Salmond Inquiry today.

The Higher and Advanced Higher exams have been cancelled again.

9 December I am getting lots of supportive emails from families of care home residents after yesterday's exchanges.

A report is out today on the new CalMac ferries being made by Ferguson's in Greenock. They are £100 million over budget and four years late.

Murrell's evidence from yesterday is being ridiculed in the newspapers. He claimed he and his wife were too busy to discuss her role as First Minister and that when he came home to find Salmond, Salmond's lawyer and chief of staff in his house, he said hello, then went for shower without asking why they were there.

10 December At FMQs, Ruth Davidson gave Sturgeon a torrid time over Murrell's evidence. Sturgeon struggled badly and had to resort to 'you are dragging my husband into this.' Well, yes, because he just happens to be the Chief Executive of the SNP.

11 December Boris Johnson was in Brussels over the last few days for talks, which went very badly; we could be on World Trade Organisation terms if no deal is struck soon.

My daughter Chloe and her boyfriend Ryan got the keys to their flat today. They are moving into Glasgow.

13 December Despite assurances from Jeane Freeman that she would have urgent talks with me on care home visiting, I have heard nothing.

Michael Sharpe resigned as Scottish Labour General Secretary. One of the most decent, committed people I know, he has been forced out by a cabal of self-entitled right wingers who made his job impossible.

15 December 1,264 Scots died last year because of drugs. I went into the chamber to hear Joe FitzPatrick give his statement. As he started Sturgeon and all other government ministers left him on the front bench on his own. The SNP benches were almost empty. His speech was abysmal. Monica Lennon called for him to resign, the Tories and Liberals attacked him and I said:

There has been a 55 per cent cut in drug and alcohol budgets over ten years. The situation in Scotland is three-and-a-half times worse than anywhere in the UK – with the same legislation, minister. Working-class communities are in crisis. We will have working groups and take pill presses off people and think that that will resolve the issue. The minister is a nice man, and I believe him, but we do not need a nice person in charge – we need a competent person in charge. Please stand aside and let somebody drive the change that we need.'

Still no contact from Freeman about our 'urgent talks'.

16 December FitzPatrick is taking a pasting in the media for his abject performance yesterday.

My 'urgent' meeting with Jeane Freeman is to take place on 21 December.

Tom Gordon in *The Herald* ran a story saying I was looking for a job in the lobbying sector. The implication is that I brought in the Lobbying Transparency (Scotland) Bill and now want to join the lobbyists. What he didn't say was that I have always said lobbying is a legitimate part of the democratic process and that I want to work in the charity, union or not-for-profit sector, and not for the big bucks business lobbyists.

I spoke to Michael Sharpe. He was sickened by what was going on and has had enough. I can't blame him.

Heard from a number of constituents who have been contacted by Track and Trace telling them to isolate as they had come in with a Covid contact on 6 December, a whole ten days ago.

17 December The coverage of the drug deaths crisis is all over the media. At FMQs, all the opposition leaders went on the attack. Sturgeon put on her sad face. I was called last and asked her to reverse the 25 per cent Alcohol and Drugs Partnership cuts of the last ten years, stop the prosecution of Peter Krykant, bring someone in who would drive change and for FitzPatrick to be sacked.

Spoke to Lyn McMath from the Labour press team. She has had enough of the internal battles and is off to work at Edinburgh University. Another good person bailing out.

18 December Former MSP Drew Smith is to take over from Michael Sharpe as the Scottish Party General Secretary. He has clearly been lined up for this.

After Labour tabled a confidence motion in Joe Fitzpatrick, he resigned a short while after to be replaced by Angela Constance, who was previously sacked by Sturgeon. I checked the official report: she has barely raised a word about drugs in her time as an MSP.

Andy Wightman MSP resigned from the Green Party. He had been threatened with deselection over his views on the trans rights issue. Andy has been an excellent MSP, bringing knowledge and substance to Parliament. He has clearly upset Patrick Harvie, who doesn't like people challenging him. The collective sanctimony of the Greens will be their undoing. I think Andy will stand as an independent. If he does, he will lose.

Later, Johnson and Sturgeon announced we are going into Tier Four after Christmas. Instead of five days of respite over the festive period, it is now Christmas day only.

21 December Went out with some of my staff team to help the West Calder Community Development Trust to deliver Christmas parcels to residents. Over 250 people received food and presents.

My so-called urgent meeting with Jeane Freeman was cancelled at two hours' notice.

22 December Met with Pax Christi, the Catholic human rights organisation. They raised concerns about Police Scotland's role training the Sri Lankan Police, who are notorious human rights abusers. I agreed to work with them on this.

23 December The family got a letter saying that visits to my mum's care home have been cut back to one person, outdoors – outdoor visits in Scotland in December? I raised this with Sturgeon at FMQs and got the usual blah,blah answer.

24 December The big news today is that a Brexit deal has been struck. Boris Johnson is celebrating and spinning it like it is the greatest achievement ever, Starmer says Labour will vote for it. Can you imagine if it had been Corbyn telling the PLP to vote for a Tory Brexit. He would have been crucified, yet there is radio silence from Ian Murray, Jackie Baillie, Daniel Johnson and the right wing at Westminster. After years of being lectured about how EU membership was a point of high principle for the New Labourites, it appears their principles have disappeared.

Had my long delayed 'emergency' meeting with Jeane Freeman. Along with the Tories, Lib Dems and Greens, we called for emergency legislation to protect the rights of older people in care homes, similar to what has happened in Canada, but she gave zero commitment.

25 December Had a lovely, quiet Christmas Day with Fiona, Chloe and Ryan.

28 December Parliament is to be recalled on the 30th to discuss Johnson's Brexit deal.

30 December Last night, Labour put out a shambolic press release which basically adopted the SNP position of refusing to give consent at Holyrood, while supporting the Brexit deal at Westminster. All hell broke loose, with party members appalled by what is going on and the SNP having a field day at this contradictory position. Later there was a Labour Group meeting to decide what to do. As soon as the meeting had finished, a full account was reported in the *Daily Record* and *The Times*.

31 December Last night, the Brexit Bill went through the House of Commons with a 448 majority.

2021

AS MY TEN years as an MSP drew to a close, the Covid pandemic was still with us. The mass vaccination programme reduced the death toll, but the aftermath of the pandemic put even more strain on public services that were creaking at the seams before the crisis.

The fallout from Alex Salmond's court case erupted with the former SNP First Minister launching blistering attacks on his successor Nicola Sturgeon and launching a new political party.

Keir Starmer, who was elected on a programme of ten pledges that would build on the policy programme of Jeremy Corbyn, set about dropping almost every one of them, launching repeated attacks on the party's left.

1 January Fiona is working at the hospital and Chloe is in Glasgow so I had a quiet day to myself.

Reflecting on the past year, it has been really difficult. It's now been over 12 months since my mum had her stroke and had to go into a care home. She has shown remarkable resilience, but it is very tough for everyone in this situation. I hope that we see changes soon.

The rate of Covid infection is now higher than ever and people are afraid. All hope is pinned on the vaccine. The economic situation is uncertain. Many fear a major recession. The Salmond case will bring few problems electorally for the SNP. The situation for Labour is dire, Richard Leonard's days are numbered. The wreckers' long game will pay off with electoral oblivion or a last-minute leadership change before the May election. Keir Starmer has the charisma of house brick and has rolled back on almost every commitment he gave when he was elected. All in all, it is very depressing.

3 January The *Sunday Mail* carried a piece from me calling out those who were responsible for the internal sabotage of the last few years. I urged party members to replace them when the candidate selections come.

Here is an excerpt from the piece:

The people doing this are not inexperienced politicians, they're some of the longest-serving members of the parliamentary group.

They have never accepted responsibility for failed political and strategic direction.

They couldn't accept it when their anointed candidates failed in their role as leader or lost internal elections.

Like the spoiled brat who thinks he or she has the divine right to all the spoils, their destructive tantrums have caused repeated and lasting reputational damage.

Labour faces a fundamental choice – change or die. It is that serious.'

Findlay pointed to significant political victories for Scottish Labour including its recent Period Poverty Bill, along with campaigns for victims of mesh implants, the scrapping of the Offensive Behaviour at Football Act and helping expose the Covid-19 care home crisis. But he urged members to use their vote for regional list candidates to get rid of 'arrogant' MSPs.

Findlay added: 'Imagine how much more we could achieve without those directing an internal campaign of self-harm. Scotland needs an effective, campaigning Labour Party delivering real change. But it's clear to me this can only come with a change of personnel.

4 January Parliament was recalled for a statement. We are going back into full lockdown until February.

5 January Covid cases are soaring. I am being inundated with hundreds of inquiries about every area of the economy and society.

Spoke to Peter Krykant is considering standing as a candidate at the election.

6 January Had a meeting today with Jim Sillars, Alex Neil, Kenny McAskill, Pauline Bryan and Tommy Kane to discuss how we might put aside our differences on the constitution and cooperate on a cross-party, anti-austerity, pro working class agenda in the run-up to the election. We agreed to keep talking.

In the US, pro Trump protesters stormed the Capitol building. The scenes are extraordinary. Four people are dead.

Heard from NHS staff who can't get appointments for Covid vaccinations. I will try to help them.

7 January The gloves are well and truly off in the Salmond/Sturgeon civil war. He has released an 11-page statement claiming Sturgeon repeatedly misled Parliament.

8 January Lots of speculation that the Scottish election could be delayed. I really hope not as I am ready to go and want to see out the end of my term.

10 January Covid rates are now 1 in 50, 80,000 people have died.

11 January I put out an email and social media post asking parents to get in touch if their kids were having difficulty accessing IT to do school work or if they did not have a computer or tablet. Within a few hours, over 100 people have been in touch. All were passed on to councils to follow up.

12 January Still getting emails about kids with no IT access. A significant number of kids can't have been learning during the pandemic because of this. Why has this not been proactively addressed?

Did a Zoom call with John Hendy, Shami Chakrabarti and Pauline Bryan about the abhorrent Covert Human Intelligence Sources Bill. A legislative consent motion is likely to come before the Scottish Parliament. I will speak against it when it does.

13 January At FMQs, I asked Nicola Sturgeon if she would bring in emergency legislation to provide care home residents with enforceable rights, she gave no commitment. At the education statement I raised the issues of the 100 children who have no IT access.

Trump has been impeached for the second time.

14 January Well, well. What a day! After the committee, I spoke in Monica

Lennon's members' debate on the drug deaths crisis. Just after I spoke, I received a text to say Richard Leonard had resigned. They have finally got him. Apparently there was a meeting between Jackie Baillie, Ian Murray, Angela Rayner, Lord Willie Haughey and other wealthy donors who said they would not donate to Scottish Labour unless Richard was replaced by Anas Sarwar. Richard was then called by Starmer, who asked him to stand down.

From the outset, we told Richard not to make the same mistakes as Jeremy and he made them several times over. He tried to hold his enemies close and they stabbed him in the front. He has endured attack after attack and leak after leak from private meetings and conversations. Sarwar and his supporters never accepted his defeat and did everything to make sure Richard failed. Like Corbyn, a decent, honorable man has been deposed by a bunch of snakes. I tweeted 'Looks like those who have led a three-year campaign of briefings to journalists, leaks of private conversations and the constant feeding of stories to the media to bring down a decent and honest man have succeeded, These "flinching cowards and sneering traitors" make me sick.' I did clips for the media and appeared on *The Nine*.

So where do we go from here? People are urging me to stand but there is no chance of this. I am going back to the real world. There will be a big push for Sarwar to get a free run on a hard unionist ticket. Monica Lennon might stand but there is really no one else. What a state of affairs.

15 January The fallout from yesterday's events goes on. I did GMS at 7am, the BBC, Novara Media and numerous newspaper interviews. At least my intervention helped stop the narrative becoming about Richard standing down for the good of the party.

Got to see Mum today, it was great to see her and have a nice chat.

Had a text exchange with Richard tonight. He thanked me for my support.

16 January Chloe's 25th birthday today.

The Scottish Executive of the Party met today to agree a truncated leadership contest to end by 29 February. Monica Lennon will stand, but if she wins she will get the same treatment as Richard. If she needs my nomination to get on the ballot I will support her, but only if she commits to a credible third option on the constitution as a priority.

17 January I spoke to Monica Lennon about her candidacy and what she will need in place for the campaign. Sarwar has his supporters lined up.

Later, Monica Lennon declared her candidacy.

18 January I submitted my nomination for Monica Lennon.

19 January Spoke with Monica's team and went through a number of pressing campaign issues. I am happy to offer occasional advice but won't be getting too involved.

I spoke in the debate on the Legislative Consent Motion on the CHIS bill. Thankfully, SNP and Labour agreed with my position and the LCM was not granted. It is an atrocious piece of legislation that gives undercover police officers immunity from committing crimes up to rape and murder in the course of their duties. Unbelievably, Starmer who was a human rights lawyer, is not opposing this.

20 January Went with Ian McPhee and Barry Sheridan from University of West of Scotland and Aidan Martin to meet the new drugs Minister Angela Constance. We called for an independent commission into decriminalisation of drugs and offered a list of other ideas. She showed interest in the issues and the meeting was reasonably positive. Later, Sturgeon made a statement basically accepting that the government has screwed up on the drugs crisis and said they would increase funding or more likely reinstate the money they previously cut.

Biden was inaugurated today. Trump didn't attend, staying in Florida in the huff – tosser.

21 January Anas Sarwar launched his five-point plan for his leadership. It was all vacuous fluff such as 'we will listen to workers', whatever that means.

The SNP, Tories and Lib Dems voted down Claire Baker's Corporate Culpable Homicide Bill.

22 January It is being reported that a senior official connected to Nicola Sturgeon tried to get the wording in a key document relating to the Salmond case changed. This is very serious.

Spoke to staff at the TESCO distribution centre at Livingston who advised that 250 staff members are being threatened with fire and rehire and a £3,000– £15,000 pay cut. These were the people who were told a few months ago they were key workers, they are now being shafted by a company that has made huge profits during the pandemic. I wrote to the company, put down a motion and questions and will do all I can to help those affected.

I spoke to Gordon Brown today about devo max and the constitution. He asked why I wasn't supporting Sarwar for leader so I told him that it was because he was involved in the machinations against Richard and that I knew what had been going on for the last few years and could never support him.

23 January Almond Valley CLP nominated Monica Lennon and selected Craig Smith as the election candidate.

25 January People over 70 years old have received their appointments for vaccinations.

Met Jeane Freeman with a cross-party group of MSPs to discuss care home visiting. There has been little progress.

26 January Covid deaths in the UK have reached 100,000.

Met with care home residents' families to advise on our meeting yesterday. We are all exasperated by the lack of action.

Journalist Neil Mackay wrote a blistering column in *The Herald* on the abject failings of the government's approach to the pandemic. He said: 'The most dreadful of all the scandals goes straight to the heart of the bogus claim that the SNP has somehow dealt well with the pandemic... any investigation should go to the heart of government and include the First Minister and the Health Secretary Jeane Freeman.' Nail hit on head.

28 January The Scottish budget was announced. It will give the low paid 1p a month but the wealthy £30 a month of benefit. The housing budget is being cut in the middle of a housing crisis and public sector workers will get 1–3 per cent.

29 January Met with Jim Sillars, Alex Neil, Kenny McAskill and Tommy Kane to continue our discussions. These are interesting and stimulating sessions. They might not go anywhere but they are refreshing and respectful with everyone accepting we have different views on the constitution but that we could come together across party on an anti austerity agenda, holding the UK And Scottish Governments to account.

1 February The SNP sacked MPs Joanna Cherry, Kenny McAskill and Angus McNeil from front bench positions.

Labour List selection results are out today with decent results for the left, Alex Rowley, Carol Mochan, Mercedes Villalba, Katy Clark and Paul Sweeney all in good positions to be elected. We could have a broad left grouping of around seven or eight which is decent.

2 February The Joanna Cherry story rumbles on. It seems she had to call the police due to threats made to her. There is also a running feud between Patrick Harvie and Andy Wightman over trans rights. Remarkably, to some this seems to be the defining issue of times.

Paul Hutcheon of the *Daily Record* called me about an astonishing story. Prior to Boris Johnson's visit to a Livingston vaccine plant last week, Downing Street was advised that there was a Covid outbreak and that there were 14 cases affecting workers. Despite this and the fact he is the PM who has overseen 100,000 deaths, the visit went ahead.

3 February The Johnson story is out. Ian Blackford raised it at PMQs.

At FMQs I asked Sturgeon if she would follow Oregon, where this week all drugs have been decriminalised. To be fair to her, at least she accepts that the war on drugs has failed.

4 February Went to my last meeting of the RMT parliamentary group. Elaine Smith has chaired it for years and has done a huge amount of work for the union. It's the end of an era. The RMT officials have been great to work with.

I was contacted by some of the mesh women, who advised that one of the most enthusiastic implanters of mesh has been recruited to head up the new Glasgow mesh centre. The very person who advocated women have this horrible stuff inside them is now leading the team who they will have to put their faith in to remove it.

6 February I spoke to Monica Lennon's team. They are struggling with a lack of personel, so we will reach out to a few people to try and help.

7 February Alex Salmond says he will only attend the parliamentary inquiry if it publishes all evidence.

8 February Peter Murrell, the Chief Executive of the SNP, Nicola Sturgeon's husband, was recalled to the Salmond Inquiry. He looked shifty, uneasy, unable to answer questions and he stretched credibility at many times. At one point, he kept looking to his side as though he was speaking to someone in the room beside him but claimed he was 'looking at a magpie out the window'.

9 February Salmond has refused to go before the Inquiry because of its failure to publish his unredacted account. The parliament's lawyers are advising if it was published then the Chief Executive could potentially be prosecuted. This is typical of the conservative approach taken by the Parliament. The lawyers are there to give 'advice', MSPs can decide whether or not to take it. Later, the committee voted against publication with Andy Wightman of the Greens supporting the SNP position. Murrell's evidence from yesterday is being savaged.

In the chamber, the Lord Advocate made a statement about the payment of over £24 million in compensation to two former directors of Rangers Football Club who were subject to a malicious prosecution. It is an extraordinary case of corruption or incompetence.

Ballots went out for the Scottish Labour leadership election today.

10 February *The Spectator* magazine published the information the Salmond Inquiry wouldn't. There is a big stushie about this.

I raised the case of the TESCO workers at Livingston at FMQs.

I watched a debate on STV between Anas Sarwar and Monica Lennon. Sarwar stretched credibility when he claimed he never briefed against Richard Leonard. He had no position on the constitution. Monica did well.

11 February The Salmond Inquiry shambles goes on. *The Spectator* won its case at the Court of Session and can publish the unredacted evidence. This should pave the way for Salmond to give evidence.

14 February I spoke to Mesh campaigners. They are very concerned that the Scottish Government has announced that a panel has been appointed to review mesh patient's case notes with the potential to amend them. We will need to look into this closely.

16 February Into Parliament to take part in the debate on the Feeley report into social care reform. Jeane Freeman made grandiose statements about this being similar to the establishment of the NHS. In reality it will be a centralised commissioning process purchasing services from the private sector. Ownership of care homes and the employment of staff will remain with companies like HCI, who pay no corporation tax, and pay low wages. Feeley proposes leaving all of this in place. The report says some good things on fair work and collective bargaining but overall the proposals are very timid.

17 February Audit Scotland published a report saying that over the years there have been several plans developed to prepare for the coming of a pandemic but they were ignored.

18 February The Scottish Parliament Corporate Body eventually published the Salmond evidence. It is farcical stuff, Salmond is loving the attention.

19 February Met with Professor Alison Britton today to discuss the mesh review process. It was a good meeting and she took on board our concerns.

Had another meeting with the group of senior SNP old guard and Labour people to discuss a possible common proposal to put to all candidates at the election. It was another very good discussion but I fear the election may just come too quickly for us to make an effective intervention.

21 February Our campaigning is paying off, we are now getting two care home visits a week. It's pathetic we have to campaign for such basic things.

22 February There was a big push from the SNP to try and stop the Corporate Body reversing its decision to publish the non-redacted Salmond evidence but it was later published. He named senior civil servants, Special Advisers, the husband of the First Minister and others as being part of an organised conspiracy that has cost the taxpayer millions of pounds, without anyone being held to account or having to resign.

Reflecting on all of this, I recall Henry McLeish resigning over an office let and Wendy Alexander resigning over a £950 campaign donation. It seems the standards they were held to don't apply to members of the SNP leadership, past or present.

23 February What an utter shambles. The Corporate Body, under pressure from the Crown Office, has advised the Salmond Inquiry to withdraw the contested evidence. I raised a point of order in the chamber calling for the Lord Advocate or Corporate body members to come before Parliament to answer questions. The Presiding Officer arrogantly dismissed my request then later when it was taken up by the Tories and Jackie Baillie he changed his tune becoming more sympathetic. Salmond later withdrew from tomorrow's hearing. This a real crisis for the Parliament, Salmond is loving it.

24 February Jackie Baillie was granted permission for an emergency question to the Lord Advocate about yesterday's fiasco. James Wolffe claimed he had no role in it and that it was others in the Crown Office who made the decisions and he had only seen a note about it. This stretches credibility. As I first raised the issue of the Lord Advocate coming to Parliament I had hoped to get a question but was not called by the Presiding Officer.

Former SNP Deputy Leader Jim Sillars has said that he will not vote SNP at the coming election as the higher echelons of the party are corrupt.

25 February At FMQs, all sides attacked Sturgeon over the Salmond Inquiry and she lashed out at Salmond. She is poking the bear before his appearance tomorrow at the committee. It promises to be a dynamite session.

26 February At 12.30pm Salmond began his evidence. He had obviously been coached and advised not to be his usual arrogant, bombastic self. It worked. He gave a very in-depth and credible performance. He was all over the detail, having lived and breathed this for the last few years. Jackie Baillie and Murdo Fraser did well with their questions. Andy Wightman was OK, Alex Cole-Hamilton was rubbish and Stuart McMillan and Alisdair Allan nonexistent.

Salmond claimed the Scottish Government have withheld 40 documents that should have been handed over under a police warrant. Disgracefully, he refused to apologise to the women he harassed and claimed senior figures in the Crown Office, the civil service and government had failed and should consider their position. The session went on for over six hours and was at times as excruciating as it was compelling. As soon as the session was over, the committee issued an order to bring previously withheld evidence before it.

Starmer gave an unequivocal commitment to Trident.

27 February Fallout from Salmond's evidence is all over the media.

Anas Sarwar was elected the tenth Scottish Labour Leader since devolution, defeating Monica Lennon by 58 to 42 per cent. He is the first Muslim and first member of the black and minority ethnic community to lead a UK political party.

The left is in retreat. In just over a year, we have gone from having Jeremy Corbyn, Richard Leonard and Mark Drakeford leading their respective parties, to just having Drakeford in Wales. I gave an interview with the media and offered him my congratulations and said that he had the opportunity to unite the party but couldn't do this if he took a hard unionist line.

Following on from the Salmond Inquiry, the Tories have submitted a motion of no confidence in John Swinney as he is the political lead for the release of information to the hearings. The question will now be will they release the information or will the Green party come to his rescue in any vote?

I got a surprise phone call from Anas Sarwar this evening. He wanted to advise me he would not be taking a 'hard unionist line' and that he wanted to build a credible package of further devolution. I will believe it when I see it. He also said he wants to follow through on the drug policy reforms that Monica Lennon got through the policy forum. Again, let's see if he delivers.

1 March Anas Sarwar announced his Shadow Cabinet today. Monica Lennon is taking over the Economy brief with Jackie Baillie doing Health; Colin Smyth has responsibility for the Constitution.

George Galloway announced he would be voting Tory at the forthcoming election. We really are 'through the looking glass'.

2 March What an extraordinary day. The Scottish Government was forced to publish their legal advice on the Salmond case. At topical questions, John Swinney said it would be published later in the afternoon and would clear up any remaining questions. I asked him what was the most serious offence, an undeclared campaign donation of £950 (this is what caused Wendy Alexander to resign), a muddle over an office lease (which caused Henry McLeish to resign as First Minister), or the failure to release 40 documents demanded under a police search warrant? Just like the old Two Ronnies *Mastermind* sketch, Swinney answered a completely different question to the one I asked.

When the legal advice was published it was remarkable. Government lawyers expressed their anger about documents being withheld and said they were embarrassed in court when they were eventually produced. There was a letter from Salmond's lawyers, who said they were told by a senior civil servant the name of one of Salmond's complainants (Sturgeon denies this happened), and in another document lawyers, two months before the government pulled the judicial review, said they had no chance of winning the case and the government should concede but they ploughed on regardless, wasting over a million-pound of taxpayers' money.

3 March Nicola Sturgeon appeared before the Salmond Inquiry today in a marathon eight-hour session. She handled herself very well, however some of the committee were absolutely woeful in their questioning of her. There was a coordinated effort on social media to support her every word with a running commentary throughout the session. Given the case goes to the very heart of the justice system, it was appalling to see Humza Yousaf, the Justice Secretary, repeatedly commenting like a lovestruck fanboy about proceedings.

Jackie Baillie was very strong in her line of questioning and gave Sturgeon a very tough time. Murdo Fraser was OK but as a lawyer I would have expected more. Margaret Mitchell spouted incomprehensible gobbledygook and Stuart McMillan and Maureen Watt were embarrassing.

4 March As the internal warfare in the SNP continues, they are claiming that their membership has increased by 7,000. So it appears people are inspired to join a political party mired in a sexual harassment case.

I went into the chamber to hear my long-standing friend and comrade Elaine Smith make her final speech as an MSP. Elaine has been a huge support throughout my time in Parliament. She has been a stalwart of the left since her election in 1999, often attacked and marginalised by the New Labour element for her views, but she never faltered and stuck to her principles. She is a brave politician and a committed socialist. Her speech on international women's day was excellent and the tributes to her well deserved.

A poll out today has Starmer 15 points behind.

6 March My 52nd birthday today.

7 March The *Sunday Mail* led with a story about the Scottish Government trying to cover up the number of care home residents who have died of Covid by not including those who were being treated in hospital at the time of their death. This story came from a constituent of mine.

8 March The media is full of Prince Harry and Meghan getting stuck into the royal family in a TV interview with Oprah Winfrey.

Hollie Cameron, the Labour candidate for Kelvin, has been dropped because of her support for another Independence referendum. She voted Yes last time and supports self-determination and the right to hold a referendum (as do I and many other Labour members). What does this say to those who share her views and whose votes we want to win back? I texted Sarwar who denied any involvement and said it was an SEC decision – I don't believe that.

9 March I watched a bit of the Prince Harry interview, it was compelling stuff. They were ripping into the royal family with accusations of racism, bullying, people feeling suicidal etc. It left a rotten, corrupt institution looking even more rotten and corrupt.

10 March We had a marathon session at Stage Three of the Hate Crime Bill, I didn't get home until 11.30pm. There were excellent contributions from Johann Lamont, Adam Tompkins and Humza Yousaf. Johann was very powerful and effective on women's rights, Tomkins gave his best performance in five years on free speech and Yousaf defended the bill skilfully. It was a real debate about big issues. I commended each of them afterwards for their contributions and said to Tomkins who is standing down at the election that I thought he had been a disappointment and that the Tory position on Brexit where he was the spokesperson and had to defend the indefensible had knocked the stuffing out of him. He said, 'That is exactly what happened.' He will now return full-time to lecturing in Constitutional Law. Parliament will be poorer without him and Johann.

11 March Attended my final committee meeting today where we tidied up a few loose ends and thanked the excellent clerking team.

I moved amendments to the Redress bill to give survivors of abuse more rights in seeking compensation. These were defeated by the SNP.

12 March Got to see Mum for the first time in ages.

March 15 Attended my last Cuba CPG as an MSP tonight.

18 March I made my final speech in Parliament today. The opportunity came up during a debate on drugs policy. in the debate on drugs policy. In it I reflected on the experience of a young constituent whose family gave me permission to talk about his experience of drugs, addiction, prison and a system that failed him. I also spoke about my time in parliament and some of the campaigns I have had the honour of being involved in:

He was in Polmont twice: for ten days at the age of 16, and then for seven months at the age of 17. He got more drugs in prison than he did in the community. He took an allergic reaction in prison – his mouth swelled up, but he was left that way. His lawyer had to write to the governor to ask for better care. He had brittle asthma. At times, due to staff shortages, he was locked up for 23 hours at a time, with little outside time for fresh air. He needed rehab and treatment instead of being locked up. He died on Tuesday, aged 20, at Carmondean in Livingston, in mine and the minister's constituency, having used heroin and benzodiazepine. He was one of the three people to die a preventable death in Scotland that day.

We have the worst drugs death rate in the developed world – worse than that of the US. That is a shameful, damning indictment of 20 years of this institution being in control of justice and health policy. The government cut the drugs budget and then wondered why the number of deaths rose. Peter Krykant is forced to go out each day in an auld van that he had to buy at his own expense to save lives, while ministers pretend that they are powerless to provide the same services, and instead engage in constitutional games.

The simple fact is that people cannot access the services that they need. The waiting time for an appointment to see a psychologist in Lothian is between 18 and 24 months just now; it is supposed to be 18 weeks. Are we not all ashamed of what is happening on the streets, yards from us, in every one of our constituencies? We bloody well should be.

It was watching Thatcher's class war against communities like mine that sparked my political interest and awakening. Today, in those very same communities, working-class lives are ending unnecessarily because of a failed drugs policy. Think of all the families who have lost a child or a partner, lying in a manky alleyway with a needle in their arm or a fake benzo in their belly – and then think of the footballer, the nurse or the tradesperson that they could have been. Think of that waste of talent – of the deaths of people like me, my family, my pals and my community. That is what drives my campaigning on this. I have said it many times, but if this carnage was happening in the leafy suburbs or commuter villages, it would have been sorted a long time ago.

There will be no political leaders canvassing homeless drug users at the election, and they will not be in here getting canapés and warm wine. But we will walk past them on the way to the train tonight – I will – and the minister and her colleagues will drive past them on their way home in their ministerial cars. We need a revolution in drugs policy: decriminalisation, massive investment in care and treatment, and an all-out attack on the inequalities that feed despair and hopelessness. If we do not have that revolution, the bodies will pile higher and higher and higher.

With your indulgence, Presiding Officer, I will say a wee bit about my time in Parliament. I have to say that no-one was more surprised than me when I made it through the Labour Party vetting process, never mind got elected. People from the left were not particularly welcome then; I am not sure that they are particularly welcome now. I had been in this building only twice before becoming an MSP, and the only member I knew was my pal Elaine Smith, but I made a pledge to have a go, and others can decide whether I succeeded.

I thank my parliamentary team of Caitlin, Mary Theresa, Jordan, Mhari and Tommy – they are wonderful colleagues and friends. I also thank my family and pals, who have kept my feet firmly on the ground, and my wife, Fiona, and daughter, Chloe.

I do not think that it is a surprise to anybody that I have enjoyed myself most when on the back benches, working with, for example, the magnificent Scottish mesh survivors. Together, we secured a suspension and a fund to support injured women.

I also worked with the Scottish miners and secured the independent review and a commitment to a pardon after almost 40 years. I worked with the families of the children who will continue to use the children's ward at St John's because we prevented its downgrading. I worked with the communities that successfully stopped the expansion of Edinburgh airport's flight path. I worked with the blacklisted construction workers – this week, we mourn the loss of Francie Graham, who was a stalwart of the campaign.

I worked with the then political editor of the *Daily Record*, David Clegg, to convince the newspaper to take up the cause of drugs, and to go a step further and call for decriminalisation. I am so pleased that it did so, as it has been very influential.

I have enjoyed every day that I called for well-funded, publicly owned services and an end to the madness of privatisation; every day that I worked with the families of care home residents, exposing the human rights abuse of our older people; every day that I worked with the trade unions; and every day that I represented my constituents on a huge range of issues.

I even enjoyed the 60-odd public meetings at which I spoke during the independence referendum, arguing for devo max. I will continue to argue that that is the best option for Scotland's future.

I enjoyed chairing my friend Jeremy Corbyn's two leadership campaigns in Scotland – by God, how I wish we had won the 2017 election and radically changed our country for the better.

I even enjoyed standing for Labour Leader – well, we have all had a go at some point – on a socialist platform. I enjoyed the times that I screwed up by sending my entire budget speech to Derek Mackay minutes before the budget or sending everybody in the Parliament a reply to a confidential email from Mike Russell. Information technology was never my strong point.

I have a saying that a person cannot be a socialist and a pessimist. I remember using that line in a debate and David McLetchie intervening to ask, "Well, if that is the case, why do you all look so bloody miserable?" I liked debating with McLetchie. However, I am not miserable and I am not pessimistic. More than ever, I believe that socialism is the answer to the biggest questions that we have to deal with: poverty, climate change, hunger, conflict and exploitation. It is because of free-market capitalism that we are here, on the precipice of a disaster for our planet. Those questions can be addressed only by a planned economy, public ownership and international solidarity. Irrespective of our political views, we are all brothers and sisters, and we have as much of a duty to feed and educate a child in war-torn Yemen as we do a child in the school next door, but those principles are alien to anyone who believes in capitalism.

I make a plea to those who follow me: speak up, challenge others and your own party, be awkward, do not accept the line that that is how it has always been done, take up issues, do not be afraid to be rebuffed, and come back again with the same issue until you win. Finally, I say to them, 'Enjoy yourself' – I certainly have.

Following the speech, I got a lot of nice comments from MSPs, texts and emails from constituents and messages friends. It was quite satisfying to bring my time in Parliament to an end in this way. I have had an experience many covet. I gained this not through any planned career path, brown-nosing or burning ambition but through sheer luck and I enjoyed every second of it (almost).

19 March Keir Starmer was in Scotland today talking ill-informed rubbish about drugs. As a former Director of Public Prosecutions, he of all people should understand that the war on drugs has failed, but apparently not. He was talking up the law-and-order approach that has self evidently failed.

20 March Lots of speculation about Nicola Sturgeon's future in the newspapers today and whether she will be found guilty of breaching the Ministerial Code in a report out tomorrow. I don't think there's a chance of this happening.

21 March James Hamilton QC's report into Sturgeon was published today. It concluded Sturgeon did not break the Ministerial Code. The least surprising news I have heard all year. The Tories are stupidly going to pursue a vote of no confidence.

22 March Brilliant news today, the court of appeal has quashed the case of the Shrewsbury pickets who were convicted 47 years ago. The group includes actor Ricky Tomlinson, they were stitched up on falsified charges during a national building workers strike. Tomlinson and two colleagues went to jail and refused to wear prison clothes claiming they were political prisoners. Their case has been supported by a number of trade unions and the left.

The committee report into the Salmond Inquiry was published. It made a number of serious points but yesterday's report which said Sturgeon did not breach the Ministerial Code was the crucial one in the PR battle. The Tories mishandled this badly. Labour and the Lib Dems abstained in the Tories confidence motion.

24 March My last day in Parliament. I went to the Petitions Committee and successfully argued for them to keep the mesh petition open. Later, I received a letter from Jeane Freeman who advised the next Parliament will legislate for women who have travelled abroad for treatment to be reimbursed. This is brilliant news and something we have campaigned on. I said farewell to staff in the canteen and postroom and went home after FMQs. A bit of an odd feeling, to be honest.

25 March I got a letter from Humza Yousaf on the renewal of Covid regulations. I had raised with him the need for regulations to ensure safe picketing following some heavy-handed action by the police at a picket in Edinburgh. The good news is the regs are to be amended. Another little but important victory.

First day of election campaigning.

26 March Alex Salmond launched his new political party, Alba. He called for people to vote SNP in constituencies and Alba on the list.

I was invited to take part in the 172nd Earl Marshal debate hosted by Aberdeen University – the motion was 'This house has no faith in the Scottish Govt'. It was quite good fun.

27 March Kenny McAskill MP has defected from the SNP to Alba.

28 March Neale Hanvey MP for Kirkcaldy defected to Alba. Tommy Sherdian has joined too – what a line up.

29 March Campaigning in Stoneyburn today.

30 March I watched the Scottish election debate. Douglas Ross was terrible, no matter the question asked he rabbitted on about independence. Sturgeon looked well out of sorts. Sarwar put in the best performance by some way.

1 April Alba are on 3 per cent in the latest poll, Labour have overtaken the Tories into second place.

Sturgeon is now taking failed policies and recycling them as new announcements, she also said that Salmond gambles on horses every day. I wonder why this never merited a mention all the years she was his besto?

2 April Got to take mum out for a seat in the sunshine today. It was lovely to be out with her in the fresh air. Three people came over and spoke to her, which was nice.

3 April Panelbase polling today has Alba on 6 per cent and Galloway winning a seat in South of Scotland, god forbid.

8 April Jeane Freeman admitted in a radio interview that her decision to discharge untested residents from hospital to care homes was a mistake. I am seething at this. I pursued her for over a year on this very matter and she repeatedly denied it, attacked me for even suggesting it, blamed others, and now that she has left office she admits it was a mistake. Damn right it was a mistake and one that cost many people their lives. She admitted this on the day the 10,000th Scottish citizen died from Covid.

9 April Out leafletting all day until news came through that the Duke of Edinburgh had died and all campaigning was suspended. Parliament will be recalled on Monday for tributes. I think I'll pass on that.

10 April Got my Covid vaccination today, all very quick and efficient. After about an hour I felt groggy, then got shivers, sore head and limbs.

11 April With Parliament being recalled on Monday following the duke's death, I wrote to the Presiding Officer calling for time after the tributes to question the First Minister about the 10,000 Covid deaths in Scotland and the care homes admission by the Health Secretary. I have no doubt this will be refused but I had to do it. I have published my request and sent it to all Labour MSPs in the hope they will support my call.

11 April There is radio silence from Labour MSPs following my call for time to question Sturgeon after tributes to the Duke of Edinburgh. Eventually, Elaine Smith and Johann Lamont offered support. Shortly after, the Presiding Officer refused my request, claiming it would give candidates in the election an advantage, a really rubbish excuse.

12 April 12 Since Parliament was sitting today, I emailed a motion to the chamber desk regarding the admission by Jeane Freeman about care home policy failings and the 10,000 deaths in Scotland. The chamber desk advised they were closed and couldn't accept it. I then emailed the Presiding Officer, who also refused to accept it. So, Parliament is open but no business is being accepted. Later, party leaders spoke for five minutes to pay tribute to the duke and that was it, what a waste of time.

13 April Went to see Mum. We sat outside and did a crossword in the sun.

15 April The SNP published their election manifesto today. It is full of free things, including bikes and computers for school pupils, a move to a four-day week, a minimum income guarantee and no income tax increases. There is no accompanying document setting out how these policies will be paid for.

16 April Covid restrictions have been lifted.

17 April The funeral of the Duke of Edinburgh was held today.

Had pals round for a drink in the garden, it was great to see people again.

18 April The *Sunday Times* ran a story on the Red Paper Collective submitting a petition to Parliament demanding a third option on the ballot in any future referendum.

19 April There is a big outcry about Celtic, Rangers and other big football teams seeking to join a European Super League. The backlash from fans is huge and the chief executives of the clubs are backtracking and denying this is what they want. The reality is that when MSPs played a football match at Celtic Park almost ten years ago, Peter Lawwell, the Celtic Chief Executive, told us unequivocally that this was what they aspired to.

22 April The BBC published figures for undeclared care home deaths. They are truly shocking with several West Lothian homes having 10–20 deaths.

The Scottish Labour manifesto was published today. The headlines were a jobs guarantee for under 25s, an NHS recovery, an education catch-up plan, action on climate and a community recovery fund.

23 April SNP South of Scotland MSP Emma Harper said the creation of a border would create jobs. This follows previous claims that you get more money for a Scottish pound than an English one.

25 April Boris Johnson's lying and sleaze is finally catching up with him.

26 April Johnson is reported as saying he would 'rather the bodies pile higher than see the country go into another lockdown'. What a horrible bastard he is.

27 April DUP members are circulating a letter proposing a confidence vote in Arlene Foster, the First Minister of Northern Ireland. She is in big trouble.

30–31 April Spent a few days in London tidying up some political and constituency business before I finish up.

4 May Campaigning in Fife with Alex Rowley. He is worried about retaining his seat but I think he will be OK.

Poll today has Scottish Labour down to 18 seats and the Greens on 13. I can't see it myself.

5 May Last day as an MSP. Up early for another election campaigning session.

May 6 Polling day. Out at 6.30am to drop off boards at polling stations then a leafleting round before door knocking. The turnout has been good.

May 7 Election results started to come through. Labour lost the Hartlepool by-election – a disaster for the hapless Starmer.

As the Scottish results came in it was clear the turnout was good. The SNP took back East Lothian. Lib Dems Willie Rennie and Alex Cole-Hamilton had excellent results in Fife and Edinburgh. Tories Jackson Carlaw, Oliver Mundell and Rachel Hamilton retained their seats. Daniel Johnson increased his majority for Labour in Edinburgh South and Jackie Baillie won again in Dunbarton. The Greens saw their seats go up to eight. Alba failed to make any impact and Galloway lost.

The good news for the Labour left is that Carol Mochan, Katy Clark, Mercedes Villalba, Richard Leonard, Alex Rowley, Monica Lennon and Paul Sweeney were all elected.

The SNP fell short of an overall majority.

In England the results for Labour were very poor but in Wales Mark Drakeford's socialist programme was very popular, they had a great result.

With the election over and me no longer a Member of the Scottish Parliament – let's see what the real world brings.

Postscript

AS A NAIVE 16-year-old living in a community ravaged by deindustrialisation, Thatcher's pit closure programme and the war on trade unions, I could never in a million years have imagined that my interest in politics and my developing awareness of socialism might end up with me first becoming a councillor for my home village, and then a Member of the Scottish Parliament.

Class is a hotly contested and much-debated concept. Many people try to convince themselves that it is no longer relevant and that everyone aspires to be middle class these days. But for me, class and class identity are central to who I am and my worldview. I am working class; I always will be working class. Over time, my job role and income may have changed, but my views, politics, culture, beliefs, values and relationships have remained constant. Class to me is not simply about the role each of us plays in the economy. It is not just about whether you own and control the means of production or whether you are employed by those who profit and enrich themselves by your endeavours. It is also about what you feel, your outlook on life, your sense of community and the culture you are immersed in.

My community was built on coal. The connectedness, the feeling of shared danger, responsibility and effort and the way of life have diminished but to this day a sense of solidarity survives, and will survive for many decades more.

Our families, communities, relationships, environment and history shape us. The decline of the coal, steel and car industries left parts of West Lothian with an unemployment rate of 26 per cent. I was lucky, my da took me on as an apprentice bricklayer. The building trade is a hard game, but I worked with some of the smartest, funniest, most streetwise people you could ever meet. I learned more from them about life and what is important than I ever did in school, college, university, or parliament – life lessons that will remain with me forever.

During my apprenticeship, my interest in politics and social justice campaigns grew. This led me to return to night class to get an education and I went on to university, before working in housing and education. All this gave me a solid base from which to begin to analyse and understand the world.

In my early 30s I was approached to stand as a council candidate. I spent eight happy years representing my home patch and surrounding villages, a very rewarding time. Then, a series of chance events saw me elected to the Scottish Parliament in 2011. My attitude to this was, well, it will only last for four years, so I better get stuck in, enjoy it and do the very best for the people I represent. I have never been an ambitious person, but I felt if I proved myself I might, just might, survive my party's notoriously byzantine and rarely fair or democratic candidate selection process, and then the small issue of another election. So, I set about doing what came naturally to me – campaigning.

Initially racked with imposter syndrome, I was now working among people I perceived as intellectuals, skilled communicators and talented debaters. I had only been inside the Scottish Parliament twice before being elected. I did not mix with the political classes who inhabited the place. I worried about making a fool of myself among all these clever, confident people.

It took a few months for this crippling self-doubt to dissipate. This happened for several reasons, not least because I had recruited a great team. Tommy Kane, as my researcher and confidant encouraged and supported me but did not flinch from telling me things I might not want to hear – a vital attribute. Marion Kirk ran my office and handled the constituency casework with skill and compassion. Frank Toner was a good all-rounder who mucked in, doing whatever was required. As a team, our first priority was always the constituents we served. People don't come to their MSP when all is good, they come when they have tried to resolve things but have hit a roadblock. The role of an elected politician advocating on behalf of constituents is for me the most important part of the job and often the most satisfying.

I loved the variety, dealing with people from all backgrounds on a wide spectrum of issues. It might be helping someone who has been in severe pain for a long time to get a date for their operation; or assisting the family of a disabled child to secure appropriate accomodation, reducing the stress on them all; or enabling an asylum seeker with a traumatic past to get settled status. Such outcomes can be truly life-changing and to be involved is hugely satisfying for those who advocate on their behalf.

Across the country, politicians from all parties work to secure positive results for their constituents. The media, rightly at times, portray politicians as free-loading chancers ripping off the taxpayer, junketing and cheating their expenses. But in my experience, the vast majority genuinely do their best. No one can succeed in every case, but they can try. Not to try is unforgivable.

I loathe the way the establishment conspire and collaborate to protect and enrich their own, while trampling over the lives and rights of the rest of us. Many of the issues I became involved in as an MSP were so obviously unjust that it is sickening that we had to campaign on them at all. An outstanding example of this is the Mesh campaign. I worked with women who had been fed a pack of lies and maimed by health-care multinationals, surgeons and public bodies, in a ten-year war of attrition to uncover the truth. These women are some of the bravest, most determined, caring, and compassionate people I have ever met. I am proud that together we secured a ban on mesh implants in Scotland and exposed the scandal to the world. I am proud the women received compensation and that we secured a fund to help them with some of their daily costs. I am proud that women who paid for treatment abroad will be refunded and that others will have this poison removed from their bodies by a world-renowned expert. But I am angry too – angry that across the world so many women had their lives ruined unnecessarily to satisfy shareholder greed.

I am proud to have worked with former miners, their families, their trade union, solicitors, and supporters to drive the campaign for a pardon for those who were convicted during the great strike of 1984–85. I punched the air with delight in 2022, when the bill we fought for was finally passed.

I am proud to have campaigned for health and social-care services, for the retention of the threatened children's ward at St John's Hospital, for the community at Stoneyburn who have been left with no GP service for the first time since the creation of the NHS and for investment in social care.

The NHS is the greatest social policy implemented by any government. It is practical socialism in action. The current state of it is such that I genuinely fear for its future. Both my wife and daughter work in frontline services, the pressures on them and their colleagues are immense. We cannot allow the abject failure of the present government to destroy it. Will the people see through the polarised constitutional stand-off and demand change?

The Covid pandemic brought unprecedented pressures on governments, public services, workers, and families, but some of the decisions made by those in charge were unforgivable. As an opposition politician, it was my duty to do what I could to ensure that policy-makers were held to account for the abject failure on testing, inconsistent advice and repeated U-turns. The callous treatment of our older people in care homes represented to me another great injustice.

Worst affected by Covid were the poor, the low-paid and the vulnerable. Decisions made in Edinburgh and London by those with little understanding of the lives of ordinary people resulted in tens of thousands dying unnecessarily. I do not for one second regret holding ministers and their advisers to account during the pandemic. I took abuse for it from their supporters, but I live in hope that the forthcoming public inquiry will see those responsible held to account and my position on many of the issues vindicated. I have offered this diary to the inquiry as part of their evidence gathering. To date I have had no response.

In my day-to-day work as an MSP, I always supported workers in their struggle for better pay and conditions. I refused to cross the picket line at the Scottish Parliament when staff were on strike over pensions. I visited hundreds of demonstrations and picket lines to offer support and solidarity. I see this as part of any Labour politician's duty.

Tabling questions in the Scottish Parliament, I did my best to expose Scotland's appalling record on drug deaths and repeatedly called for drugs law reform, including decriminalisation.

Again and again I dedicated my energies in support of workers in their efforts to save their jobs. I have worked with communities on local planning issues, backing them in their opposition to flight path expansion, train and police station closures, bus service cuts and the cull of bank branches.

Some of these campaigns resulted in success, others sadly not, but with each campaign we brought people together, helped them organise and elevated their voice in the media and inside and outside of parliament.

I enjoyed every bit of it.

Surveying the political scene at the start of 2023, we are in the midst of the greatest period of industrial conflict since the 1970s. Trade unions in almost every sector are or have been on strike. Workers, having experienced a decade of service reductions, job losses and pay cuts (in real-terms) have said in huge numbers 'enough is enough'.

The war in Ukraine, fallout from Covid and post-Brexit chaos have resulted in soaring energy costs, food bills and interest rates.

The Tory Party, having gone through four prime ministers in the space of just a few years, looks to be in line for a 1997-style drubbing at the polls. For Labour, Keir Starmer has the personality and charisma of a house brick. The manifesto he put before party members to be elected was a fraud and has been well and truly buried. His shameful failure to stand in solidarity with nurses and postal workers is part of a strategy to woo the right-wing media and corporate funders, and allay establishment fears. Starmer and his party managers are engaged in an all-out attack on the left with mass expulsions, routine rule-breaking and attempts to deselect socialist MPs. His purge is far from finished.

In Scotland, the constitutional debate continues to polarise and dominate our politics. Every issue is seen through a constitutional lens. Loyalty to either side of the Yes/No debate determines one's position on everything from dog shit to international diplomacy.

Across all portfolio areas, the Scottish Government's mismanagement is there for all to see. The NHS is in crisis with record waiting times, a huge recruitment problem and a social care system not fit for purpose. Blaming Covid is a smokescreen – the NHS has been in crisis for over a decade.

Education standards are falling, class sizes are rising and teachers have been on strike for the first time since the 1980s.

New ferries for the Scotland's island communities are six years late and hundreds of millions over budget. The latest orders for new boats have gone to a Turkish shipyard. 'Standing up for Scotland', indeed!

Councils having been hammered year on year by a government that appears to have nothing but contempt for local government with more swingeing cuts on the way. We are seeing the very services that civilise us a society dismantled.

Scotland is now behind the rest of the UK when it comes to meeting climate change targets and a government which includes the Greens cannot even bring in a bottle return scheme on time without it becoming a fiasco.

The justice system is creaking at the seams, child poverty and social inequality are rising, food insecurity and hunger soaring and the drug death crisis getting worse. Indeed, it is hard to identify a policy area which can be spoken of as a genuine success.

The divisions following the Salmond trial saw the SNP remain well ahead in the polls. One major reason for this is Scottish Labour's abject failure to develop a radical and credible alternative to independence, nine years after the 2014 referendum. I find this as incomprehensible as it is indefensible. It has been my view since 2011, that a 'Home Rule' proposal that devolves the powers necessary to bring about radical, progressive change to our economy and society but shares power where it makes sense to do so would secure widespread support. It would offer an alternative based on pragmatism and what is best for the country, not what is best for any particular political party. It would challenge both Scottish and British nationalists, who both gain from a 51 per cent – 49 per cent strategy that pits friends, relatives and neighbours against each other, instead of seeking common ground and building unity.

As this book goes to print, a political earthquake is hitting Scotland. Just a few weeks after declaring she had 'plenty in the tank' to carry on, Nicola Sturgeon resigned as Scotland's longest serving First Minister. Soon after, her Deputy John Swinney, Chief of Staff Liz Lloyd, Head of Communications Murray Foote and Party Chief Executive (her husband, Peter Murrell) all resigned. The race to succeed her broke the SNP's rigid code of discipline and descended into farce and recrimination. Just days after Humza Yousaf was sworn in as Scotland's new First Minister, Murrell was arrested and viewers across the world awoke to TV footage of Police Scotland officers raiding both the home he shares with Nicola Sturgeon and SNP headquarters. There is little doubt the tectonic plates of Scottish politics are shifting.

Is this a time of hope or of despair? Time will tell.

In my own life, after leaving parliament myself, I joined with my friend and former researcher Tommy Kane and former Scottish Labour General Secretary Michael Sharpe to establish a not-for-profit social enterprise. We work with trade unions, community groups and voluntary organisations, helping them with research, campaigning advice, media and social media, report writing and events planning. It is very satisfying to be able to continue working on a day-to-day basis with organisations that seek to make the world a better place.

We are currently in the midst of the most intense period of industrial action in over 40 years. It is interesting, exciting and rewarding to be supporting so many trade unions in their fight for fair pay and job security.

As a socialist, I am an optimist and live in hope and have a belief that tomorrow will always be better than today.

Also published by **LUATH PRESS**

If You Don't Run, They Can't Chase You

stories from the frontline in the fight for social justice

Neil Findlay

ISBN 978-1-910022-43-6 PBK £9.99

These inspiring portraits will move you to continue the struggle.
OWEN JONES, author of *This Land: The Struggle for the Left*

If You Don't Run, They Can't Chase You

stories from
the frontline
in the fight
for social
justice

Neil Findlay

In this book Neil Findlay brings together first-hand testimony from people who have played crucial roles in social justice campaigns. Their stories are personal, political and unforgettable. They say a lot about dignity, integrity, courage and humanity. We can apply what we learn from them to build a sustainable and fair society for generations to come. Activists, social justice campaigners, trade unionists and environmentalists will find this collection inspirational, emotional and educational. And they will understand why it is titled *If You Don't Run, They Can't Chase You.*

These inspiring portraits will move you to continue the struggle. OWEN JONES

Details of books published by Luath Press can be found at:
www.luath.co.uk

Luath Press Limited

committed to publishing well written books worth reading

LUATH PRESS takes its name from Robert Burns, whose little collie Luath (*Gael.*, swift or nimble) tripped up Jean Armour at a wedding and gave him the chance to speak to the woman who was to be his wife and the abiding love of his life. Burns called one of the 'Twa Dogs' Luath after Cuchullin's hunting dog in Ossian's *Fingal*. Luath Press was established in 1981 in the heart of Burns country, and is now based a few steps up the road from Burns' first lodgings on Edinburgh's Royal Mile. Luath offers you distinctive writing with a hint of unexpected pleasures. Most bookshops in the UK, the US, Canada, Australia, New Zealand and parts of Europe, either carry our books in stock or can order them for you. To order direct from us, please send a £sterling cheque, postal order, international money order or your credit card details (number, address of cardholder and expiry date) to us at the address below. Please add post and packing as follows: UK – £1.00 per delivery address; overseas surface mail – £2.50 per delivery address; overseas airmail – £3.50 for the first book to each delivery address, plus £1.00 for each additional book by airmail to the same address. If your order is a gift, we will happily enclose your card or message at no extra charge.

Luath Press Limited
543/2 Castlehill
The Royal Mile
Edinburgh EH1 2ND
Scotland
Telephone: 0131 225 4326 (24 hours)
Email: sales@luath.co.uk
Website: www.luath.co.uk

ILLUSTRATION: IAN KELLAS